A CHILD'S PLACE

Ellen Ruppel Shell

A CHILD'S PLACE

*A Year in the Life of a
Day Care Center*

LITTLE, BROWN AND COMPANY

Boston   Toronto   London

FIRST EDITION

This is a work of nonfiction. Some names and one relationship have been changed for reasons of privacy.

"The Talking Migrant Tot Lot Blues" used with the permission of Cambridge Children's Center.

Excerpt from "We Live in a City Built by Human Hands" from *Little Boxes and Other Handmade Songs*, Oak Publications, 1964.

LIBRARY OF CONGRESS CATALOGING-IN-PUBLICATION DATA

Shell, Ellen Ruppel, 1952–
    A child's place: a year in the life of a day care center / by
Ellen Ruppel Shell. — 1st ed.
      p. cm.
    ISBN 0-316-78376-5
    1. Day care centers — Massachusetts — Cambridge — Case studies.
  I. Title.
HV859.C36S49 1992
362.7'12'097444 — dc20   91-39218

10 9 8 7 6 5 4 3 2 1

RRD-VA

Published simultaneously in Canada by
Little, Brown & Company (Canada) Limited

PRINTED IN THE UNITED STATES OF AMERICA

*To Martin and
to our children,
Alison and Joanna*

Contents

A CHILD'S PLACE

Introduction

OTHER PEOPLE'S CHILDREN

IN October 1989, Marion Wright Edelman, the founder and president of the Children's Defense Fund, presented the keynote address at the annual conference of the National Alliance of Business, in Washington, D.C. Having endured four days of lectures, workshops, and cocktail parties, the audience was restless — several dozen left the auditorium before Edelman had a chance to step up to the podium. Once she began to speak, however, the room fell silent. Edelman spoke of children: unwanted children, sick children, abused children. "The future which we hold in trust for our own children," she said, "will be shaped by our fairness to other people's children." She then recited a prayer. The room rose as one in a standing ovation. Not a few members of the audience brushed aside a tear. The next day, President George Bush announced through a spokesperson that he intended to veto any act of Congress that included provisions for federal quality standards for day care centers. Setting standards for the care of young children, it was implied, was a job for parents, not for society.

While we Americans are known for our reverence for youth and the sanctity in which we hold the family and especially our own children, we have, as a people, little patience or tolerance for the children of others. Our fierce defense of personal freedom extends to our allowing families who abuse, neglect, or ignore their children to carry on as if nothing abnormal were happening. We are, if nothing else, discreet, intruding in family life only if and when a child is so physically or psychologically battered that he becomes disruptive or mean or a painful eyesore. Even then, our help is not offered unconditionally. On the whole, we do not give with grace.

Several years ago, I wrote a magazine article that concluded that day care centers in this country, like butcher shops, should be required to abide by a set of minimum standards of safety and competence. I suggested, for example, that training requirements be set for teaching staff and that the number of children per teacher be limited. To me, this seemed like an entirely reasonable proposal, akin, perhaps, to the notion that a surgeon attend medical school or that a police officer be trained in the use of firearms. But the mail I received in response to that article was eye opening. Many of those who wrote accused me of being naive and uncaring, of ignoring the needs and rights of two-parent families that struggle and sacrifice to live on one income so that one parent (usually the mother) can stay home and "do the right thing by" her children. These people quite explicitly did not want to squander a single dollar of their hard-earned money on taxes to enforce standards for day care centers. Day care, after all, is a service for other people's children.

But we all know the statistics. More than half of all mothers of preschoolers work outside the home, and by the turn of the century, that figure will increase to 70 percent. Roughly three out of five women in the work force have children too young to care for themselves. Millions of mothers are single and cannot, except under the rarest and most fortunate of circumstances, afford to stay home full-time with their children. While there are an estimated thirty-five million children under the age of fourteen whose mothers work, there are only five million licensed or registered day care slots to put them in. Certainly, many of the children not in one of these slots, more than one-fifth, are cared for by a relative, and another 6 percent are cared for by a babysitter at home. Almost 15 percent are cared for by their fathers, most of them sharing split shifts with the children's mothers. Nine percent are cared for by mothers while they work, an experience that I, who have cradled a nursing baby in one arm while typing with the other and talking on the phone, can only compare to a feat of extreme athleticism.

But this does not account for all the children. We have heard about those other children, left to fend for themselves or worse while their parents work. And we also know that, as a nation, we're pretty much ignoring them. Few employers offer special breaks or benefits to working parents. We do not have a national parental leave policy, and few employers feel moved to provide adequate ones on their own. We hurry most women out of the hospital within forty-eight hours after they give birth, provide their families with little or no support when they return home, and then demand that they go back to work within weeks or risk losing their jobs. What these "other people," these working parents, do with their children, we seem to have decided, is their business.

My purpose in writing this book is to take a closer look at these "other people," these working parents, and their kids. I chose to focus my attention not on the families struggling outside the system, who are forced to abandon their children to unsafe circumstances, but on families who were lucky enough to have found not a reprieve but a niche. I have focused my sights on a day care center because organized, center-based care is the fastest-growing segment of the child-care industry. One out of four working parents with young children use day care centers, nearly twice the number that did so just a decade ago, and the percentage is growing. There are, after all, fewer grandmothers free to mind grandchildren, and fewer homebound moms willing to baby-sit for a neighbor. Center-based care is clearly the most practical and efficient way to serve large numbers of families. Indeed, many parents who are, in principle, resistant to institutionalized care for their young children find themselves with no alternative but to use it.

I am one of those parents. My oldest daughter, Alison, was just over two years old when I thrust her full-time into a day care center. Like many parents, I was frightened, confused, guilt-ridden, and a little desperate at the time. Alison had, from the age of eight weeks, been in the care of Lee, a family day care provider who had taught high school mathematics in China before following her husband to this country as he pursued a Ph.D. at the Massachusetts Institute of Technology. It seemed, at first, like the perfect arrangement. My husband was working at MIT at the time, and I was studying there on a journalism fellowship. Lee lived and worked just a few steps away from my office, and I could visit Alison whenever I liked. But after Alison celebrated her second birthday, Lee seemed to lose interest in her, preferring instead to focus most of her energy on her own four-year-old daughter. When another mother pointed out that Alison seemed bored and a little listless in Lee's care, I was shocked into action. I decided to get Alison into a day care center within the week. (Now I recognize the absurdity of that overreaction, but at the time it made sense.) I made a few frantic phone calls and made an appointment to visit one day care center, the only center with an opening, the next day.

Like many parents, I had read little and knew less about day care and day care centers. I had never set foot inside a day care center before, and my evaluation of this one was based entirely on intuition. The place felt good to me. Unlike many centers, it was not housed in a basement. It was sun drenched, well equipped, and cheerful. The kids seemed happy and constructively occupied. The director was a trained pediatric nurse who had two kids of her own. The head teacher was well educated, energetic, and compassionate and had ten years of experience with young children. She was warm, easy to talk to, and also had a daughter. We seemed to share the same values and goals for our children. In less than an hour of stumbling about asking uninformed questions, I became convinced that the center was all that I had hoped for: a stimulating, loving, secure environment for my daughter. I quickly forked over two months' tuition, and Alison began school the next day.

Of course, that morning's introduction gave me not a clue to the inner workings of the place where my daughter was to spend forty hours a week for the next two years of her life. As it often turns out, things were not what they seemed. The head teacher who so impressed me left less than a month after my visit to join her boyfriend on a cross-country peace march. She was replaced by a far less sympathetic young woman who had a master's degree in early childhood education but little teaching experience and less patience. And although the center's tuition was high, even by Boston's exorbitant standards, the teachers were poorly paid. This forced several of them to take night jobs, which, combined with their daytime duties, brought them near to collapse by day's end, just when the children were closing in on meltdown.

I watched all this nervously from the sidelines, hoping the smoke would clear and that my daughter would emerge unscathed, maybe even made stronger by the exposure to imperfect people in an imperfect organization. It never occurred to me to take action or to spend more than thirty minutes at the school after my initial visit. I looked to Alison to let me know if anything was really troublesome, never really bothering to consider the wisdom of giving such a weighty responsibility to a two-and-a-half-year-old child. Indeed, Alison seemed to thrive in day care. But "seemed" is the operative word. Like many working parents, I was too busy, too caught up in my own struggles, to get deeply involved in the details of my child's daily life in day care. Most of what she did there, and how it affected her, will remain forever a mystery to me.

Researching this book has, among many other things, given me insight into that mysterious world, albeit not my daughter's particular corner of it. It has allowed me to be the eyes and ears for working parents who, as I do, spend countless hours each month reconsidering and worrying about their child-care decisions. I have focused my attention on one center, Cambridgeport Children's Center, having spent the better part of the 1989/90 school year observing and talking to children and teachers and parents there. I was given pretty much free access to the school, which is the hub of a few troubled and many fascinating lives.

Cambridgeport Children's Center, or "Tot Lot," as it is more commonly known, is perhaps best described by what it is not. It is not a gourmet center, catering to families who demand and can afford the best of everything. It is not a model, university-based center, bustling with Ph.D.s in early-childhood education and fawned over by eager graduate students. It is not a municipally funded center or a church-operated center. It is not a corporate center. It is not a chain center. It is not entrenched in some utopian past; it has changed with the times and with the needs of its clientele. It is, for better or worse, a community center in a neighborhood that is diverse, complex, and contentious; a neighborhood of poor, middle-class, and affluent families, some of whom have careers, aspirations, and commitment, some of whom just have bills to pay. Cambridgeport Children's Center is not meant to be representative; it is, as all places where children spend their time should be, a special place, like no place else. But the struggles here, for power, for love, for survival, are basic and universal. No parent, no family, will fail to identify with at least some of them.

Cambridgeport Children's Center is a most deliberately multicultural school, a crazy salad of ethnicity where differences among children and families are not minimized but celebrated. Like an increasing number of Americans, the families of Tot Lot have not immersed themselves in the melting pot to be simmered down into so much bland stew. In Cambridge, as in many urban centers throughout the country, populations have voluntarily segmented into subgroups that cannot and will not blend. For millions of families, the day care center has become the first line of entry into American life. Accommodating the needs, customs, and values of these different cultures is an enormously difficult challenge, an experiment in socialization of which the outcome is yet unknown.

The children and parents and teachers I highlight in this book were chosen because I found their stories both telling and compelling. They are mostly unalike, but they do share one thing: an unwillingness to allow the system to wash over them. While not necessarily winners in the conventional sense, they are most definitely survivors in the best sense. The families in these pages share with all working families the terrible and relentless pressures of time, yet they were incredibly generous in their willingness to share a bit of this precious commodity with me. With some, like the Torroella and Thompson Barth families,

I spent many hours, at work, at school, and at home, and, more rarely, at stolen moments of leisure. With others, like the Brissetteses, I spent what time they could spare, squeezing in cups of coffee at odd moments or spending an evening with them at their church. For allowing me entry into their busy lives, I am grateful. But it was not for me that they agreed to this enormous intrusion. Their hope, and mine, is that our time together will illuminate the larger issues of families and work and the care of children that have been the center of debate in this country for decades and will, most likely, continue to be the center of debate for decades to come. Their hope and mine is that this glimpse of "other people's children" will help us all to recognize these children not only as others', but as ours.

Prologue

PESTO AND PLUMBING

Summer

SUSAN Boisen tiptoes out of her office, past the row of overflowing cubbies, and into the kitchen. She often comes to this room for the excellent view it affords of the preschool classroom. Positioned strategically between refrigerator and dishwasher, she is almost invisible to the teachers and children. Standing here, she can feel the voyeur.

But this afternoon, her eye is not on people but on plumbing. She watches grimly as brown water drips steadily from the faucet into a sink full of milk-rimmed cups and scummy bowls.

"I called the water department this morning," she says. "They say the water often turns brown on street-cleaning days."

Street-cleaning day in this part of Cambridge is the first Monday of every month. Today is the second Tuesday in July, but Susan doesn't quibble. She knows, given that two of the toilets in the preschool room are clogged, that a plumber will have to be called anyway. She'll worry tomorrow about where the money will come from to pay for it. Cambridgeport Children's Center is open year-round, but September is the psychological starting point. Susan would like to give the impression by then that things are under control.

It's 1:15 P.M., fifteen minutes into naptime, and the littlest ones, the one-and-a-half- and two-year-olds, are already asleep in the toddler room, huddled into their mats like newborns. Susan casts her eye over the older children, the preschoolers, squirming in twisted clumps, doing battle with their blankets. They are three and four and five years old. Linda, Marina, and Margaret, their teachers, lie beside them, rubbing backs and stroking heads, coaxing them to quiet. The teachers, their eyes half-closed in vacant daydreams, appear somewhat more fatigued than the children.

Susan leaves the kitchen and slips into her office. As director, she is entitled to a private space, but her office is not private. Everyone who walks in the front door detours there to complain or question or chat. Susan doesn't mind; the place brightens with people. It is small and cramped with a window overlooking the neglected backyard of the MIT fraternity house next door. There's a gray metal desk, a black metal vertical file cabinet and a dirt-colored plastic-and-metal chair, the bulging guts of which are bandaged with multiple turns of silver duct tape. There's a bulletin board heavy with notices from various state agencies. Susan stares at her desk. Is it possible that the pile of unanswered mail and forms has deepened since she stepped out less than fifteen minutes before? She sits down halfheartedly, her hands hovering over the mess, as if willing it to disappear.

Susan is small boned and slim and always well dressed, better dressed, one might think, than a person in her line of work needs to be. She wears skirts and dresses and sharply pressed trousers with pleats and, often, patent leather shoes. Susan says she dresses formally because her work clothes are in the laundry, but that explanation only goes so far. The truth is, Susan would as soon leave the house in a pair of men's striped pajamas as she would in a wrinkled T-shirt or ragged jeans.

Susan's mother is half Mennonite and half Amish, but you wouldn't know it from looking at her daughter. Susan is swarthy like her father, who is Jewish and was born in Brooklyn. She has her father's sense of humor, which is droll and secret. When she smiles, which is often, her whole face gets into the act, her large eyes narrowing into crescents and the bridge of her nose crinkling into laugh lines. Her thick, kinky brown hair is usually

11

pulled back into a ponytail that bobs and flicks at her waist. The ponytail looks out of place hanging down the back of a thirty-four-year-old woman in pressed linen slacks.

Susan has worked in day care centers for nine years, mostly as a director. She has a master's degree in elementary education, but she tries not to let it get in her way. Anyone who took graduate school too seriously, she says, wouldn't last a week in this job. So far, she has lasted two years.

The phone rings, and Susan picks up the receiver. It's the father of a three-year-old boy who is on the waiting list for a slot in the preschool room. Susan listens, fiddles with a paper clip, rolls her eyes toward the ceiling, and gently informs the caller that a September opening looks highly unlikely. She reminds him that it is already July and the waiting list hasn't budged. The father says he suspected as much. He's called before and more than once. He was just hoping that there had been some change. Susan says no, things are the same, but agrees to take down his phone number and address in case an opening somehow materializes. Susan hates to disappoint people, but lately that's seemed like a big part of her job.

It's 1:25 P.M. Molly Fontaine walks into the office to ask whether Susan wants to split a cheese pizza from Stephani's, the Greek sub shop around the corner. Molly is lean, with straight brown hair pulled back with a force that seems to have arched her eyebrows. She is forty, older than the others, nearly twice the age of the two other full-time toddler teachers. She has lived in the Boston area all her life and speaks in the native drawl with the voice of experience. She has come to Susan's office to talk toilets. Today's clog problem, she ventures, has something to do with trees. Last night's thundershower made the towering chestnuts of Chestnut Street sprout new roots that have poked their way through the center's aging water pipes. There's only one solution that she can see, and it's a damn expensive one — Roto-Rooter. Roto-Rooter, Molly knows, charges something like a hundred dollars a clog. It's a lot of money, but what choice do they have? Unless that toilet gets fixed soon, they'll be putting diapers on the preschoolers. The thought of four-year-old Luke strapping on a diaper makes Molly laugh out loud, and Susan's worried look collapses into a grin.

Marina Bonie pops her head in the door, interrupting. Marina is twenty-six, a teacher in the preschool room. Marina was born and grew up in Italy, in a villa just outside of Florence. She is striking, with delicately freckled white skin and long, wavy red hair. She wears baggy harem pants, a tank top, and black high-top sneakers. She is dramatically slim yet voluptuous. It's easy to imagine Marina out on the town, turning heads.

Marina makes the proud announcement that there is no need to order pizza, that she has made pasta with pesto for lunch today. Her smile is crooked and gleeful. Susan and Molly leave Susan's office and join the other teachers in the preschool room at two Formica tables. The tables are crusty with dried finger paint and modeling clay. The chairs are tiny, driving the teachers' knees nearly to their chins. The preschoolers toss and turn in the red-rug area just steps away, well within earshot. Marina lugs the green-coated spaghetti from the kitchen in an oversized metal bowl, mentioning that the oil for the pesto was pressed from olives picked from trees in her family grove in Italy. She says she plucked the basil just moments ago from the center's roof garden.

José, a new part-time toddler teacher, seems impressed. He immediately mounds a huge portion of pasta and sauce on his plate and eats in silence. Between bites, he munches on a hot chili pepper. José is from Mexico. He wears a red bandanna around his neck and carries a chili pepper with him at all times, as protection against bland food.

Julia Hogan, another part-time toddler teacher, is encountering pesto for the first time. She is twenty-six and has worked in the center for five years, longer than anyone aside from Molly. Generally speaking, she is leery of novelties. She had never heard of rice crackers or tofu before coming to the center. But now she finds that she actually likes some of those things. She's decided to be a sport about the pesto, washing down dainty bites with raspberry ginger ale. But, unlike the other teachers, she gets no gratification from the homegrown aspects of the dish. The fact that the oil came from Marina's family orchard and the basil from the center's roof garden leaves her cold: she'd just as soon eat sauce from a jar.

"See, day care workers are so poor," she says, smirking slyly into her plate, "that they have to grow their own food."

Susan cranes her neck to steal a glimpse at the wall clock. It's 1:45, less than an hour until wake-up time. Susan pushes her plate aside and gets down to work; the first order of business is what to do about Ben.

Ben is twenty-eight, soft spoken, intense, and committed. He is patient, precise, and consistent. He is an active listener. He is a lively, imaginative storyteller. He is, all agree, a gifted teacher. He resigned from the center last month.

"How are we are going to replace Ben?" Susan asks. It is less a question than a lament.

Ben has a master's degree in early-childhood education and was the only full-time teacher on staff with an academic grounding in the field. The other teachers used him as a resource, someone whom they could count on to know about child development and psychology. He could talk Piaget and Erikson. But Ben also had an undergraduate degree in economics, and it was that background that got him thinking about changing careers.

"I love working with children," Ben said before he left. "I love their openness, their egocentricity, the freshness they bring to everything. I enjoy forging bonds with them and with their families. But as an economist, I can't help having a graph in my head, and that graph includes wages. My salary here is very low, but that's not the whole issue. There is no pension plan, no career ladder. As things stand now, day care is not a career."

Ben is getting married next month and will start a doctoral program at Tufts University in the fall. Susan is happy for him. But she is also worried. She scatters a handful of résumés like playing cards among the half-empty plates of pasta. The teachers scan the neatly typed papers and eye each other ironically. Not one of the applicants has had any experience with young children. Those who can write coherently give clear clues that day care is not their career of choice. One applicant, recently graduated with a science degree from a local university, writes that she thinks she might enjoy dabbling in day care before applying to medical school. Another, with a degree in business administration, lists frying up chicken at a fast-food franchise as her only work experience and her career goal as "doing something good for other people."

Susan sighs. The state, she says, used to pay for courses to help qualify people as day care teachers, but those programs were cut back because of lack of funds two or three months ago. As of now, things don't look promising. Good teachers are getting harder and harder to find.

"Maybe the budget cuts are inhibiting people from applying," she says. "Maybe they are afraid that the job will get pulled out from under them."

Marina and Molly nod their heads. They've been fielding questions from frantic parents all week. Everyone wants to know what's happening with state funding. Susan says she doesn't know when or by how much or even if the center's budget will be cut. She hasn't heard anything beyond what's been in the newspaper. What's getting her, she says, is Michael Dukakis. The governor says he cares about kids. In his failed bid for the presidency, he was extravagant in his support of federal aid for day care. But now the state is broke and there is no money to put where the governor's mouth was on the campaign trail: the previous month, more than $250 million was cut from children's services, and more is slated to be cut in the coming year. Of the state's eight thousand subsidized day care slots, three thousand are on the cusp of extinction.

Eight of Cambridgeport Children's Center's thirteen toddlers are subsidized by the state, as are ten of the twenty preschoolers. In fact, fewer than half of the kids pay full tuition. The center isn't cheap — $175 a week for toddlers, $145 a week for preschoolers. Still, Susan says she could find private payers to fill all the vacated slots. The man on the phone, for one, would be delighted. But filling the place is not the point. The point is, Cambridgeport Children's Center is committed to having a multiracial, multiethnic group of kids — and not one of the African-American or Hispanic or Haitian children at the school is a private payer. If the state makes good on its threat to cut the

15

subsidized slots, the center will lose its ethnic and economic diversity.

"The day care centers in the suburbs won't mind that at all," Margaret sneers. "Most of them haven't even filled their subsidized slots."

Julia squirms in her seat. Margaret lives in one of Boston's swankiest suburbs, driving her beat-up old Volvo to the city each morning and retiring to the quiet of her garden each night. Yet her disdain for the middle class sometimes spills over into her treatment of the children. Parents have complained that Margaret's values sometimes overwhelm her compassion. And Julia, who grew up and lives in one of Boston's toughest neighborhoods, sees right through her.

Still, no one would argue that Margaret is wrong on this point. Suburban centers have subsidized slots, but they aren't always filled with needy kids — sometimes they are just left open. The bulk of the burden of caring for children of the working poor falls on urban centers like Tot Lot. Susan says that if Tot Lot's budget gets cut, she won't be able to take on the toddlers she's admitted for the fall. That means that Claude and Marcia and Carlos will go.

Marina is incensed — she feels the need to do something. She talks of organizing a march on the state house to demand that the cuts be reconsidered. Molly looks cool; this is not a new idea. Marina and some of the other teachers escorted eighteen kids to a rally at the state house the previous April. The effectiveness of that protest, if anyone wondered, was made pretty clear by this year's cuts. Marina suggests a shutdown. Susan leans forward, her hands folded on the table. She's only half-listening. She knows there will be no shutdown. There has been brave talk like this before, talk of teachers walking out of day care centers across the state. Why not? Public school teachers do it. Even nurses do it. But day care teachers have never done it, and they probably never will. They fear for the children. If they close the centers, they know some children will be left home alone.

Julia checks out the paint job on her fingernails. There is, she thinks, nothing she can do about all this, and she sees no point in getting involved in a philosophical discussion. She changes the subject. She wonders out loud if it's really necessary for the center to keep saving bottles and cans. They clutter up the place, she says, and they are unsanitary. With all there is to do, do they really have time for recycling? It is obvious that the question is directed at Margaret.

Margaret is twenty-seven, a graduate of Wellesley College with a master's degree from Harvard University Divinity School. She is an ardent feminist, a strict vegetarian, and a committed environmentalist. Every week, she dutifully packs her Volvo with center refuse and carts it to the recycling center near her home. She promises Julia that she will make sure that things don't pile quite so high, and she requests that they all be careful to rinse cans and bottles so that the garbage doesn't, as Julia suggests, serve as cockroach fodder. Julia shrugs. She'll be damned if she's going to waste time rinsing out old juice bottles and cottage cheese containers.

In a rare stab at tact, Margaret lightens the tension with an amusing announcement: the Massachusetts Department of Nutrition has finally designated yogurt as a "meat." Tot Lot can now serve yogurt in place of cheeseburgers or hot dogs and still pass nutritional muster. This is good news, given the center's vegetarian policy, a policy set years ago and maintained out of habit as much as conviction. Someone asks about tofu, and Margaret's smile dims. Tofu, she says, remains in nutritional limbo — as far as the authorities are concerned, it is not a food. Putting a palm to the side of her face, Marie breathes "amen" in Julia's direction, and Julia chuckles. Julia and Marie are both partial to pepperoni pizza and ribs.

Susan reminds everyone that there will be thirteen new kids starting in the center in the fall, making parent orientation particularly important. Then, bracing herself but trying to look offhandish, she mentions that several of the parents have asked for a few changes — for example, they want teachers to post the day's activities. The silence lasts about twenty seconds. Julia is the first to boil over.

"They think we got that kind of time to waste?" She bristles. "Why don't they ask their own kids what they do every day?

17

Why don't they ask us? Most of them don't even bother to take home their kid's art work. They just leave it in the cubby or toss it in the trash on their way out."

Molly can't abide this kind of talk, the kind that puts blame on the parents. She cuts in, saying that kids aren't always in the mood for a chat when they get home from preschool. She says young children are more likely to say that they did "nothing" rather than deal with the hassle of remembering the details of their day. But Molly doesn't like the idea of activity charts either. Posting a daily activity list is something the day care center chains do, to reassure parents that the children's every waking moment is spent in constructive activity. Lists don't mean anything — to Molly they are window dressing at best.

"You know, I don't think it's so great, parents knowing every little thing their kids do all day," she says. "They need privacy."

It's almost 2:30, time to wake up the few kids who aren't already whispering and giggling and poking at each other. Marina and Marie push away from the table and head toward their charges. José, his shift over, gets up, rinses his plate in the sink, and leaves. Molly, whose shift began at eight o'clock that morning, is also supposed to go home, but she stays on to help rouse the sleepy toddlers. She'll stay until the kids find their bearings and Julia has started the afternoon activity. She never lets the toddlers wake up without her if she can help it.

Susan reluctantly steels herself to dig into the pile of paperwork in her office. What with the uncertainty over state funding, she has no idea what her true operating budget will be for the fall, no idea whether the center can afford to hire the new teachers she's trying to recruit or even the classified advertisements to lure them. She's worried about Linda, a preschool teacher who said nothing at that day's staff meeting. Linda is often silent. It seems she will do anything to avoid confrontation. Even so, Linda appears to be having trouble getting along with Margaret, and Susan is braced for an explosion. Ben had issues with Margaret, too, as do some of the parents. Margaret can be harsh sometimes, but she is a creative, intelligent teacher, particularly good with the minority kids, and Susan can't afford to lose her, especially now, with Ben's job to fill. And soon there will be another vacancy: Heather, another toddler teacher says she's leaving at the end of August to join a friend in southern California. But, who knows? Maybe Mother Teresa will waltz in tomorrow, begging for a job. Or maybe, Susan thinks out loud, she'll be on to something new herself. "You know," she says dreamily, "I'm not about to spend my entire life in this place." She smiles, looks wistful and then worried. She gathers her calendar and papers and heads back to the office. On the way, she stops at the kitchen. She glares at the sink as though at an old enemy. She gives the faucet a yank. The water gushes fast and brown. Molly was right — time to call Roto-Rooter.

THE third week in August, José comes into Susan's office and closes the door. He tells her he is taking a sabbatical. He's going home to Mexico to help his mother and brother straighten up some family business. He doesn't know when he'll be back, but he promises to return, probably in October. Susan fiddles with some papers. José is not yet entitled to a week's vacation, let alone an open-ended "sabbatical." But she doesn't tell him this. Clearly, he is not one to negotiate. She is fairly sure that José will not return, anyway.

José is short and strongly built, with straight black hair and deep black eyes that are alternately flashing and hooded. He does not measure his Indian blood in drops. He wears a cap, even in summer, and a black leather jacket with studs on it. He prides himself on being a man of mystery.

When he was hired, José claimed to have had plenty of experience with kids, but now no one is quite sure how far that experience extended beyond caring for his own two children, one of whom, Julio, is a student in the preschool room. José says he is working toward a master's degree in ethnography at Boston University, but that, too, is cloudy. As far as Susan knows, he has no training or coursework in early-childhood education. Because he is only a part-time teacher, this is not considered critical. The center's hiring committee, made up of Susan, a few parents, and two other teachers, selected him in late spring partly because he seemed okay with the kids but mostly because he is a

Spanish-speaking man. There are several Spanish-speaking boys at the center who they thought would benefit from a strong father figure. Unfortunately, it's gradually become clear that Julio is one of these boys. He is skittish and has the odd habit of pulling his hair out by the fistful.

There is no pasta today at the staff meeting, just sandwiches and yogurt from the convenience store down the street. It's too hot to cook, and besides, the basil is long gone.

There is good news. Cambridgeport has been awarded a $3,000 grant to develop a work curriculum for preschoolers, to be written up and published in journal form for the Cambridge Literacy Curriculum Connections Program. The purpose is to teach children about different kinds of jobs, to give them some idea of what grown-ups do all day and of how this relates to the world around them. Molly, especially, is excited about this.

"Most people I've met don't like their jobs," she says. "So they see no reason to tell their kids what they do."

Years ago, Molly says, she had a two-year-old in her group whose mother worked downtown in a pillow factory. The mother wasn't proud of what she did and never told her daughter about it.

"All that child knew was that her mother took the subway," Molly says.

So one day Molly asked the woman to come and talk about her work. The mother balked at first — how interesting could pillow stuffing sound to little kids? But eventually she came. She explained to the kids about sewing machines. She told them what pillows were made of. She even brought pillow cases for the children to use as covers for their sleep mats. Everyone had a good time, and from that day the little girl knew that her mother didn't just ride the subway. She learned that the subway took her mother to work.

Molly relishes this parable, and she tells it slowly, repeating bits and embellishing as she goes along. As she talks, Margaret and Linda look increasingly tense; they've heard the story before. Both Linda, who is trained as a kindergarten teacher, and Margaret are hungry for structure. The work curriculum promises to help fill that need. It is their pet project, and they'd just as soon get on with it without the benefit of Molly's two cents.

Susan runs her eyes down her yellow pad to the next agenda item: personnel. There hasn't been a single applicant for Ben's job worth interviewing, she says, and Heather will be leaving soon. The center is sorely understaffed. Marie has kindly offered to extend her commitment from working part- to full-time in the preschool room, juggling her courses at the University of Massachusetts at Boston to make room for the additional hours. Margaret and Linda seem pleased, but Susan knows that Margaret is secretly unnerved at the prospect of spending six hours a day with Marie. Marie is large and boisterous and given to speaking her mind. Susan hopes that Marie will be the one finally to put Margaret in her place.

Fortunately, one staff position, at least, has been filled. Nancy, a recent graduate of a state-sponsored program that trains low-income adults for jobs in day care, will work mornings in the toddler room with Molly. Nancy has taken courses in the Montessori method of preschool teaching and, the teachers agree, seems eager to learn. She lacks direction and organization, but that will come with experience. She is also the mother of a three-year-old daughter, whom, for now, she is raising alone. The teachers want her to have this job.

Susan mentions that José is leaving the following week for an extended leave. Molly is not afraid to glare. It is the toddlers, her kids, who will have to deal with the loss. She tells José not to forget to say good-bye to the children well before he goes. José looks at her as though she were crazy. He says he would never forget.

Susan takes a bite of egg salad, clears her throat, and gets on to a bit of difficult news: Zack will not be at the center in the fall. Zack is a kid in the preschool room. He is large for his age and beautiful, with huge brown eyes and sandy brown hair that falls just below his eyebrows. Susan has told Zack's mother that the center could do nothing more for her son. He doesn't do well in groups. He's disruptive. The other children are afraid of him.

Marina interrupts. She says she thinks Zack is neglected,

perhaps even abused, at home. No one looks surprised — they all know this. But there is no proof and it would be futile to report mere suspicions to the Department of Social Services. Zack is angry and sad, but he is not starved or visibly beaten by his parents. His clothes are not ragged, and his lunchbox is always packed. There is no case to be made to the authorities.

The teachers agree that things will get worse for Zack, much worse. His father is a drug addict and alcoholic, and his mother is chronically depressed. When she is between jobs, which is often, she drops Zack off at the center and goes home to bed. Susan thinks she sleeps most of the day. Susan knows the mother won't be able to get her act together to deal with a child at home. But Zack has run out of options. "I hate to see a child with nowhere to go," she says. "I know that he is in danger. But I have no choice."

Marie looks up from her sandwich. She teaches preschoolers in the afternoons, and she sees Zack's mother at pick-up time, groggy and disoriented. Marie knows what it's like to be poor and misunderstood. She was three when she moved to this country, the same age as Zack is now. Her parents fled Haiti because there was no longer anything to hope for there. They moved to New York City where they found jobs and the means to educate their children. But sometimes Marie wonders if things are all that much better here. In Haiti, there is outside trouble, political trouble, but here the trouble comes from within. Parents who treat their own children like strangers — this, to her, is beyond imagination. Even though she is twenty-four, her parents' eyes follow her wherever she goes. Even here, two hundred miles away, she can feel them watching over her.

"Sometimes I look at some of these parents and think, hey, just give me your kid, I'll take him home," she says. "We'll write you postcards and send snapshots, and you can have him back when he's old enough to defend himself, say, when he's twenty-one."

One

SIT AND SPIN

WHAT was odd about the first day of school was the peace. There were no tantrums, no fights, barely a whimper when parents left, many reluctantly, heading for subway or car or bike. The children, shy and swaggering, delicate and bold, milled among each other like puppies. But most of them did not cry. Crying and tantrums, Molly said, would come later. They have to feel a bit braver for that. It's now a month later, the first week in October, and most of them are feeling brave enough.

Thirty-three children aged fifteen months to five years attend Cambridgeport Children's Center, and the youngest of these, the toddlers, are in Molly Fontaine's charge. Molly's job is to see that thirteen children under the age of three are toileted, changed, and fed, comforted and disciplined, entertained and enlightened. Her days are spent settling property disputes, negotiating tiny deals, bolstering bruised egos, and nursing wounded feelings. In between, she teaches. She has worked at Cambridgeport Children's Center for six years and in day care for twice that number. That makes her a rare veteran in a field where 40 percent of people leave their jobs in less than a year. More than one person has characterized her as a martyr, but

Molly doesn't see it that way. The way Molly sees it, she's simply doing her job.

"My number-one priority is helping kids learn self-esteem," Molly says. "Once they've got that, the rest is easy."

She points to a long, low bench made of varnished wood. It stands poised at the far end of the toy-strewn toddler room, anchoring one end of a torn, mud-colored rug. Each year, on the first day of school, Molly lays out a plan. Her goal is to have every squirming toddler bottom planted squarely on that bench before snacktime each morning. The purpose is to introduce the concepts of self-control and cooperation. Each child will learn to sit a few moments to listen and share. Given the confused mass of small bodies bouncing around her this morning, the challenge appears Herculean.

It is before nine o'clock, free-play time. A Raffi recording of "Mr. Sun" spins on the record player. Raffi is a preschool music idol who specializes in rocked-up versions of old nursery favorites. Most of the children pay the music no mind, except for Claude, who bounces to the beat. Claude is two, and he doesn't talk much, but he dances with abandon. Dancing and tickling are the two things that he seems to like best. Claude is so independent and private that the teachers can only speculate about what goes on inside his head. But when he is dancing or rolling around the floor enjoying a good hard tickle, his African mask of a face cracks open, and the little kid peeks out.

Free play is almost over when Carlos's mother arrives. It is cool, well into autumn, but Carlos's mother has walked to the center bare legged, wearing only a wispy housedress and bedroom slippers. Monica, her daughter, a student in the preschool room, is also lightly dressed. But Carlos is more than snug. He wears jeans and two shirts, and the hood of his sweatshirt is pulled tightly around his face. He is half-asleep and, cradled in his mother's arms, looks even younger than his seventeen months.

Carlos's mom makes no apology for being late. She smiles shyly at Molly and then carries her son straight over to José, who stands, hands on hips, in the back of the room near the windows. José speaks Spanish to Carlos in low, soothing tones. Carlos appears both comforted and confused. José is only recently returned from his two-month sojourn in Mexico, and Carlos is as yet uncertain of what to make of him. When his mother tries to pass him over to José, the boy's back stiffens, and his eyes open wide. His mother immediately takes him back, tickles him, and holds him close. She, too, is ambivalent, not because she mistrusts José, but because Carlos is her youngest, her baby. She gives Carlos a hug and a look of longing. She smooths his hair with her fingers. She promises to pick him up early. She stays and stays. And then, suddenly, she leaves. She closes the door behind her.

Carlos lets out a scream that would wake the dead. It is a scream to wrench hearts. All heads turn toward him. The children stare, not out of empathy, but curiosity. Carlos's performance is instructive. He has put himself in the limelight. Later, perhaps, they will do the same. José wraps his arms tightly around Carlos and whispers to him softly in Spanish. The scream dies into a wail and then a whimper. Carlos curls into José's arms.

Dawn stares blandly at Carlos and returns to her play. At two and a half, she is one of the oldest toddlers, and she looks it, with well-defined features and no baby fat. She is delicate, with thin legs and a concave belly and fair hair that stands out in wisps around her tiny, puckish face. Dawn is a little girl with a mission, that being to collect every stray toy in the room and place it in a mound. Dawn decides what qualifies as stray, and her definition is quite liberal. Any toy not tightly clenched in the fist of another child makes the cut. Not that Dawn is above unclenching a fist or two to get what she wants. It's just that there are so many toys to gather, and so little time to gather them before a teacher takes notice, that Dawn chooses not to waste precious minutes squabbling. Her usual ploy is to wait quietly until another child drops a toy and then to claim it as her own.

Once Dawn has amassed a really big pile, she likes to sit down beside it, not to admire it, but to guard it. Other kids who dare to come near are quickly rebuffed, sometimes with a kick. At naptime, she stuffs as many things under her mat as she can. Molly and the other teachers try to limit her naptime stash to a book or two, but often Dawn manages to squeeze in a half-dozen toys before they take notice. She stays awake as long as possible in order to keep an eye on the loot. Usually, she's the last child in the room to drift off. Sometimes, she'll sneak another child's blanket or personal sleep toy into the pile. This causes extreme distress to the victim and throws the teachers into a frantic search. When the toy or blanket is discovered under Dawn's mat, Dawn looks blank and innocent, as though she's never set eyes on the thing before in her life. She shows no remorse.

No one is certain just why Dawn adopted this habit of hoarding. One teacher suggests that perhaps it's because Dawn feels the need to possess things now that her parents have left each other. Dawn, she thought, has somehow gotten caught in the cross fire of their separation, which is sometimes so noisy it can be heard even at Tot Lot. But Molly is not convinced by this reasoning. Maybe Dawn is just a greedy kid, she says. You can't blame everything on the parents. In any case, Dawn is only two — she's not doomed to a life of crime just yet.

Free play is over, and it's time for morning circle. May doesn't want to sit in circle today, and she hovers, lower lip quivering, on the periphery. May is chubby, with black-brown eyes and hair riddled with cowlicks that resist taming with comb or brush. She and her twin sister, Felise, who has just finished with a puzzle, couldn't be less alike. Felise is calm and sure of herself. When something worries her, she gets a puzzled look, as if attempting to work it out. May is physical and impatient. When something worries her, she falls apart. Felise can talk fairly fluently. May can barely get out a word. Felise enjoys looking at picture books. May likes pushing furniture around. The sisters are ten weeks short of their second birthday, which falls on Christmas Day. They are Chilean, born of a farm laborer who couldn't afford to keep them. They live in Cambridge with their adoptive parents, Patricia and Bruce Weissman, who flew with them here from Chile just over a year before.

At breakfast this morning, May spilled milk all over herself and then fell backward out of her chair. She has a cold, and her nose hasn't stopped running all week. Patricia felt a little guilty bringing her to the center, but if she kept May home for every cold, she'd never get any work done. May seems to have the sniffles most of the time. During free-play time, May was teary eyed and uncooperative. And now she simply refuses to join the other toddlers in morning circle. She cries and cries. Nancy, the new toddler teacher, has lost patience. She hoists May up as though she were a weepy rag doll and carries her to circle, propping her up next to Dawn. May lets out a scream to rival that of Carlos, who now sits sweating in his hot clothes, still clinging to José. Molly's eyebrows arch and a pair of parallel lines streak across her forehead. She grabs a strand of hair and twists it around and around her index finger. She believes that Nancy has done exactly the wrong thing. But she doesn't say so. Instead, she gets up slowly, casually skims her palms over her jeans as if to brush off cake crumbs, and crosses the circle to May's side. She silences the scream with an embrace. The room relaxes.

Molly has planned a special activity. She has brought a tube of hand cream. The children squeeze a bit of cream into each of their own palms and then rub it into the palms of the children sitting next to them. This lesson in sharing and gentle touching is a smash hit with the kids. Even aloof Claude manages to smear a bit of goo on Christopher before breaking down into a fit of hilarity.

After circle, the children have a choice. They can scoop cornmeal with spoons and plastic cups or build with thorny-looking plastic objects called Bristle Blocks or string beads on a thong. Each activity focuses on fine motor control, the bringing together of the fingers and the mind; each is a tiny lesson in cause and effect. Not all the children are able to string beads, so Molly encourages them to treat the square beads like blocks by piling them into towers. Not all the children can get the cornmeal back into the bowl, so Molly puts down a tray to catch the overflow. There is no right or wrong way to do anything; each child is allowed to find his own way, even if it means standing by and watching while another child plays. In any case, fine motor activities require coordination and concentration, qualities not found in abundance in most toddlers. Molly knows she has twenty minutes at most to get them ready for another circle and then lunch. Meanwhile, Nancy circulates stealthily, scouting out kids one by one for a diaper change. Molly swabs the changing table with disinfectant. Nancy swoops a toddler into the changing room and dumps him or her playfully onto the table. Molly unsnaps the overalls, whips off the old diaper, tosses it into a pail, whips on a new diaper, snaps up the pants, gives the child a hug, and lowers him or her to the floor. The entire process takes about sixty seconds, and, all the time, Molly is talking and smiling. Some teachers resent changing diapers, and many day care centers won't take children until they are toilet trained. But Molly enjoys the chore — it gives her a chance to get close to each kid every day.

Molly steals a glimpse at her watch, notes that it's almost time for lunch. She sits down in the center of the thin gray rug, crosses her legs swami style, and begins an incantation. "Sit on the bench, the bench says sit on me." She chants in a gravelly, mechanical monotone that she calls her robot voice. The kids are mesmerized. Gradually, they untangle themselves from the beads and cornmeal and Bristle Blocks and, as if possessed, toddle over to the famous bench. Each takes a seat expectantly, like a tiny patron at the symphony. Only Claude and Marcia remain standing, shaky and uncertain, waiting to be guided to their seats. It will be some time before they manage to find their places at the bench alone.

Molly has the children regroup after every activity. She knows from experience that many toddlers find transitions scary and disorienting. During transitions classrooms break down; it's when children wander off or get in fights or start crying for no reason, when teachers lose their tempers, when, as Molly puts it, "all hell breaks loose." So Molly softens the blow of change by giving the kids a haven, a place to go, time and again, for instruction and support. To an older child or an adult, all this routine might seem boring. But for toddlers, it is critical.

After the children have found their places, Molly leads them in a counting game. They count together in English, Haitian Creole, and Spanish, at least one of which each child hears spoken at home. They sing "The Wheels on the Bus," showing with their hands how the driver on the bus gestures the riders to "move on back" and how he makes the horn on the bus go "beep, beep,

beep." Then, from out of nowhere, Crystal breaks into a song all her own. Crystal, a cherub in corn rows, loves to sing. Her voice is precociously pure and tuneful. The other children stop in mid-verse to listen. Molly listens, too. When Crystal is finished, Molly applauds, and the other children look slightly confused. Crystal pulls her dress over her head.

Molly calls the children, one by one, to the lunch table, not by their own names, but by the first names of their mothers. The sound of their mothers' names makes the children's faces light up, as though the women themselves had suddenly walked into the room. For some, the ability to fix a name to their mother's face is still in the making. Marcia has yet to master the association, and, when her mother's name is called, the other children push her to her feet.

Dawn lets out a whimper. Molly looks up to see her standing, her eyes fixed on nothing, a thin stream of urine running down her leg. Dawn bites her lower lip in a futile effort to hold back tears. Molly comforts her and then leaves to check her cubby for spare clothes. There are none. Scowling, Molly rummages through the lost and found and digs out underwear and a pair of pants. She makes a mental note to remind Sharon, Dawn's mom, to bring extra clothes tomorrow.

Dawn is not wearing diapers today because Sharon has decided that it is time that she be toilet trained. But Dawn continues to wear diapers at home. Sharon is twenty-one and in school and usually a little frantic; she says she's simply not up to dealing with soggy pants. And when Dawn's dad picks Dawn up after school, he swings her onto the changing table and slaps on a Pampers. He, too, wants his daughter toilet trained, but he has the upholstery in his van to think of — he can't imagine letting her into his car without a diaper. All this cracks Molly up. She says she has a cousin who had the same attitude. This cousin had a two-year-old, and he also had a fancy car, some kind of souped-up Camaro that she thinks cost him something like four-teen thousand dollars. Molly calls it a rich man's car. Anyway, the guy was so picky about his car that he never let his daughter inside without a diaper, even when his wife was trying desperately to toilet train her. This battle went on for months, and then one day the family was driving along, and the kid, still wearing diapers, threw up all over the back seat.

"When I heard that story, I thought, 'good for you, kid' " Molly says. "I mean, at some point, you've got to start being a parent."

The children are not allowed to bring toys out of the play area to the lunch table, but sometimes the teachers make an exception. When Dawn asks for an extra chair for her dolly, who, she says, "needs to eat, too," the teachers oblige, partially because of her accident and partially to make up for the fact that Sharon has, once again, forgotten to pack her a lunch. Nancy goes to the kitchen to whip up a peanut butter and jelly on white bread for her, while Molly helps Max. Max is a robust child, one of the largest kids in the toddler group. His fine brown hair is clipped in Buster Brown bangs straight across his forehead, and his pale skin reddens easily. He is wearing a striped T-shirt and red sneakers and a Little Slugger baseball cap. Molly opens his lunchbox, and he bursts into tears. Molly is not moved; she knows that the sight of food makes Max sad. He hasn't eaten lunch at the center since he started three weeks before. He needs breaking in. Besides, Max has a new baby brother, always trouble for a two-year-old. Molly knows that he won't starve, that he'll eat his sandwich and fruit on the way home with his grandmother or baby-sitter. He feels safe then. Right now, he's not so sure. Molly hands Max a tissue and leaves him to his introspection. There are some things kids have to work out for themselves.

Marcia sits staring blankly at her lunch. Her mother has packed some canned green beans and a cold boiled potato. The potato looks glassy, and the beans are tinged with brown. Marcia stares and stares at the food, as if not quite sure what it's there for. Her huge eyes are bleary, and her head gets heavier and heavier until, finally, it falls to her chest. She's asleep in her chair.

Crystal opens her lunchbox. Inside are peanut butter crackers, apple slices, cheese sandwiches, bread sticks, and juice, enough for a high school athlete. Crystal reaches for a bread stick, takes a nibble, then returns it neatly to its place. Grinning smugly, she closes the lunchbox and, walking on cat's feet, puts it back on the shelf.

Lunch is over. The children line up to brush their teeth, or at least chew on the brush and swallow a little toothpaste, and get a wet paper towel smeared across their faces. Nancy laid out the sleeping mats at lunchtime, and everyone knows his or her place. Felise, May, and David fall asleep almost before they're prone. David sucks so hard on his pacifier that he looks in danger of inhaling it. He is eighteen months, barely out of infancy, and has been fighting off sleep all morning. Others begin to fight now. After sleeping through lunch, Marcia is wide awake. Every time a teacher gently pushes her down on her mat, she pops up again, like one of those plastic blow-up clowns with weighted bottoms.

Max cries, pleading with Molly to rub his back. Molly tells him that she can't now, that it's Rosa's turn to have her back rubbed. Rosa is new to the center, too, and although she doesn't make a fuss, Molly knows she's in need of special attention. But Max doesn't care. He cries louder, and Molly tells him to take a deep breath and count to three. He breathes dramatically, counts quickly, and lets out a sob. Molly frowns, considering her options. If she gives in to his cries, she'll reinforce the behavior, but if she ignores him, he's liable to wake the whole room. She settles on a compromise. Another fifteen seconds and then on to Max, whether Rosa is sleeping or not. Max is asleep almost immediately after Molly stretches out by his side. At ten minutes after one, the room comes to a fitful rest.

Molly pushes herself to her feet. She feels stiff. She is tired and hungry for a smoke. She is also a little worried. Her doctor told her the day before that her constant bouts of coughing added up to a mild case of asthma. He said that, from now on, every time she gets a cold, she's likely to get an asthma attack. Looking around fondly at the room of snoring, sniffling children, she has to laugh. Expecting to avoid a cold at this job is like a prostitute expecting to keep her virginity.

At 1:30, three members of the toddler staff, Nancy, Molly, and Julia, settle down to lunch with Edith, a social worker with a master's degree in early-childhood education. Edith is paid by the city to help young children and their families. She has an office in North Cambridge, but she also makes school visits. She comes to Tot Lot once a month. This year she's working only with the toddlers. The preschool teachers have decided that they no longer require her services. Edith is miffed at their apparent rejection. In private conversations, she says the preschool teachers will feel helpless this year for lack of either experience or a mentor to show them the way.

"They need to seek help outside the center," she says. "Those children cannot be managed entirely within the classroom. The teachers need to reach out to the families, and they need help with that."

Edith meets with the toddler teachers around the short-legged table that has just been cleared of the children's lunches. She sits at the head, eating a sandwich she has pulled from a brown paper bag, her notebook open in front of her. The room is kept dark, so as not to wake the children sleeping just a few yards away. The atmosphere is slightly spooky, more that of a séance than of a professional consultation. Edith lets the teachers do most of the talking.

Molly has a number of concerns. She mentions Max's lack of appetite. She says that Marcia grunts rather than talks and that Christopher hits and pushes his mother when she comes to pick him up at the end of the day. She describes how some of the kids sobbed uncontrollably the day Heather left for California and voices concern over Dawn's toy hoarding.

Edith listens carefully, waiting for Molly to finish. Even after Molly is done, she waits, thinking and nodding her head. Edith has heard all this before, and she has a ready explanation. What most of this boils down to, she says, is separation anxiety.

"Children really worry about what their parents do when they're gone," she says. "It's your job to validate their feelings. You can't just say, 'don't worry, Mommy's coming back soon.' They do worry, and Mommy is not coming back soon."

Edith explains that not all kids deal with separation in the same way. Some don't seem angry or sad but may, like Christopher, punish their parents by putting up a fight when they get picked up in the evening. Some have other, more subtle ways of expressing anxiety.

"You mustn't make light of their fears," Edith says. "You must deal with their sadness and anger and help them move on from there."

She recommends that the teachers paste photographs of the toddlers' parents on the wall. She also suggests that the children bring in transitional objects, things that they can carry between home and school to help link the two places in their minds. But she warns that separation anxiety can plague children for months, even years. Some young children, she says, just aren't built to be away from their mothers all day.

Molly nods her head thoughtfully and twists a strand of hair around her index finger. She would never make light of children's fears. The photograph idea has already occurred to her, she has done it before, and this talk of separation anxiety makes her nervous. She believes that children, no matter how young, can adapt to a variety of environments, as long as the environments are safe, welcoming, and stimulating. She remembers her own childhood, thirty-odd years before, when she spent a lot of time wishing she had some place other than home to go to.

Molly's mom quit her job as a public school teacher to stay home with her children. But Molly says she doesn't remember anything particularly heartwarming about that time. She doesn't remember long afternoons baking cookies or reading or even shopping with her mother. What she remembers most clearly about that period is being shooed out of the house so that her mother could clean in peace. Molly's mother pretty much left her kids to their own devices, but she was a bug about shining up her toaster. It wasn't enough that you could see your face in it; the entire kitchen had to shimmer in its reflection.

"Imagine a woman with seven children and time to polish a toaster," Molly says.

Molly says she wishes her mother had gone back to work and put her in a day care center, a place like Tot Lot where people paid attention to kids, where children were regarded as something other than nuisances. Molly's deep sympathy for children stems in part from her memories of a childhood in which children were kept at bay.

Edith finishes up the meeting by giving the teachers her office phone number and telling them to call if they have specific questions. Then she smiles empathetically, bunches up her lunch bag, closes her notebook, and tiptoes out the back door. Edith has little time to spend hanging around observing children in action and relies almost entirely on secondhand reports from Susan and the teachers. This forces her to generalize rather than to tailor advice to the needs of individual children. Despite her expertise and excellent intentions, she is less helpful than the teachers would like her to be. To an extent, Molly finds the advice soothing, an affirmation of her intuition. But the preschool teachers, Margaret, Linda, Marina, and Marie, regard Edith as a distant presence, someone who comes in once a month, makes vague suggestions, and leaves. They want more than this and, being young and inexperienced, they need more.

It's nearly 2:30, and the toddlers are making wake-up noises. They grunt and fart and rub their eyes, and a couple cry a little. Molly goes in to help them find their shoes and socks. Julia is here for the afternoon shift, but as usual Molly sticks around anyway, making sure that the kids are okay before she leaves. She thinks it's a little weird for children to go to sleep with one set of people and to wake up with another. Besides, Molly doesn't feel much like walking the half-mile to her house: Pat Weissman comes in early to pick up the twins, and Molly knows she can always hitch a ride home with her. About a third of the toddlers are picked up after nap, usually by mothers who have the luxury of working part-time. Those left behind look groggy. For many toddlers in day care, the afternoon is an afterthought, a long, slow winding-down of the day, when part-time help, often high school students, come in to spell morning teachers. Tot Lot is fortunate to have Julia, who works part-time so that she can finish off a degree in elementary education and is experienced, dedicated, steady, and focused.

The afternoon is clear, with sun shining through a bit of a breeze. It's perfect outdoor weather. Julia and a teacher's assistant prod and tease the kids into motion, joking while deftly dressing those who are still too dreamy to dress themselves. It takes close to twenty minutes to get the kids wrapped in sweaters and Jackets and headed out the door for their walk.

Outside, Christopher points to his house proudly. "That is where me and my mommy live," he says, his entire body gesturing toward the first floor of an enormous and graceful mansard-style structure, just half a block from Tot Lot. Julia smiles and acknowledges his excitement, but the kids pretty much ignore him. They kick through the piles of fallen leaves and collect sticks. They stuff half-rotten chestnuts into their pockets. They linger to stare at a mangy brown mutt relieving himself on the chipped bark of a chestnut tree. The dog sniffs a few kids from crotch to toes as though scouting out its next target. Christopher giggles at this, but Claude stiffens. His eyes open wide, and he backs off slowly, as though edging away from a wild animal. He grabs Julia's hand and hurries along.

The walk around the block takes forty-five minutes. Julia says she would have taken the kids to the park, but that it's just not worth it these days. I ask if she's concerned about bad influences, about drug dealers, and she laughs. It's not drug dealers she's worried about, it's dangerous trash, broken bottles and cigarette butts and rusty nails. Trying to keep toddlers away from that stuff is like trying to keep a moth from a flame. The teachers have called the park "Trash Park" for so long now that they can't recall its actual name.

After the walk, it's time for afternoon snack, crackers and peanut butter. Claude picks at his cracker, but Christopher consumes a pile. He stuffs in one after the other, following each with a big swig of milk. Then he hikes up his overalls and saunters down to the play area to browse through the book collection, settling on a well-worn copy of *Peter Rabbit*. His mother has read him this book so many times that he knows it word for word. But Christopher has no plans to recite *Peter Rabbit* today; he chose the book for comfort. He tucks it under his arm and walks over to the Sit and Spin, a sort of giant top. He sits down on the Sit and Spin and starts the thing whirling. His brown hair flies away from his face, and his large eyes close into slits. His head tilts back almost to the floor. He holds *Peter Rabbit* tightly clenched in his armpit. Julia sits with her legs stretched in front of her, watching Christopher.

"A lot of kids work out their angry feelings on the Sit and Spin," she says. "Zack used to spend a lot of time on that thing. I hope it works better for Christopher."

Two

GUILT

CHRISTOPHER Torroella is big for a two-year-old. Holly, his mother, guesses he's outgrown five pairs of sneakers in the past eight months. His jeans are a size four. He's fair skinned with beautiful eyes the color of smoky brown topaz and thick, long lashes that fan almost to his brows, the kind of lashes that people say are wasted on a boy. They are not wasted on Chris.

The first day of school Chris wore overalls and a white plaster cast on his right arm. The arm broke when he slipped off the first rung of a ladder on a playground slide. Holly wasn't there to see it happen. She was at work. Her brother Ted was watching Chris that day. But Holly made it home in time to take Chris to the hospital for X rays. The arm doesn't seem to bother Chris anymore, but it bothers Holly a lot. She wonders if she should have gotten him to the hospital sooner. She wonders if he should have been on that ladder in the first place.

Words come more easily to Chris than to most kids his age, and he's not shy about using harsh ones. He is, in fact, not shy at all. Already, he has a thick Boston brogue that seems to give his many pronouncements added weight. At times, he is so charming that it's hard to resist doing what he says. At other times, his stabs at manipulation are all too obvious. His eyebrows rise up, and his mouth firms into a pout, and, sometimes, his fingers curl into a fist.

Chris's mother works for the phone company. She is twenty-nine years old and looks a lot like Chris. Her eyes are gray edging toward hazel, and her brown hair curves gently to her shoulders, except at the forehead, where it is cropped straight across, Cleopatra style. She is of medium height, though when dressed for work, she often appears inches taller. She hates wearing heels, but the phone company has a dress code, and Holly feels dowdy wearing flats with dressy clothes. The heels don't seem to interfere with her stride, which is long and confident. Holly figures she walks about eight miles a day on the job, which involves the monitoring and maintenance of a large chunk of computer system. Her brisk pace combined with a steady stream of anxious moments conspires to keep her slim.

Holly works on the third floor of a six-story brick building. The building spans the better part of a city block on the edge of East Cambridge, a corner all but obscured by the architecturally ambitious office complexes of the Kendall Square waterfront a few blocks to the south. A dozen or so years ago, Kendall Square was nothing more than a back alley to the Massachusetts Institute of Technology, a random sprinkling of consulting and high-tech firms enlivened by the F & T Deli, a noisy, smoke-filled joint that served liquor to the neighborhood drunks and blue plate specials and hamburger club sandwiches to students and slumming MIT faculty. Urban renewal brought gleaming hotels, glass-fronted high rises, and hordes of young professionals in a hurry — eager, hard-hitting go-getters who wear stiff white shirts and red suspenders and shoes imported from Italy and England. The F & T is long gone, but there are health clubs and any number of places to pick up croissants or Black Forest cake and capuccino.

At the phone company, capuccino is not served. The employees do not appear to spend much time in health clubs. And they don't look eager or bright eyed or ambitious. They look like they'd rather be someplace else. The phone company building is a flat, dull place in a dismal corner of the neighborhood, without much to recommend it save its proximity to both the subway and a handful of decent Portuguese sausage vendors. There is little to catch the eye here and nothing to hold it. Holly says the chief distinction of the building she works in is its remarkable resemblance to Attica State Prison. It certainly is secure. There is a uniformed guard at the entrance, and the door leading to Holly's area is bolted and can be opened only from within or with a special card. Inside, it is cavernous and cold. In winter, Holly sometimes banishes her high heels to the back of her closet and wears thermal underwear under her slacks. Still, she says, she never feels warm. The thermostat has been set not for human comfort but for the machines: row upon row of whirling disk drives and chattering printers that require a hefty dose of air conditioning to keep from burning themselves up. The din of these computers is not menacing, like the piercing whines in a dentist's office, but it is constant, a cloying hum that adds up to a headache after a few hours. Holly's office, a three-walled cubicle built of room dividers, offers no relief from the sound, but Holly says she doesn't mind. She's worked here so long that the noise is almost a comfort — and it helps keep her coworkers out of earshot of her personal telephone conversations.

Holly shares her cubicle with a colleague who has become a good friend. Sometimes, if they can find baby-sitters, they go out for a drink or dinner together after work. Between them they have plastered nearly every inch of partition wall with mementos, mostly snapshots and school photographs of their children. There are more photos of Chris on the walls than there are of all four of Holly's friend's children. Holly keeps even more photographs of Chris in a pile on her desk, along with wedding photographs of herself and her estranged husband, Frank. On the floor in the corner, there's a stack of *Rolling Stone* magazines and a thick novel from the Central Square branch of the Cambridge Public Library. Holly loves to read, and she prefers good, long mysteries. Often, if she doesn't have errands to run, she reads straight through her lunch hour.

Tacked up at eye level on Holly's cubicle wall, there's a message written in large letters formed by a dot matrix printer. From a distance, the sign looks like a piece of Op art. Up close, it reads "If Assholes Could Fly, This Place Would Be an Airport." Pointing to it, Holly ducks, as if to avoid a low-flying 747. "Truer words," she says, "have never been written."

Lately, Holly has spent twelve hours a day, six days a week, pounding the linoleum of the computer room. The telephone company strike started August 6, and since then Holly has been under orders to work both her own hours and those of the striking union members. The strike was called after the company announced a cut in employee health insurance benefits. Management got the idea that workers should pay a bigger chunk of their health insurance costs because the soaring cost of medical care was cutting into their profits. But the workers say they can't afford to buffer the blow of higher insurance rates, and, for nearly a month now, more than sixty thousand of them have stayed off the job to drive home the point. They march around the company's Boston headquarters, chanting slogans and carrying picket signs with messages like "Millions on commercials. Nothing on employees."

Stuck in Cambridge, Holly feels trapped and guilty. She thinks the union is right.

"The company thinks it's making a really critical point, bearing down against the workers," she says. "But I think it's a royal screw job. These people spend more time at the company than they do with their families. They deserve respect. Health care is a basic human right."

Holly wishes she, too, could march in the picket lines. But she can't — she is a manager herself. "They call me management, but what does that mean?" she says. "Slave would be a more appropriate title."

Holly says she was promoted to management not because she has anyone to manage but because of her access to computer networks that, if sabotaged, could disrupt phone systems from Maine to Connecticut. The company needed nonunion workers to monitor these lines. Or, as Holly says, "They needed people they could run around."

But the sabotage has begun nonetheless. The phone company hired four hundred retired operators to handle the phone lines, paying them roughly twice the wages of regular employees. Union workers retaliated by cutting a cable and disrupting phone service in fourteen communities around the state. Still, the company shows no signs of weakening.

Four weeks of double shifts are beginning to show on Holly's face. She has deep lines under her eyes, and her skin hasn't looked this bad since puberty. Her hair hasn't been trimmed in ages, and she has trouble keeping her bangs out of her line of sight. Anyway, her life has been a blur since the strike began. There is no time to go shopping or call friends. There is no time to watch television or read the paper. There is no time to think. There is barely time to do the laundry and make sure Chris hasn't outgrown his latest pair of sneakers.

One of Holly's fondest hobbies is baking, especially when Chris is around to help her. Chris sifts the flour and spoons in salt and mashes the butter. They bake brownies and Key lime pie and apple pie and cookies. If there is extra pie crust, Chris cuts it into shapes with a cookie cutter. Baking, Holly says, is her way of being with Chris and letting off steam at the same time. She does it instead of smoking or drinking. She would get fat if she ate a fraction of what comes out of her oven.

But Holly hasn't had much time for baking lately. She spends so many hours at her office that she barely knows when one day is over and the next begins. Long hours mean more money, which helps. But Holly misses sunlight. And she figures that at least part of her overtime pay will go straight to a psychotherapist to help her work through the guilt once the strike is over.

Holly feels guilty about a lot of things but especially about not being able to spend more time with Chris. She sees him in the afternoon, after school, but not in the morning, when she stumbles around in the dark getting ready for her 4 A.M. shift. Holly's mother, her younger brother Ted, and Kevin, an old friend, take turns sleeping on the pullout couch to cover for her in the morning. Chris sleeps in her bed.

Chris doesn't understand anything about unions or strikes, but he knows he misses his mother. Sometimes, when she picks him up from school at 4:30 or 5:00 in the afternoon, he'll kick her, then grab the hem of her skirt in his fists and hang on for dear life. Holly is embarrassed by this, and, when she has the strength, she reaches down and uncurls his fingers. When she's too tired to deal with it, they walk home stuck together like a pair of mating dragonflies.

When Holly finishes up one of her twelve-hour days, she longs to make a cup of herb tea and put her feet up. She has a pile of books she'd like to read. Instead, she picks Chris up from school and focuses every ounce of what energy she has left on him. Today, since the weather is good, she takes him for a walk along Chestnut Street, where they live. True to its name, the street is littered with squashed and squirrel-chewed nuts. Chris is fascinated and yanks his mother's hand every step or so to alert her to another treasure. Holly gets on her hands and knees to retrieve a particularly well formed specimen that has rolled under a parked car. Chris says he will plant it in a pot next to his bed. He says it will grow into a bean stalk and that he will climb it. Holly beams and then, straightening up, grabs her back with both hands and winces. Today, she feels about fifty years old.

Holly considers herself lucky to have the apartment on Chestnut Street. It's a friendly building; the people who live there look out for each other. Holly rents the apartment from her older brother, who is married but doesn't have children and can afford to dabble in real estate. Holly plans to buy the apartment from him, or, better still, a larger apartment in the same building, as soon as she can scrape the money together. The place she has now is really much too small. There's a cramped living room, a windowless bedroom entirely filled by Holly's double bed, a kid-sized bathroom, and a kitchen that only a real estate agent would describe as "eat-in." The rooms are dark and crowded with toys, books, and clothes. There is no possibility of privacy. When Chris starts drilling with his toy drill in the living room, Holly feels as though she's on a construction site. When Holly gets a telephone call, Chris listens to every word. Still, the apartment is rent-controlled, which means the market can't force the monthly rent to ridiculous heights, even if her brother were mean enough to want it to. And Holly has done a fine job of spiffing it up with wallpaper and paint and other little touches, such as a window box in the kitchen. One of the first things she did after moving in was to rip up the wall-to-wall carpet, which was stained and reeked of a previous tenant's cat. Holly has asthma and is allergic to cat hair, and it looks like Chris has asthma and allergies, too. (She's noticed he's been coughing a lot lately, even during the rare times when he doesn't have a cold.) The carpet had to go. But the linoleum underneath is torn and dull, and it looks awful. Holly plans to rip it up herself and replace it with a hardwood floor after the strike is over.

After their walk, Holly sticks a videotape into the VCR to entertain Chris while she forages through the refrigerator for dinner. Chris has seen the movie, *Bambi*, plenty of times before, and he watches it with half an eye, calling out from the living room for chicken noodle soup. Holly is proud of her cooking, and she usually makes Chris hearty, balanced meals, but today she capitulates. She pulls a packet of soup from a box in the cupboard, puts a pan of water on to boil, and, deciding she's probably too tired to eat much anyway, puts on the kettle for tea for herself. Just as she's pulling out a kitchen chair to sit on, the doorbell rings. It's her mother, Betty Michaels.

Betty is a slim, attractive woman of fifty-five, with graying brown hair and gentle blue eyes. Dressed fashionably in slacks and a sweater, she has come straight from the classified advertisement department of the *Boston Globe*, where she has worked part-time for seventeen years. She spends Monday and Wednesday nights with Chris. Holly says her mother does that at the risk of her own marriage. It is Holly's impression that her father wouldn't cook if he was starving.

Betty Michaels has always worked at one job or another, but when her five children were young, she kept to night hours so that she would be free to stay home with the kids during the day. The rare times she needed a baby-sitter, she called on her mother-in-law, who lived in the neighborhood and was happy to be of use. Betty has big misgivings about working mothers. She thinks that they should find a way to be with their children most of the time. She worries about Chris and Holly.

"Really, it makes me very sad," she says. "I'm not saying it's great to be poor and home with kids; it's very, very difficult for children to be poor. But Larry and I were poor, and I managed to raise my own children. Larry worked twelve hours a day, seven days a week. We didn't have day care centers. We didn't even have Laundromats. Lots of times, I did the laundry by hand. I know I'm old-fashioned, but I took care of my own kids."

Holly remembers those times, and the memories are mixed. She remembers having to work a paying job all through school and not being able to read and study and think as much as she would have liked. She remembers having to drop out of the University of Massachusetts during the second semester of her senior year for lack of money. She remembers having no choice but to take an entry-level job with the phone company to pay off her loans — a job she hated.

"If I came back in another life," she says, "my wish would be to go to school and not have to work. I want that for Chris."

Betty says she'd rather see her daughter go on welfare than put Chris in full-time day care. She simply can't stomach the idea of a two-year-old being cared for by someone other than his mother. Holly has heard all this before, and she's ready with a rebuttal. She reminds her mother that she didn't plan it this way, that she wants passionately to spend more time with Chris, but that, at this point, there seems to be no reasonable alternative to working full-time.

"I want to do more than just scrape by," she says. "I want Chris to have a good background, to go to college. Anyway, I feel like I spend more time with Chris than a lot of mothers who stay home all day with their kids. And we can do what we want when we want to. We eat when we want, go to the park when we want; it works out."

Betty smiles. She loves her daughter, and she is uncomfortable passing judgment on her, especially now, with things being so rough for Holly. She just wishes things were different, wishes there were more that she could do.

Holly pours her mother a cup of tea and sits on the edge of the couch, keeping one eye on Chris, who is pawing through a pile of books, deciding which one to have his grandmother read aloud. Holly says the telephone company has talked about setting up a day care center for sixteen years, but so far it's only been talk. One of the company vice presidents is a woman with two kids who, Holly says, goes around saying things like "If I can do it, you can do it; figure it out for yourself." What this vice president doesn't say, Holly says, is that she has a salary large enough to support both a nanny and a housekeeper.

Holly's experience with baby-sitters has been erratic. The first sitter she hired seemed okay at first, but then Holly found out that she was warehousing Chris in a playpen all afternoon while she watched the soaps. When Chris cried in protest, the sitter screamed so loudly at him to shut up that the neighbors complained. Holly says, "I got rid of that one fast." The next sitter, a friend of a friend, was reliable and kind and had two little girls of her own whom Chris loved, but she wasn't officially in the day care business and agreed to keep Chris only for the summer. Holly put Chris in family day care with her cousin that fall. The arrangement worked well, but Holly was worried that the sight of her cousin's husband coming home each night would be unsettling to Chris, who rarely saw his father. By that time, Holly and her husband were living apart. Besides, her cousin was thinking of giving up doing day care anyway, and while Chris seemed to take changes well, Holly was certain that all this jumping around among sitters wasn't doing him any good.

"I knew he needed some consistency in his life," she says. "So I started calling day care centers. I called thirty-five centers, and most of them wouldn't even let me come for a visit. Some wouldn't even put my name on a waiting list, said the list was too long already."

The few places with openings didn't feel right to Holly.

"There were too many kids, or the place didn't feel safe," she says. "I was a little desperate, but I wasn't so desperate that I'd put Chris just anywhere."

Holly discovered Tot Lot while taking a walk with her mother. She couldn't believe she'd missed the place, given that it was right down the street from her apartment. She'd passed it many times before and seen kids going in and out but hadn't thought anything of it until her mother spotted the small, hand-painted sign hanging lopsided on the wire-mesh fence. Even then, Holly had to crane her neck to see it. When she did, she marched right up the boardwalk and through the blue door and checked it out on the spot. It was rough and tumble, with lots of kids and lots of noise. There were blob-shaped art projects hanging from the ceiling, and teachers running around doing fifty things at once and still managing to laugh. Holly liked it immediately. She talked to Susan, the director, and liked her, too. She especially liked Molly, the toddler teacher. Molly seemed so calm and controlled, exactly what Chris needed. The place seemed good, so good that Holly wasn't surprised when Susan told her there were no openings and that there probably wouldn't be any in the fall.

"So I called and hounded them every week for nine months and dropped by every chance I could," Holly says. "I just made a nuisance of myself and they must have taken pity on me, because when another family dropped out, we got the slot. It was the first piece of good luck we'd had in a long, long time."

Three

HALLOWEEN DREAMS

IT'S 5:45 A.M. when the clock radio goes off. Molly leans across the bed and stabs the snooze button. Her head falls back onto the pillow, and her right hand fumbles on the night table for her Marlboros. She finds one, grabs a pack of matches, and lights up. The first cigarette of the day is always the best.

Molly has tried to stop smoking more times than she cares to think about. Every time she stops, something happens to make her start again. It's her one bad habit, now that she's all but given up sweets and alcohol and, through no choice of her own, men.

Molly's room is dark, the street light muffled by pulled shades behind lavender curtains. Dusky light sneaking in from the kitchen window illuminates a rocking chair, a bureau, a television, and two baskets, one for laundry, the other for old clothes too good to throw out but not good enough to wear. The radio clicks on again, and this time Molly lets it run. She gets up, shrugs on a robe, and crosses the threshold to the kitchen. It's a large, airy room with a polished hardwood floor, a wall of varnished wood cabinets, and a small wooden table covered carefully with a cloth. Molly turns on the tap and packs four scoops of Maxwell House into the percolator. She pulls back a curtain and stares dreamily out the window. When the coffee's ready, she fills a mug and takes it back to bed. She pulls the covers up, lights another cigarette, and settles down to listen to the radio.

Molly wakes up to the Joe and Andy Show on WROR every morning. She likes the music, mostly contemporary soft rock with a sprinkling of golden oldies she can dance to in her mind. But often Joe and Andy piss her off, especially Andy, who is sometimes rude to the point of being offensive. Sometimes, Molly thinks, Andy talks like an overgrown toddler with a bad case of garbage mouth. Molly says that if she had little kids around, she'd switch radio stations rather than expose them to Andy's lip. But her only child, Patrick, is twenty-one. Molly turns the radio up a notch. Joe and Andy are kidding around, poking fun at Michael Dukakis again. Molly winces. She doesn't trust any politician, but she kind of feels sorry for the governor. What with a wife who can't stay off pills and booze and his bad luck in the elections, he's become pathetic, really. It took time, but it seemed that Dukakis had finally learned to be smart about issues she cares about, like equal rights and antipoverty programs and, of course, child care. To her mind, the fact that things seem to be falling apart in the state right now really isn't his fault.

At 6:30 Patrick gets up and gets ready for work at the laundry. Molly can hear him from her bedroom. She gets out of bed, pulls the covers taut, and then goes back to the kitchen to pour another cup of coffee and wash the previous night's dishes. She takes a quick look at the clock on the stove. If she hurries, she'll have time to iron her favorite blue workshirt, maybe even pay some bills. Patrick comes into the kitchen, opens the refrigerator, and pulls out a carton of juice and a quart of milk. He is small to medium height and strong looking, and he walks with a rolling gait, as if on a ship. He wears his hair in a modified Mohawk, a wide strip of crew cut flanked by swathes of shaved skull. Patrick nods in Molly's direction and then pours juice and a bowl of Cap'n Crunch cereal and sits down at the kitchen table to eat. He eats two brimming bowlfuls, his eyes fixed on the back of the cereal box. At 6:45, he's out the door.

Molly, still in her robe, ducks into the bathroom. She brushes her teeth carefully, thinking with horror about the dentist appointment she has next week. Molly's gums are close to shot, and her teeth are a mess. She delayed going to the dentist as long as she could, until a roaring toothache brought her crawling to his chair. The estimate he quoted comes to roughly one-third of her yearly take-home pay. She'll be in debt to him for years. She wishes the center could offer dental insurance, but she knows that's a pipe dream. In fact, there are mumblings at budget meetings about eliminating family health insurance coverage. One parent kindly explained to Molly that a little day care center like Tot Lot was in no position to offer employees family coverage. Molly kindly replied that a teacher making what she is making working in that little day care center is in an even worse position to afford it. Molly brings home less than $280 a week, less than half the monthly rent on an average studio apartment in Cambridge.

Back in the bedroom, Molly stands in front of the mirror and combs impatiently through her hair, brushing it away from her face, tucking it behind her ears, and tying it back in a no-nonsense ponytail. She pulls on jeans and buttons the stiffly ironed workshirt over a powder blue turtleneck. The shirt skims her narrow shoulders and billows out behind her. Molly says that she was heavy at one time, but that's hard to imagine. What is easy to imagine is her shoulder blades bony and nearly touching. She wears gold hoop earrings and a thin gold band on the ring finger of her left hand. She was married once, but that was a long time ago, a very long time ago.

Molly tries to be out the door no later than 7:20 on weekday mornings. Usually she leaves earlier than that. School doesn't start until 8:00, but Molly prefers to get there before anyone else. Once the kids are in, there's no time to think. Molly goes in early to get her bearings.

It's less than a half-mile walk to school, and usually Molly relishes the solitude and exercise. But today it's pouring. The sky is muddy with rainclouds. The puddle running from her driveway into the street is large enough to float a bathtub in. Molly resists the urge to go back inside for more coffee. She can't believe this weather — it's been raining cats and dogs for four days now without a break. The kids will be climbing the walls. She'll be lucky if she can keep Christopher from killing Marcia, and if Max starts with the crying again, she's going to go nuts. Max is a darling kid but so weepy. And Claude has been having such a hard time lately. Once or twice she's had to pin his arms to his sides to keep him from slugging her.

Molly pulls her blue rain poncho tightly around her and yanks up the hood, tying it under her chin. She's got boots on, too, not rain boots, but black winter boots with furry insides. Here it is not even November yet, and she's dressing for winter. She feels a bit foolish, but better that than get her sneakers soaked. Anyway, she's no fashion plate. Gathering courage, she jerks open her collapsing umbrella and sets off through the near dark. She picks her way down William Street, which is slippery with a skim of matted leaves. She takes a right onto Magazine Street, then cuts through Dana Park to McTernan Street and then to Pearl through the Blessed Sacrament churchyard, down Putnam Street to Sid's International Market. She shakes the water off her umbrella, closes it, and ducks inside, standing just inside the door for a minute, letting her eyes adjust to the glare from the refrigerator case. She nods hello to Suzy, who's ringing up a strip of lottery tickets for a regular customer. Molly used to work behind that cash register herself, ringing up lottery tickets and cups of coffee and quarts of milk. She worked from 6 P.M. until 9 P.M. during the week and full-time on weekends. That was years ago. She enjoyed chatting with the customers, and the money came in handy, but she couldn't bring herself to do it for long. She lost the energy for moonlighting.

Molly grabs a napkin, fishes a bagel from a plastic tray of breakfast pastries, pays for it, and heads back out into the gloom. She doesn't bother opening the umbrella this time; the center is less than a block away from Sid's. She dashes down the street to the high white fence that separates Tot Lot's rear exit from a stack of formidable-looking condominiums, unlatches the gate, and runs up the path to the back door. She unlocks the door, takes off her poncho, and shakes it out before heading inside. She switches on the lights and walks past the row of toddler cubbies, through the toddler room, and into the diaper-changing area, a dingy grotto with a hospital smell. She spreads her poncho out to dry across the back of a broken chair. She takes off her boots and, still standing, slips into a pair of sneakers. All the time, she's thinking strategy. Activity today is going to have to be particularly absorbing, to keep the kids from getting nostalgic about the playground. The usual stuff, Play-Doh and markers and bead stringing, won't do. She settles on papier-mâché and finger paints — they're messy but distracting. José's not one to get down in the mess, but Nancy will certainly be willing. Sometimes Nancy seems like an overgrown kid herself, what with her braids and her crafts projects — those fuzzy balls of yarn she rolls and cuts during staff meetings. Sometimes it's hard to believe that she's as old as Molly and a mother herself.

It's ten of eight when Molly's growling stomach reminds her of her bagel. She carries the paper bag to the kitchen and opens a cupboard to get a plate. There's a faint knock on the front door; Molly closes the cupboard and goes to open it. Marcia is there with her mother. There's no telling how long they have been waiting. Rain drips from the hood of Marcia's raincoat onto her face, which is broad, wide eyed, and vacant. Under the hood, her hair is done up in tight braids, with tiny bows clipped to the end of each skinny twist. Molly smiles and lets Marcia in. Marcia's mother gives Marcia a little push and turns back into the rain. She will take a taxi home. Molly walks Marcia to the toddler cubbies and helps her strip off her coat and stash her lunchbox. She thinks with longing of her breakfast, realizing sadly that, once again, it has become lunch.

At eight, Mary Martin comes in with her daughters, Crystal and Delia. Delia, who is four, heads for the preschool room while Mary takes two-and-a-half-year-old Crystal in to Molly. Mary is pale, slightly built, and pretty, with short, wavy red hair and freckles. She is twenty-one years old and has just started a new job, working in a state welfare office. Between the job and the kids, Mary finds herself running short of energy sometimes, and today is one of those times. Crystal is all over the place, slippery and contrary. Mary yanks her by the arm, barks at her to calm down, to take off her coat and act like a civilized human being. Crystal takes this as a cue to freak out. She wriggles out of her mother's grip and, lithe as a monkey, scrambles up the indoor climbing structure. Mary takes a deep breath, hauls Crystal down from the top rung of the structure, and holds her firmly against her hip while she peels off the coat. Crystal howls and kicks. Marcia, her nose running like a faucet, stands transfixed by the performance. Crystal, stripped down to her T-shirt and crisply pressed blue jeans, makes a dash for the "dramatic play" area while her mother, eyes rolling, heads gratefully out the door.

At 8:15, Lucien Brissettes comes in trailing Luke, Marcel, and Claude. Luke and Claude are brothers, Lucien's sons. They are neatly dressed in hats, sneakers, corduroys, and rain slickers over plaid shirts buttoned to the throat. Marcel, their friend, is also buttoned up, but the fly on his jeans is open, and one of the earflaps on his hat is torn and hanging, like the ear on a mangy dog. Marcel's mother is in the midst of a difficult pregnancy, and his father, Michel, is in Florida or Haiti, the teachers aren't sure which; at any rate, he's not around to take Marcel to school, so Marcel usually drives in with Lucien. Marcel looks furtively around the toddler room and then follows Luke into the preschool room. Lucien smiles warmly at Molly and shakes her hand in both of his before bending down to free Claude from his raincoat. Claude stands rooted, his eyes fixed in a blank stare, waiting for his father to finish. He stows his lunchbox in the corner shelf and then shakes his father's outstretched hand before striding confidently past the activity tables and into the gray-rug room, which is by now filled with toddlers. Claude marches past Dawn, who has already mounded up a pile of plastic food, and Crystal, who is threatening blue-eyed, blonde Samantha with a toy broom. Molly takes the broom from Crystal but keeps her eyes on Claude.

Molly has this recurring dream. She has it at least two or three times a year, and it always involves one of the children in her class. In the dream, Molly takes the child to the park, and everything is going fine until, suddenly, she turns around and realizes that she's gone home and left the kid in the park alone. She runs back to the park and looks everywhere for the kid, but he or she is gone. Molly panics, thinking about what the parents will say to her, thinking that the kid might be hurt, thinking what a bad person she is to have lost a child. Then she wakes up.

Molly says the kid in these dreams is always one who is tough to handle, a kid who she ends up having to worry about. She hasn't yet had the dream this year, but she thinks that, if she does, the child will be Claude.

LUCIEN and Madeline Brissettes have a photograph hanging on the wall of their living room of the two of them standing side by side on a balcony overlooking Port-au-Prince. Lucien is wearing a fine, light gray suit, and Madeline a lacy, white dress. Both of them are smiling. The photo was taken five years before, on their wedding day. It was shortly after that day that they left Haiti. They have never been back.

But much of Lucien's family is still there. His father continues to manage farms in Haiti and he owns several patches of land in the southern part of the country as well as a home in the mountains. Lucien's father has a second home in Port-au-Prince. When he was young, Lucien worked on his father's farms, cutting sugarcane, picking mangoes, and digging potatoes. He also helped with the horses that his father raised. When he wasn't working, he attended a series of private boys' schools in Port-au-Prince. He graduated from high school at eighteen. His dream was to become an artist.

Madeline's father was a prosperous man, too. He was an officer in the military and a successful gentleman farmer. He owned land in both the north and the south of Haiti, a home in Port-au-Prince, and another home on the ocean. Madeline's father loved Haiti. The country had been good to him and his family, and he did not want any of his children to leave it. He felt uncomfortable when his children visited friends who had emigrated to the United States. He worried that they would be seduced by America, and, of course, he was right.

In school, Madeline studied business subjects, typing, and accounting, and she also studied languages. In addition to English and Haitian Creole, she speaks French and Spanish, as well as a bit of Greek, and she can read Latin. Madeline has nine brothers and five sisters. One of her brothers is a diplomat. He has worked in Washington, D.C., and in Geneva, Switzerland, representing the Haitian government. Another brother is an obstetrician. Both of these brothers live in Haiti. They do quite well there and see no reason to leave. But the rest of Madeline's family, her other brothers and her sisters and her mother, left Haiti for Montreal and Paris four years before, shortly after Madeline's father died.

Lucien's father, too, felt strongly that his sons should not leave their homeland — so strongly, in fact, that he beat Lucien's older brother for even mentioning the possibility. Lucien's father feared the United States especially, considering it a country rife with social problems that made Haiti's difficulties seem tame by comparison. He told his sons that America was no place for a black man.

Lucien's brother was a grown man, yet he bent over to take his father's belt. But he bent over only once. Then he moved to Florida. Later he moved to Cambridge and found work fixing cars.

Lucien followed his brother in 1983. He came for a visit but decided to stay. "I really surprised myself," he says. He had studied industrial mechanics in Port-au-Prince, and his plan was to continue his studies in the United States, earn a diploma, and return to Haiti to work. He had heard that American credentials would assure him of good money back home. But then the political situation in Haiti became so bad that Lucien believed he could not go back, at least not soon.

"I was really depressed," he says. "I knew no one here; I had no car. My life in Haiti had been completely different. One hundred percent different. But I knew I wanted to learn something in the United States."

Lucien enrolled in Bunker Hill Community College in Boston to study electronics. During Christmas break, he returned to Port-au-Prince to marry Madeline. Lucien had been a school chum of one of Madeline's brothers, and their families knew each other well.

Like her father, Madeline loved Haiti, but she was afraid to stay there. She is not a political person, and in Haiti it had become impossible to go through the day without thinking political thoughts.

"At the time, I was working for the minister of the interior, and there were lots of Tontons Macoute," she says, referring to Haiti's murderous volunteer militia. "I didn't like their system. It made me nervous that they were in power. I knew something was about to happen, a coup d'état, so we moved here."

Lucien and Madeline settled into their Cambridge apartment shortly before Haiti exploded in a bloody revolt that sent "President for Life" Jean-Claude Duvalier packing and the Tontons Macoute scrambling, many unsuccessfully, for their lives. The Brissetteses had no special interest in Cambridge, but Lucien's brother was there, and it seemed like a good place for both of them to attend school and sharpen their skills before returning home to Haiti.

Lucien dropped the idea of getting a college degree and instead entered a trade school to study auto mechanics, which he says is a much sought after and well-paid vocation in Haiti. His plan was to earn a diploma and turn it into gold back home. He did quite well until a Chevrolet he was working under slipped from its jack and onto his chest, breaking several ribs and convincing Lucien that auto mechanics was not for him. The accident occurred at a particularly bad time: Luke was two, and Madeline was six months pregnant with their second son. The family's future, so carefully plotted in Haiti, became suddenly murky. And their plan of moving into a house with a backyard and trees went from optimistic to impossible. Now it seems to them that they will never own a tree. Thoughts like this make Haiti more attractive in Lucien's memories.

"On American television, you never see the real Haiti, only the poorest parts," he says. "But if you visit Haiti outside of Port-au-Prince, you would never believe the country is poor. In Haiti, my family lived in our own home with trees, a garden. Madeline could walk to the beach from her house. The mountains are so beautiful. In my country, there is no money, but the people get what they need. They have the beach. They have mangoes. And nobody is afraid of getting their house taken away from them."

Near the Brissetteses' apartment in North Cambridge, there are no mango trees. There is a strip shopping mall with a multiplex cinema, clothes stores, and fast-food restaurants. But the Brissetteses would not walk there, even if they wanted to. They are afraid to walk.

When Lucien brought his bride to Cambridge, he brought her to one of the tightest real estate markets in the country. The monthly rent for apartments in Cambridge can easily exceed what a Haitian worker earns in a year. For the Brissetteses, as it is for many newcomers, subsidized housing was the only viable option. They moved into Trois Bébés.

In Creole *bébé* is sometimes used as slang for a large, voluptuous woman. In Cambridge, "Trois Bébés" refers to the Rindge Towers, a trio of twenty-two–story buildings staggered across an asphalt parking lot in a remote corner of the city's industrialized northwest. They are not voluptuous. In a 1975 inventory of the city's architecture, the complex was described by geographer Arthur Krim in hastily scribbled notes as "the multiple unit gone berserk . . . there are not one but three such monsters . . . they are a travesty." More recently, non-Haitians have come to call the complex "the tombstones." The tombstones stand on land that at one time yielded much of the clay that fueled the Cambridge brick-making industry. Later the abandoned clay pits were filled with refuse, and the site used for what the Cambridge Historical Commission describes as "fringe activities. . . ." Among these fringe activities was the building of Rindge Towers in 1968. The towers appalled Cambridge residents, who were afraid that similar buildings might be erected closer to the heart of things. There were massive protests, and the Cambridge City Council responded by voting in a series of rulings that put stern limits on the future construction of large, imposing structures. After that, no one seemed to worry much about what was happening out at the old clay pits. It became a place for people who were in no position to exercise their aesthetic sense. Most of these people are black, and many of them are recent immigrants from Haiti. Haitians are the fastest-growing immigrant population in Cambridge.

The Brissetteses live on the twenty-first floor of the tower closest to the Alewife Station train yards, the last stop on the Red Line subway line. The station has porcelain tile wall murals and carved maple benches and a large red neon sculpture hanging over the tracks. It is assumed that people waiting ten minutes for the train need some diversion. No such assumption is made about the people who wait long stretches for the elevator to arrive at Rindge Towers. The lobby is stark.

The air in the hallway leading to the Brissetteses' front door is thick with the smell of garlic and cooking rice. The walls and carpet are dirt colored, the walls a slightly drier mud than the carpet, and the doors are covered in chocolate brown sheet metal. There are no nameplates on the doors, but there are numbers and, occasionally, bumper stickers reminding visitors to remember Jesus.

The Brissetteses' apartment is neat, impersonal, and sparsely furnished, as though on the verge of being vacated. Just inside the door, there's a round Formica table. At mealtimes, the family sits on brown upholstered chairs, thickly covered in protective plastic, pulled in from the adjacent living room. The living room also has a coffee table set with a vaseful of bright red plastic flowers. Behind it, there's a couch. Luke and Claude like to kneel on the couch and peer out the window, watching the trains. They can see freight trains and commuter trains, as well as Red Line subway cars taking the air before their descent underground. Lucien and Madeline can hear the trains every night in their bedroom, even though their windows are almost always tightly locked. When the wind blows hard, it sounds and feels as if a train is passing through a neighbor's apartment. At those times, the tower seems to sway like a palm tree.

Luke and Claude share the smaller of the two bedrooms. There is very little floor space in their room, so they spend a lot of time playing on and under the bottom bunk of their sturdy double-decker bed. Both of them enjoy rolling trucks and cars along the carpet, and sometimes Claude, who is two, just likes to lie on his back, kick his feet, and hoot. The television is usually on in the living room, and, when there is music, both boys dance. There are no bookshelves, but there are two books, the Bible and a children's book of Bible stories. Madeline is proud that both her boys can recite Bible stories from memory.

"Claude usually tells me one each night, before he goes to

sleep," she says. "He knows the story of Cain and Abel. He knows what happened to Cain, and he knows why it happened."

Madeline is compactly built, and she dresses well, usually in pumps and dresses that flow well below her knees. Her hair is black and only slightly wavy and is swept up off her face in a style that makes her appear years older than the twenty-eight she has lived. Her skin is as smooth as the inside of a conch shell and very black. She is slow to smile, her usual expression being a wry, bemused look that reveals nothing. Sometimes her look is almost mocking, a tease.

Madeline has been looking for a job nearly every day for months now but so far hasn't had a nibble. She is sick of interviews. For now, looking for a job has become her job, and it is a job she hates too much to talk about.

Lucien is tall and athletic looking, with broad shoulders and strong arms and a gracefully erect posture. He has large soft brown eyes, a strong chin, and short cropped hair that seems always to be the same length, as though its frequent encounters with clippers have caused it to give up growing. Like Madeline, Lucien dresses fashionably, in well-cut corduroys and khakis and roomy cotton shirts. Usually he wears sneakers and, in winter, a black leather jacket. He is soft spoken and courtly, the first to get up and the last to sit when a woman or an older man walks into the room. Lucien is less reserved than Madeline, and his smile, which comes easily, is unabashed and trusting.

The Brissetteses named their first son for his father, but Lucien was a difficult name for Americans to get their tongues around, so Madeline shortened it to Luke. Luke is strong and broad shouldered like his dad, but otherwise his resemblance to Madeline is striking. Like her, he keeps a hidden agenda, as though saving himself for a later life. Though he was born in Cambridge City Hospital and has gone to school with Americans for two years, his English is spotty. Madeline explains that he was "tongue tied" at birth, a condition known as *ankyloglossia*, in which a membrane traps the tongue, holding it too tightly for normal speech. The problem was surgically corrected, but Luke still finds it difficult to express himself verbally. His body language, however, is fluent. He uses slapstick, a broad and phys-ical clowning that, at times, is hilarious and, at other times, infuriating. He loves to laugh and will do almost anything to pull off a joke, often made at the expense of others. A favorite target is his best friend, Marcel, who lives just down the hall from the Brissetteses. Marcel is lanky and awkward, with big hands and feet that seem always to be two steps ahead of his thought pro-cesses. His language skills are worse than Luke's, though not because of any physical deformity. The teachers think it might be because his parents have neglected to talk to him.

Talking at length to children is not something that Haitian parents do readily. In Haiti, children are raised in a circle of fam-ily and friends, but they are watched over by older siblings and cousins and are expected to talk to each other, not to adults. Having been born in this country, Marcel has not had much op-portunity to mingle with other kids. Because of his father's fre-quent trips and his mother's difficult pregnancy, Marcel is left in the care of the Brissetteses a good deal. In effect, Marcel has become Madeline and Lucien's third son. For them, this is no problem. In Haiti, children need not be the biological offspring of adults for them to accept responsibility for them.

Madeline and Lucien speak English fairly well and say they don't necessarily single out Haitians as friends. Their friends are mostly fellow members of the Congregation of Jehovah. They have been Jehovah's Witnesses for more than a decade, and the church is the center of their lives. Madeline spends twenty hours a week doing volunteer work for the church. She goes door to door proselytizing and handing out copies of *The Watchtower* to anyone who will agree to read it. She also helps other people learn the Bible. She says she would work full-time for the church if she could afford to. But right now, she can't; she needs a paid job.

Madeline stayed home for a few months after Luke was born and then signed on to a state-sponsored job-training program. She tried several baby-sitters, but none of them worked out. They seemed to have little interest in Luke, and Madeline wasn't sure he was safe with them. She dropped out of the job-training program and decided to delay working until Luke was old enough to go to school. But then she got pregnant again, and the car fell on Lucien, and things changed.

Lucien is cheerful and forgiving, and he is not at all bitter about having had a car fall on his chest. He says his injuries still bother him sometimes, that he has trouble playing soccer, but otherwise it's no big deal. He got some compensation, though not much, and went back to school to study telecommunications. There is no telling when or even if he will graduate. Sometimes Lucien gets philosophical about school and his career — he figures there's no point worrying, really, given that life on this earth is so brief.

Madeline can be philosophical, too, but she is also quite aware that things cost money on this earth and that her children will need at least some of those things before the millennium. Staying home with Luke and later Claude, she was impatient, knowing that she had skills that, if brushed up a bit, could earn her a living in this country. Madeline can do bookkeeping and type, and she's even dabbled in accountancy. But she wasn't free to get a job; she had no one to care for her children.

"At home in Haiti, there is an extended family; everyone takes care of the little ones," she says. "But here, there is nothing like that. People move away from their families. They are alone."

Madeline felt trapped. She did not trust many of the other people in the apartment complex; she did not feel comfortable negotiating the elevator alone with a newborn and a toddler. She found the clot of unemployed men hanging out in the lobby intimidating. The play area was bleak and coated with broken glass. Teenage boys monopolized the benches and turned up their radios way beyond the comfort zone. The parking lot was lorded over by men in their twenties doing who knew what kind of business out of the trunks of their cars. Most of the time, Madeline and the children stayed inside their apartment until Lucien came home and drove them to church. While they waited, they watched television. As she watched, Madeline's low opinion of life in America got ample reinforcement. She watched talk shows in which women openly confessed to cuckolding their husbands and men admitted to dressing up like women for kicks; soap operas in which adultery was a way of life; game shows in which adults humiliated themselves to win prizes. At night, Lucien watched with her. They heard about children dealing drugs. They heard about thirteen-year-olds having babies. And there seemed to be no end to the violence. In Haiti, there is violence, terrible violence, but here the violence is different. In Haiti, the killing has to do with politics. Here, people kill their neighbors. Children turn on their own families.

Lucien was particularly horrified when he heard of a boy in his apartment complex who reported his own father to a social service agency for beating him. Lucien knows the father; he is a neighbor and, Lucien says, a good man. He beat his boy for dealing drugs. And now, for disciplining his own son, this man was being investigated by the authorities. In America, Lucien says, children laugh at their parents rather than obey them. If parents try to gain control, the children call the police.

The year before, Madeline looked out at the glass-covered playground and the teenagers dealing drugs in front of her building. She looked out at the tired mothers, exhausted from their day's work, straggling back to their apartments at five o'clock to fix dinner for ungrateful, foul-mouthed children. This was not, Madeline thought, a proper environment for her kids. She was desperate to get them out, at least during the day.

She can't remember when or who, but someone gave her the telephone number of the Child Care Resource Center in Cambridge. The Child Care Resource Center is what is called a "resource and referral agency," or, in the jargon of early-childhood specialists, an R&R. R&Rs, of which there are hundreds around the country, supported by government, industry, and private charity, serve as a liaison among families, the community, employers, and day care providers. In Cambridge, just about everyone calls the Child Care Resource Center when they need help finding child care. When Madeline called, the woman at the front desk told her to try Cambridgeport Children's Center. She'd heard there was an opening for a subsidized child there. Madeline called, and Susan said, yes, there was an opening for a child with a voucher, a child whose parents were in a work-training program. The Brissetteses had such a voucher. Madeline went to look at Tot Lot, but she'd already decided. The idea of comparison shopping for a day care center simply did not occur to her. It was clear that any place was better than the playground at Trois Bébés. Luke started school that month.

Madeline says that she was lucky, that Luke has been very happy at Tot Lot. She thinks Claude will be happy there, too. What's ironic is that now that the kids are taken care of, Madeline can't find a job. Meanwhile, Lucien has switched fields again. He's studying air-conditioning and refrigeration technology. He is not sure when he will finish his studies. But these days he is less and less philosophical. Suddenly, he needs to get on with his life. He is thirty-five years old.

TODAY is Halloween, and Marina says she wishes she had stayed in bed. In Italy, they have carnival, not all this silliness with ghosts and witches. And candy. Marina says that tonight she'll let other people deal with the greedy hordes. She's going to lock the door to her apartment and not go out after six. After spending the whole day at Tot Lot, she can't face more kids in masks and costumes shoving paper bags under her nose.

The children were encouraged to bring costumes from home today, but a lot of them came without one. The Brissetteses, for one, don't believe in Halloween and would never permit Claude or Luke to trick-or-treat. To them, Halloween is like voodoo, not a thing to be taken lightly. They refuse to discuss it, even with Susan; it is just their way. Tonight they, like Marina, will stay at home with their doors locked, and tomorrow they will go to church and pray for those who send their children out alone in the night. Marcel is without a costume, too, but not for religious reasons. Madeline says that Marcel's father, Michel, is not a likely candidate for her church.

Michel is a large man, built like a football player, and cocky. He flirts ardently with the black teachers, especially Marie, who is also Haitian. No one is quite sure what Michel does for a living, but whatever it is, it requires him to be out of town a lot. The teachers figure that's just as well. Marcel gets a hangdog, rabbit-in-a-trap look and seems to lose the use of his tongue when his father is around.

When Michel enrolled Marcel at Tot Lot, he told Susan that

his son had not attended day care before. That seemed reasonable, given that Marcel's mother was home caring for his baby sister. But soon a social worker visiting Tot Lot on a site visit mentioned that she had seen Marcel before, in another day care center across town. The teachers in that center thought that Marcel needed special help, the kind of help that would require his parents to meet regularly with teachers and social workers and speech specialists. Word has it that when Michel got wind of this, he yanked Marcel out of the school. The next fall, Marcel was enrolled at Tot Lot. Once again, there happened to be an opening for a child with financial support from the state.

When Marcel first came to Tot Lot, it was clear that his exposure to the world outside of his apartment had been limited. Television had introduced him to dancing hamburgers and talking animals and superheroes but not to trees and leaves and grass. Cruising the sidewalk outside Tot Lot on a nature walk, Marcel would stare at a stick or a chestnut as though at some strange and wondrous object.

"When Marcel started here, we really didn't know what planet he'd come from," one teacher says. "He acted as though he had been locked in a room full of nothing all his life."

On the first day of school the previous September, it took three teachers to pull Marcel off a tricycle when his turn was over, and he kicked so hard he knocked Marina over and broke her sunglasses. Finally wrestled to the ground, he lay panting and heaving, looking frantic and confused, like a deer stopped dead in the beam of car headlights. Later, when a teacher confiscated a bag of forbidden potato chips from his lunchbox, he slapped the bag out of her hand and onto the floor, stamped on it, and lunged for the crumbs.

Seeing this and other things has led Susan to the conclusion that the teachers at Marcel's first day care center were probably right. At four, the boy has the vocabulary of a rather reticent two-year-old. He has difficulty curbing his impulses and trouble paying attention or sitting still. It is also possible that he is developmentally delayed. It's certain that Marcel would benefit a great deal from some sort of intervention. But it's equally clear that Marcel's father has no interest in mixing it up with social service agencies. Susan has seen parents like Michel before, at other centers. She remembers a time several years ago, when she asked a family at one of those centers to cooperate in an effort to have an educational plan drawn up for their son, who was wild and uncooperative and seemed learning impaired. The family got huffy and then scared, withdrew their son from the center, and disappeared. Susan still gets edgy thinking about where that child ended up. This time, she is playing it cool, waiting to see what she and the teachers can do for Marcel before calling in the behavior experts. Better to have Marcel at Tot Lot where he's safe than to force his father's hand.

BEFORE circle, the preschool teachers make a noble effort to make the preschool room spooky, or at least festive. They put lighted candles inside carved pumpkins and line them up on the red rug. This is a daring move — what with Marcel and Luke and Mike and Dylan and who knows who else dying to get their hands in those flames. At circle, Linda holds Mike tightly on her lap, circling him with her legs, while Margaret outlines the concept of "witch" to the group. To Margaret, who is a feminist, the term *witch* does not mean what it means to most people. To her, a witch is a storyteller, doctor, teacher, healer. She has, she says, witches as friends. The children's eyes widen, as if imagining Margaret sitting down to brunch with some ugly old crone just in from the Coast on her broom. Susan rolls her eyes to the ceiling, thinking of what Lucien and Madeline would think of all this. Technically, Margaret is doing nothing wrong. Nonetheless, Susan is glad there are no parents around to hear. Margaret finishes her lecture on witches and opens a storybook, an Italian fairy tale. It's a story about a good witch who has possession of a black iron kettle that, upon her command, makes unlimited amounts of pasta. It is a story in the vein of "The Sorcerer's Apprentice," in which the pot gets into the wrong (human) hands and a pasta riot ensues. The story is wonderful, but it is long, and some of the children start to droop. Monica falls asleep. Dylan lies spread-eagled on the floor. Mike attacks Jacob, pulling his sweatshirt and muttering "you're bad" over and over under his breath. As Marina and Linda deal with the skirmishes, Margaret plods on, determined to finish the tale, to carry those children who want to come to the end. Samantha, Noel, and Quy are fascinated, clearly hearing Margaret's voice as that of the witch she is reading about.

At Tot Lot, as at all day care centers, well-behaved children are the ones about whom the teachers have the least to say, the ones whose names almost never come up at staff meetings. They are often adorable, affectionate, and charming, but they are also easy to take for granted. They are at risk of being overlooked. At Tot Lot, they often are.

When the story is over, the children gather in their small groups, to which they are assigned by age. Marina's group, the Bees, is not only the youngest but the wildest, and she works quickly, so as not to tax their attention spans. But Noel, Marina's star pupil, waits patiently to have her face painted. Noel is a sprite, small and gentle, generous and obliging, with a squeaky voice that sounds like a parody of little-girlhood. She requests that a heart be painted on one pale cheek, a rainbow across the other, and stands rock steady while Marina obliges. Mike pushes past Noel and plops down in front of a student teacher, demanding that she paint him as Spiderman. But Mike can't sit still long enough for a complete face job. He grabs the paint from the teacher's hand and smears it across his forehead, down his cheeks, and onto his chin. He looks in the mirror and grins at the mess he's made.

Margaret works steadily with her group, the Butterflies, making them beautiful, many-colored masks. She transforms Moses and Monica, Quy, Skip, and Luke into the demon of their choice. She asks if the children all brought their crowns home the day before, the crowns they made from leaves collected on their nature walk. Luke says, "I don't have a home." Margaret is alarmed but keeps her smile steady. "Of course you have a home, Luke. You have a home and a brother and a mama and a papa." She persists until Luke admits that he does, indeed, have a home. It's only that he's a bit nervous about going there now, what with the devil paint on his face. But he doesn't tell Margaret that. Luke keeps his home life to himself.

Peter arrives after lunch, just in time for a nap. He comes

in a bus empty save for himself, the driver, and an aide. The city has hired a school bus and two adults to chauffeur Peter to Tot Lot every day, as though he were a movie star or a dangerous criminal. It is a costly compromise. Peter used to attend Tot Lot full-time, but the previous spring the teachers agreed that he needed more than they could give, and his father was asked to enroll him in Special Start, a morning program run by the public schools for kids with behavioral problems. Peter's father did not run from their advice; he works hard to help his son. He agreed to the terms, enrolled Peter in Special Start, and tries to see that he gets there. But he is twenty years old and on his own, and there aren't many supports for young working fathers to fall back on. All too often, Peter doesn't manage to make it to school. Those days, he stays with his grandmother, and when he comes to school the next day, he's wild. Peter's grandmother, it is rumored, has questionable taste in men and a strong taste for controlled substances. Peter's dad would prefer not to count on her, but who else, really, can he turn to? Peter is blond and blue eyed and beautiful, and everyone would like to love him, but of course they can't. There's only so much that people outside of family can give.

Today, Peter is too wound up to sleep. He's had his face painted in a Batman mask at Special Start, and he's eager to live up to his makeup. He swoops around, playfully kick-boxing with Dylan and blurting to anyone who will listen that he's not going home that night, that his mother is taking him trick-or-treating. The teachers eyeball each other. Peter's mother has been known to break a promise or two. Margaret guides Peter to a mat, helps him take off his sneakers, and, lying down next to him, dreamily strokes his hair. She lies there for twenty minutes, until Peter falls asleep. And then she lies there, stroking his forehead, a little longer.

AT lunch, the teachers talk about Thea. Thea is an adorable four-year-old with the vocabulary of a streetwalker. Thea, they say, is not only foulmouthed but cruel to the other children. Jane, her mother, has no parenting skills and resents advice. Jane is young and attractive and doesn't appreciate Thea's interfering with her busy social life. The teachers have never seen Jane talk directly to her daughter — she talks at her instead. Jane told Molly, "I don't know what her problem is, but she's got this attitude. She's bad, so I don't want you hugging her. You should yell at her when she's bad." Thea isn't at school today, and she wasn't in yesterday, and Susan thinks she may never be back. Susan has tried calling Jane several times, but to no avail. Jane had mentioned to Marie that she wanted out of the center because, she said, the other parents were too old and there were too many meetings. Jane has never made it to a meeting, but even the thought of going seems to put her off. Susan says she heard that Jane had been trying to shoehorn Thea into another center across town, but Susan is pretty sure she isn't in another center just yet. At any rate, she's heard nothing from Jane, who seems not to be answering her phone. She just hopes Thea is okay. Jane is in a job-training program, and Susan worries that she's leaving her daughter home alone, or, worse yet, with one of her boyfriends. (As it turns out, Thea never comes back. And Jane, who owes two weeks' tuition, never returns Susan's calls.)

Peter wakes up from his nap so excited about trick-or-treating that he can barely bring himself to cause trouble. He makes a halfhearted attempt to rile Mike, but Mike is such an easy mark that Peter soon tires of the game. He joins Dylan in another game of kick-boxing, carefully pulling his punches to avoid contact. He's not going to blow this opportunity to spend time with his mother. He's not going to give her a reason to forget to pick him up.

The afternoon wears on slowly, the kids restless to get out and begin the night's festivities. By 5:00, most are gone, picked up by tired parents anxious to get things over with. Only Mike, Skippy, and Peter remain. Then Elizabeth, Mike's mom, arrives, wheeling Mike's baby brother, Benjamin, in a carriage. Mike tells her he wasn't able to finish making his paper bag costume so he'll do his trick-or-treating wearing a plastic garbage bag. Elizabeth smirks — Mike rarely finishes a project. She'll be damned if she'll let him walk around in a garbage bag, but she says she'll think of something. Right now, though, she's got to get the baby home for a bottle. She hustles Mike out the door. Skippy's dad comes next. He wears a blue bandanna, an earring, and a black leather jacket. Marie compliments him on his pirate costume. He thanks her, tells her it's not a costume but his work clothes, then hurries Skip off to his waiting pickup. Marie holds her stomach and rolls into one of her rapid-fire belly laughs. She was pretty sure that the getup wasn't a costume, but she couldn't resist making the remark. Some of these parents just crack her up.

Peter is getting nervous. It's closing time, and Marina, Susan, Idara, and Marie tell each other to go home, but none of them budge. They stand, pretending to tidy up, watching the gate. It gets to be 5:35, then 5:40. Susan makes noises about calling Peter's dad. Marina gets second thoughts about trick-or-treating — maybe she'll go, just this once, and take Peter with her. At 5:45, Peter's mother opens the gate. She is young, very attractive, and stylish in a neat gray suit and matching umbrella. She takes one look at Peter, whom she hasn't seen in over a week, and tells him he looks terrible. His clothes, she says, are awful, and that Batman face has to go. Peter stands, head down, submitting to the scrutiny like an ugly man on a blind date with a bombshell. His one goal is to not piss his mother off, to avoid offending her with his presence. His goal is to have his mother make good on her promise. He summons his courage, takes her hand. "We're going trick-or-treating, right, Mom?" Susan, Marie, Idara, and Marina pretend not to listen. They fall all over each other telling Peter's mother what a great day Peter had and how he is looking forward to this evening. They have not reminded her that she is a quarter of an hour late. Peter's mother looks down at her son. She tells him to stop yanking at her umbrella. And then she pushes him out the gate and into the street.

Four

A VERY OLD SOUL

NOEL'S parents, Glen Barth and Peggy Thompson, do not have a telephone answering machine. This is a great frustration to their friends and colleagues, who wonder how two such busy people can possibly get by without this most basic of tools for modern living. Peggy and Glen don't have a ready explanation and, in fact, claim that they have an ongoing plan to buy a machine. But it seems unlikely that they will. If they had a machine, they'd feel obligated to return the calls. And they don't have the time.

Two or three mornings a week, Peggy and Glen get up at 6 A.M. to jog. Glen runs his three miles first. Peggy heads out the minute Glen returns, just as his feet hit the front steps, the two passing each other like teammates in a long-distance relay. Glen pounds panting into the living room, where he drops to do push-ups and sit-ups on the worn Oriental rug. He wears thin-rimmed glasses, lifting them from his face to wipe the sweat from his forehead with his clean white T-shirt. He says he is five feet eleven or so, but he looks shorter, possibly because he is slightly built, small boned, and thin muscled. His hair is a bit shaggy over the ears but cropped high on the forehead little-boy style. He has a thick mustache and a closely shaven, hollow-cheeked face whose features are usually set in a look of deep concern overlaid with distraction.

Peggy and Glen live on a modest Cambridge side street in a restored Victorian. The house is large and flanked tightly by its neighbors, with a fence of wire mesh out front to keep the sidewalk at bay. Their daughters Noel and Kate live here, too, as do various and sundry housemates who seem to come and go at random. (The current tenant is a young woman from Guatemala who is studying agricultural economics with the ultimate goal of helping farmers in her country find a profitable alternative to growing marijuana.)

Glen is thirty-four and has worked at a string of jobs, the current one being to coordinate the high school dropout-prevention program for the Massachusetts Department of Education. The job requires that he go to countless meetings and wear a tie most of the time. It is politically charged and slippery and demands enormous fortitude. Except for the tie part, it suits Glen well. At a small dinner party, a colleague mentioned that in the several years that she has known him, she had never seen Glen doing just one thing at a time. In fact, she was surprised to see Glen sitting in his car one day recently, waiting at a red light with no pencil in his hand. But when the light turned green, Glen's car didn't budge — he was too busy reading some memo to notice.

Peggy is not exactly the yin to Glen's yang, but she is more contained, more at ease with herself. This morning, she jogs slowly down still-sleeping Erie Street, three blocks of mostly modest old residences situated halfway between the Charles River and Central Square. She turns onto Magazine Street, a once-impressive boulevard lined with churches, apartment complexes, and houses in various states of repair and decay. From here, she jogs the few blocks to the footbridge spanning Memorial Drive, which even at this early hour is reeling under the full throttled assault of rush-hour traffic. She lopes a couple of hundred yards down the waterfront on Magazine Beach, savoring the view of sculls pulling upstream on the Charles River, and then turns back over the bridge to Brookline Street and home.

The entire loop is about a mile and a half and takes her something like twenty minutes. She stands outside a moment, hands on narrow hips, snorting the late-autumn air. Still puffing a bit, she goes inside, through the entryway with its bulletin-board mosaic of family snapshots, and into the living room, where Glen sits slumped on the couch recovering from his overdose of calisthenics. Glen gives her a quick, sheepish glance, as if to apologize for the wasted interlude, and then bounces to his feet and dashes upstairs to shower. Peggy, smiling, pads to the kitchen where she makes coffee and pushes a frozen bagel into the toaster oven. In minutes, Glen, wet headed and dressed in a checkered shirt and gray slacks, joins her. His shoes are brown, thick soled and sturdy, mail-ordered from L. L. Bean. He looks at his feet wistfully.

"It would be great if I could get everything mail order, underwear, books — everything," he says. "Shopping is such a waste of time."

Glen gulps vitamins and a cup of tea standing up. Peggy eats half of a bagel, also standing up. At 7:30, both of them trot up the stairs, Peggy to change out of her jogging clothes, and Glen to wake the kids.

Noel is deep under the covers, hugging her stuffed tiger, Tigger. Glen yanks back the blankets, grabs her, and peels off her pajama bottoms in one sweeping motion, tickling her under the arms with his free hand, growling in her ear. Noel, pretending to sleep, smiles weakly and lets him get on with it. She's inured to this routine. Glen has her dressed in seconds in Minnie Mouse underpants, purple stretch pants, and red socks. At Noel's somnolent request, and to odd effect, Glen layers a short-sleeved T-shirt over a long-sleeved jersey. Noel smiles with sleepy approval; the layered look is her trademark. Her sneakers, which are pink and well worn, fasten with Velcro strips.

Noel has brown hair that is full and slightly wavy. It's coaxed rather than parted to the side of her head and falls in clumps over her forehead. She has thin arms and legs and no belly to speak of, but she is not at all fragile. She will be four years old in January.

71

Glen orders Noel to feed her fish and then points her in the direction of breakfast. He walks through the connecting door and into Kate's room.

Kate is six and less pliant than her sister. She grabs the covers back out of Glen's hand, which recoils like an ax head hitting steel. Glen strides across the room to a small plastic record player and drops the phonograph needle onto a recording of "Puff the Magic Dragon." He twists up the volume. Kate grimaces, pulls the covers over her head. Glen sweeps them off her again. Kate looks pained and then angry. She whines, arches her back, folds her legs into a fetal position. Glen shrugs, tells her to hurry, and goes downstairs to the kitchen.

The kitchen walls are yellow paint over plaster and exposed brick. Peggy and Glen pulled down a wall several years before to allow light to squeeze in through the back-door window. Otherwise, the kitchen is pretty much unrenovated. The refrigerator is peppered with political cartoons torn from the *Boston Globe*. The pilot light on the stove burned out ages ago. Glen and Peggy don't plan to get it fixed, arguing that two hundred dollars is too much to pay for the convenience of not having to light a match. For them, it's not the money, it's the principle. There is no dishwasher.

Peggy's coffee gets cold as she stands in her signature Reeboks sneakers slapping butter onto slabs of banana bread for the kids. Her hair, which is strawberry blonde and permed into a tangle, is still damp from the shower. Peggy is slim and nearly as tall as Glen, with freckled fair skin, blue eyes, and pale, almost invisible eyelashes. When she was younger, she was probably gangly or coltish. She looks as though she might have played basketball in high school, but on a club team rather than on varsity. She is dressed for work in a loden green skirt and a blue-and-green plaid shirt with the sleeves rolled to the elbows. A thick clutch of keys jingles at her waist. She wears no makeup, but her face is lit from the side by her earrings, reflective, multi-colored plastic dangles. She putters about, deep in thought, while Glen huddles behind the sports pages.

Peggy is a teacher at Graham and Parks, a progressive public elementary and junior high school. She teaches seventh- and eighth-grade language arts and social history. Her first job, right after getting a bachelor's degree in history from Oberlin College, was as a secretary at Harvard University, where she marched in a picket line in support of a union for clerical workers. She recalls this as her first overtly political act. Later she worked for a couple of nonprofit agencies and then went back to college to get a master's degree in order to teach. Peggy says Glen is the better teacher, but friends disagree. Glen regards teaching as an exercise in which one keeps one's cool, maintains control, and stays one chapter ahead of the students. Peggy is committed to teaching with an intensity that borders on self-abuse.

Peggy and Glen have many things in common, but foremost among them is a fierce sympathy for underdogs. This concern extends beyond national boundaries, and even over continents. Years ago, they traveled together to Central America to learn Spanish and ended up working as volunteer health aids at a clinic. They have been active supporters of the South African liberation movement for close to a decade. But they also fight local battles, for Cambridge's controversial rent-control policy, for instance, even though they own their home. Peggy recalls being a bit timid in her convictions when she was younger, but her mother says Peggy has always been a crusader. She works harder than most people and regrets that she isn't able to give more. Sometimes Peggy gets so caught up in the needs of others that people get the misimpression that she has none of her own.

By the time Noel gets downstairs, Glen is buried deep in the metro section. Noel smiles dreamily, sits down close to her father, and stares quizzically at her banana bread. Unlike Kate, Noel does not squander words. She didn't talk until she was nearly three because, Peggy recalls, "It just wasn't important to her."

Peggy once told an acupuncturist of a dream she had about Noel. The acupuncturist thought for a while and then said, "Your daughter sounds like she has a very old soul." To Peggy, that sounded just right.

Noel toys with her breakfast as Kate, all scowls, storms in and throws herself into a chair. Noel smiles at her brightly, oblivious to the melodrama. Kate wants an apology from Glen for invading her space in the bedroom, but she knows that she won't get one, and that makes her mad. Glen, ignoring her glares, probes further into the metro section, foraging for news of the Cambridge Rainbow, a grass-roots political group committed to the city's progressive candidates. In Cambridge, progressives are defined as candidates who support rent control and oppose commercial land development. There is a forest of Cambridge Rainbow placards in the front yards of the Thompson Barth neighborhood, and Glen himself has spent an untold number of hours haggling and campaigning on behalf of the group. He reads juicy bits aloud from the paper as Peggy hovers uncertainly over the children's empty lunch bags, trying to figure out what to drop in. Kate breaks in with a whine.

"Daddy, you always make me peanut butter and jelly for lunch, and I hate it, even on crackers. I don't make you lunch so you don't have to eat peanut butter and jelly every day." She is almost in tears.

Glen cuts her off. "Okay, we've got to leave in five minutes. Anyway, I don't make your lunch; your mother does. I hate making lunch."

Peggy pulls food from the refrigerator, chanting "I love lemon yogurt," thinking she'll cop one for her own lunch bag. But there's only one lemon left, and Kate quickly requisitions it. It's not that she's selfish; it's just that she sees no alternative. There's tuna in the cupboard, but Kate is boycotting tuna. "Tuna fishermen kill dolphins in their nets," she explains, looking stone-cold serious and coy at the same time. Peggy drops the lemon yogurt into Kate's bag.

"This is Kate's first independent political act," she says. "And it's really convenient because Kate hates tuna."

Noel smacks her lips. "I love tuna, and I love coffee yogurt too," she says. Peggy says that Noel may seem shy, but she's not — what she is is accommodating. Glen, who has no stomach for talk of food, pushes back from the table to make his own lunch: a box of crackers and a jar of peanut butter dumped in a grocery bag. He'd rather haul around a sackful of groceries all day than deal with spreading peanut butter on bread before noon.

"We have two minutes," he warns. His voice seems disembodied, like that of a flight announcer at an airline terminal. His mind is still on the elections. He stands at the sink, running water over the breakfast dishes. Kate stalks out and returns with a bicycle helmet coated with reflective stickers. She centers the helmet carefully on her head and fastens the safety strap under her chin. Glen ties his necktie. Peggy puts on her helmet and hands Noel hers — she'll need it later for the ride home on the back of Peggy's bike. Peggy rolls her bike around to the side door, Kate goes out to get her own, and they pedal off to school together. Glen grabs Noel by the hand and all but throws her into the Hyundai, which looks new. He bought it the previous year, he says, when his old car, an ancient Toyota, was ripped off. Having had his car stolen seems to bother Glen much less than having to drive around in a new one. Glen backs quickly out of the driveway, already distracted by his meetings, which today are in downtown Boston. As always, he'll drop Noel at Tot Lot on the way.

BEFORE Peggy gave birth to Kate six years ago, she didn't think of herself as the mothering type. "I wasn't one of those women who always dreamed of having babies," she says. So she was pleasantly surprised at the overwhelming joy she felt when Kate was born. She adored Kate instantly, loved her with an unexpected intensity. Still, the thought of staying home all day with a helpless newborn gave her pause. With thousands of teachers getting laid off around the state, she saw herself as becoming increasingly less employable, and she worried about getting trapped, a housewife forever. In a small, unexpected way, she began to resent her new role.

"Somehow, I got appointed primary parent," Peggy says. "Somehow, I was the one who was expected to stop working. I panicked; I couldn't see beyond the point of never working again."

But Peggy did go to work just five months after Kate was born, at Jobs With Peace, a nonprofit agency that redirects public funds and manpower out of the military and into the civilian sector. She brought Kate to a family day care home in Woodrow

Wilson Court, a low-income housing project just three blocks from her home.

This arrangement lasted three weeks. It turned out that Kate's baby-sitter had taken on more than her legal limit of children under the age of two, which, in Massachusetts, is two. The woman thought nothing of this; she said she had no problem taking care of three infants. Indeed, the Massachusetts limit is one of the strictest in the country; North Carolina, for example, allows eight infants per provider. Most states fall somewhere in between, settling on four or five infants. Still, there is pressure to ease those restrictions to lower the cost of care.

At any rate, Peggy and Glen knew that plenty of women who offered day care in their homes were bucking the requirements in order to pull in bigger weekly profits, and they could sympathize, but at the same time they didn't feel comfortable breaking a law that made so much sense to them. (The idea of caring for more than two infants at one time blew Peggy's mind.) They moved Kate into another family day care home, this time with a Korean woman whom Peggy describes as "wonderful" and whose husband was in graduate school at Harvard. Everything went splendidly for five months. Then there was the accident.

It happened Sunday, May 13, 1984, when Kate was eleven months old. It was Mother's Day, Peggy's first, and the little family spent it on a picnic with their friends Mary Teseo and George Pillsbury. That evening, after getting home and eating dinner, Peggy settled down in front of the television with a cup of peppermint tea to watch *The Dollmaker*.

Peggy recalls the opening scene of the film as gruesome. A girl is choking. Her mother, played by Jane Fonda, stands in the middle of a back country road, frantically trying to flag down a car to take her daughter to the hospital. No one stops. The mother, left with no alternative, takes out her whittling knife and plunges it into her daughter's throat, saving her life instinctively with an improvised tracheotomy. It was then, Peggy says, that she heard a "blood-curdling scream." The scream didn't come, as she first thought, from the television set. It came from the floor near her feet where Kate sat drenched in steaming peppermint tea.

Peggy and Glen tore at Kate's clothes, clawing off all but her diaper. Their hands were suddenly clumsy, unable to remove the pins. They rushed her to the bathroom, doused her with cool water from the faucet. Peggy recalls being confused by the endless layers of wet toilet paper that kept coming off in her hands. Suddenly, and with horror, she recognized the toilet paper as Kate's skin, peeling off in fine, translucent sheets. Kate, it seemed, was in shock. Somehow Peggy, Glen, and Kate got to the car, to Memorial Drive, to Massachusetts General Hospital, and from there to the Shriners Burn Institute. The doctors and nurses applied ice, shrouded Kate in layers of gauze. Kate stopped crying, went silent as a mummy. The doctors took her away and told Peggy and Glen that Kate could not go home that night, nor for the next week, or maybe two. They would see how things went and get back to them. Glen nodded. Peggy stared at them incredulously. She could not imagine going home without her baby. The doctor sat her and Glen down and gently plied them with questions about how it all happened and whether it had happened before. He needed to get to the bottom of things. Peggy understood; the doctor was looking for a place to lay the blame. She gratefully took it on herself. It was, after all, her cup of peppermint tea.

Kate was fine. The scar, a slight crinkling of skin on her neck and chest, is noticeable only to Peggy. But Peggy took the accident as a sign. How could she possibly leave her baby in the care of someone else all day? How could her need to work compare with the need Kate had for a full-time mother?

"I felt so guilty," she says. "Here I was, worrying about my career, working harder and harder, and here was this tiny, fragile life, who needed me so desperately. I was missing it all because of work. I was missing out on it all."

Peggy went home, called her boss at Jobs With Peace, and quit.

That was in May. By October, Peggy had stayed home for four months and had begun feeling once again as though she wasn't doing enough. Peggy remembered her mother, a corporate wife whose only connection to work while Peggy was growing up was as a hostess at hospitality suites at her husband's sales seminars. Peggy's father couldn't cook a hot dog. He said changing diapers made him sick. Now he was off in California somewhere near the ocean, retired and doing what amounted to nothing, and her mother was working in a real estate office in Maryland, happy and free at last.

Peggy went out to look for a job. Incredibly, a part-time teaching position "fell from the sky" and into her life, a job-sharing arrangement at Graham and Parks School just three blocks from home. It meant that she could work and divide the rest of her time between Kate and her political interests. It meant that she didn't have to miss a thing.

Peggy and Glen found another place for Kate to go each morning, the home of a former day care teacher who Peggy knew was both competent and loving. But the arrangement was short-lived, the woman moved away, and Kate was put into day care home number four, this one operated by a woman who, Glen says, "didn't really do anything but let the kids run wild." Every afternoon, Kate would come home with reports of being hit by Paula, a girl about her age who happened to be the caregiver's granddaughter. Every morning, Glen and Peggy would insist that Kate go back and turn the other cheek. Finally Kate announced that she could stand it no longer. If Paula hit her one more time, she was going to hit her back. Glen and Peggy were horrified. They told Kate no, that hitting was bad. But Kate came home that afternoon bragging about her knockdown punch. From then on, Glen says, Paula and Kate were fast friends. "That really shook up our liberal sensibilities," he says, laughing. When Glen relates this story, which he does often, he has a hard time containing his pride.

AMONG the childhood memories Glen Barth recalls most often are the Tuesday evening boxing matches his father arranged for himself, his brothers, and his stepbrothers, the children of his father's second wife. Glen recalls his brothers and himself clob-

bering his stepbrothers week after week. The fact that the stepbrothers were younger and smaller than he certainly dulls the
thrill of victory, but one imagines that, for Glen, the agony of
defeat would have been much, much worse.

Glen's parents separated when he was one, when his father
admitted to an ongoing affair with Glen's godmother, an old family friend with three children of her own. Glen's father married
the woman, adopted her children, and moved his new family to
a country town twenty-five miles north of Boston. Glen's mother,
a graduate of Radcliffe and chairwoman of the local school committee, remarried a couple of times, bringing more children and
confusion into the family. Glen spent the school year with his
mother and her second husband in a swank and woodsy Boston
suburb, and his summers with his brothers and his father's new
family on the farm. Glen's father was a World War II hero, a
graduate of Harvard University, and the president of a profitable
family business founded by Glen's great-grandfather. But he kept
his upper-middle-class origins firmly under wraps, preferring to
pass himself off as a working-class stiff. The farm was nothing
more than a rich man's conceit, but Glen's dad made his sons
work for their supper. Glen remembers tending sheep, milking
cows, slopping hogs, and testing electric fences with his bare
finger for his father's amusement. In their spare time, he and his
brothers boxed or wrestled under their father's watchful tutelage
in a game called "break the German's neck." Glen was given a
BB gun when he was ten, a .22-caliber rifle at age twelve, and a
shotgun when he was fourteen. He was expected to hunt but
couldn't bring himself to shoot at animals. He says he became a
good enough marksman shooting at rocks and his father never
knew the difference. On weekends, Glen's dad lined his sons up
in a row on the front lawn and hosed them down with the garden
hose, like horses. He said he did it to save water, but Glen knew
better even then.

"My dad loved poetry, and he taught me my love of the
woods," Glen says. "He'd be up every morning at five to work.
But he would also get plastered every night. He was an alcoholic
and explosive and could be violent at times. When he was feeling

particularly angry at the world, he would line me and my brothers up against a wall, make us bend over, and beat us one by one with a belt. Violence really decimated my family."

Glen's father spent the last five years of his life silently toughing out a bleeding ulcer because, as Glen puts it, "real men don't go to doctors." The ulcer was discovered the day his father came home dizzy from the lumber mill, shooed away offers of medical assistance, and proceeded to have a massive heart attack. The attack required a quadruple bypass, and when the doctors opened him up, they found what they said was the most thoroughly damaged heart they'd ever seen beating in the chest of a living human. Later, they also discovered the ulcer. The doctors told Glen's dad to slow down and stop drinking. The night he got home from the hospital, he pushed back from the dinner table, strolled over to the liquor cabinet, and poured himself a Cape Codder, a stiff dose of vodka set blushing with a hint of cranberry juice. It was his favorite cocktail. Glen says his dad died with the glass in his hand.

Glen did not go unaffected by his family's unfolding drama. He grew up restless, impatient, and vaguely troubled, with a proclivity toward drink that often went beyond the playful. He dropped out of Bennington, the elite Vermont college, at nineteen and moved in with a girlfriend in Somerville, a blue-collar town just north of Cambridge. He worked as a stock boy at the largest manufacturer of automobile covers in the world, as a rug hauler at a carpet factory, and as a builder of slate roofs. At twenty, he got a job as a mental health assistant at McLean Hospital, near Boston. He worked on the adolescent ward, with young men who, he says, "were at the same developmental level as me. Working with crazy kids helped me struggle through my own issues. It was the first job I had ever enjoyed."

Peggy and Glen met that summer on the playing field during a community soccer game. They are both strong soccer players. Peggy had a boyfriend at the time, but that didn't stop her from getting together with Glen on the sly to go skinny-dipping in Sandy Pond Reservoir. Peggy remained faithful to her boyfriend that summer, but she found herself increasingly intrigued by Glen's flat-footed, forceful style. Glen was drawn to Peggy's gentleness and to her quiet and persistent strength. By then, he had decided to become an educator. He talked himself into a job working with poor inner-city children in an afterschool program. From there, he jumped from job to job, one year working six different jobs in a row while at the same time earning a master's degree in education at night. Finally, degree in hand and hungry to teach full-time, he marched into Charles River Academy, a small school about a mile east of Harvard Square.

Housed in a well-kept Victorian on a quiet side street in central Cambridge, Charles River Academy had the look of an expensive training ground for students with aspirations toward the ivy-covered halls to the west. It was not. On the whole, the boys who attended Charles River Academy did not intend to go on to Harvard. On the whole, the boys who attended Charles River had more immediate concerns on their minds, such as keeping out of jail. In less enlightened times, these boys would have been labeled delinquent. In 1982, they were called troubled or learning disabled or, more likely, both. Glen considered the school a perfect place to ply his talents. He told the director he'd heard there was an opening, though, of course, he'd heard no such thing. The director's jaw dropped: as it happened the science teacher, a man of delicate sensibilities, had stormed off the job just that morning. Regaining his composure, the director sputtered that, yes, a position was available. He interviewed Glen, determined him qualified, and hired him on the spot. Glen began teaching the boys of Charles River Academy the next day.

"The fact that I'd never taken a science course in my life tells you something about where special-needs education was at that time," Glen says.

Glen stayed at Charles River for three years, longer than he'd stuck with any job. He and Peggy were living together by then, thinking about having a family, and debating whether to marry. They knew full well that Glen's dad would disown him if he had a child out of wedlock. But the deciding factor was health insurance. Charles River offered it, and Peggy needed it, but to get it she needed to marry Glen. It was that simple. The morning of the wedding ceremony, Peggy discovered she was pregnant with Kate.

*　　*　　*

IN September 1985, Kate was twenty-seven months old, old enough, Glen and Peggy decided, to enter day care. While Peggy was somewhat apprehensive about putting Kate in with a large group of children, Glen was more concerned about the inconsistencies in care that she had already experienced.

"The transitory nature of our experience with family day care certainly fueled our fire," Glen says. "If it had been up to me, I would have put Kate into day care sooner."

Kate was a bit timid, a follower rather than a leader, and her parents thought a more social environment would bring her into her own. Tot Lot was their first and only choice. They knew a lot of people who sent their kids to Tot Lot, notably their best friends, George Pillsbury and Mary Tiseo, whose son Nicolas seemed to love the place. Tot Lot was part of the neighborhood — Peggy and Glen had jitterbugged many a night away there at community fund-raising dances. They liked the space, they liked the teachers, and they liked the mix of kids. They liked Tot Lot's history of commitment to integration and intercultural education. And Tot Lot remained one of the few day care centers in the area that had managed to maintain a semblance of its original cooperative philosophy. While parents no longer worked as assistant teachers as they had in the school's early days, they were required to serve on committees and to attend monthly general meetings. At Tot Lot, parents were not encouraged, as one teacher put it, to "just dump their kids and run." They were required to participate. Peggy and Glen regarded parental participation as critical.

"The more decision making you allow people, the more empowered they feel and the more innovative they become," Glen says. (Glen has spent enough years in school administration to talk like that with authority, at the decided risk of sometimes sounding like a sloganeer.) Tot Lot allowed as much input as parents had the time to give. In theory, it seemed perfect. In fact, it was a mess.

"We didn't find out that Tot Lot was in crisis until four days after Kate enrolled," Glen says. "Actually, it was falling apart."

For starters, Tot Lot's building — originally an oversized garage — was up for sale, and there was some doubt that it would continue to exist. Glen and Peggy felt ripped off, betrayed. Couldn't the teachers see that Kate had already been through more transitions than any child should have to tolerate? How could they let her risk yet another change? The answer was that no one believed that the landlord would really do what he was about to do — evict Tot Lot from the space where his own seven children (two from his first marriage, three from his second marriage, and two from his second wife's first marriage) had attended preschool for free. They couldn't believe that the man was taking no consideration of the hundreds of hours of sweat equity Tot Lot families had put into that structure. They couldn't believe that the guy had changed so drastically from the easygoing counterculture type he once had been. But he had: this was serious money, and he was holding firm. The landlord gave the parents an ultimatum: either they bought the building outright for $125,000 and guaranteed a price of $275,000 for the home that fronted it, or they were out of there.

Mary Tiseo and others worked frantically to save the center. The fund-raising went on for months and, thanks at least in part to Mary's connections in the world of philanthropy, was surprisingly fruitful. Tot Lot raised about $90,000, starting with a $25,000 grant from the Boston Foundation (described by one parent as "a place where guilty old Boston Brahmins leave their money") and followed by contributions from alumni and several anonymous donors. The school took out a mortgage for the remaining $35,000 and bought the garage. The landlord was unable to sell his house at the price that he wanted, so George Pillsbury quietly pulled $275,000 out of his trust fund and bought the place. Most parents were not aware of the transaction, but some of those who were were shocked: they hadn't realized that George Pillsbury, the shaggy-haired, lanky young man who favored well-worn sweaters and faded corduroys was THE George Pillsbury, heir to the bakery empire. George quickly sold the house, recouped his investment, and went back to posing as just another parent.

Unfortunately, as Glen and Peggy were soon to find out, Tot Lot's problems were not solved in this transaction. What they didn't know, what they hadn't wanted to know, was that the school was starting to crumble from within. Most of the blame for this was put on the director, a middle-class woman and mother of two who had pretensions toward the proletariat. Though on some levels well meaning, the director had alienated most of the white, professional families in the center. She had also alienated every social service agency in the city. As a result, Tot Lot had ceased getting referrals of prospective students and, for the first time in its existence, was underenrolled. Glen and Peggy sized the director up as a clear burnout case. She came to work late and left early, eventually clocking in as few as fifteen hours a week in a job requiring fifty or more. The teachers felt abandoned. Staff turnover was so high that the hiring committee was in continuous session. There was never not a teacher vacancy at the school.

Glen and Peggy were determined to come to the rescue. They had been in enough politically and emotionally charged situations in their lives to expect conflict and to know how to deal with it. They had no idea why the current director had been hired in the first place — by the time they entered the school, she seemed totally devoid of interpersonal skills — but they had heard that when she showed up she was good with the children and with the center's poorer families. They decided to try to establish a constructive relationship with her despite her obvious hostility toward them and the other middle-class parents. That spring, Peggy, who was by then on maternity leave with Noel, joined the coordinating committee, the center's main advisory body, to work toward setting some guidelines. It took nine months for the committee to agree on a document, and by then the director had left in a huff, leaving a legacy of bad feelings and bad management that would take two years for Susan, the new director, to sort out.

Meanwhile, Kate was enrolled in a class of toddlers that turned out to be the most difficult in Tot Lot's history. Glen says that five of the thirteen children in Kate's group had serious problems, problems that they sometimes chose to take out on his daughter. One of the boys was so violent that Molly thought he might have some kind of seizure disorder. The child had a habit of sneaking up on other kids from behind and yanking out fist-fuls of their hair or clobbering them with any object within reach. This child set a tone of violence that was picked up and carried by several other boys in the class.

"One kid was always dressed like GI Joe, and his parents would come in high every day of the week," Glen says. (Tot Lot has no explicit policy about parents who come in intoxicated, although teachers do not release children to anyone who appears drunk or stoned.) "But you have to expect at least some of this at an inner-city school that is open to everyone. Special-needs kids have special-needs parents. You can't expect everything to be easy and pristine when you make a commitment to urban education. We thought it was healthy for Kate to deal with ad-versity early in life — we figured she'd have to face it sooner or later, why not from the get-go?"

But Peggy recalls moments when she thought that Tot Lot might be doing Kate more harm than good. "I have to admit that we almost withdrew her a couple of times," she says. "There's a fine line between letting children deal with difficulties and en-dangering them. But Molly held the room together. She was wonderful. We decided to let Kate guide us. And she loved the place. She was really growing."

At two and a half, Kate and the other toddlers were com-posing stories, learning songs in Spanish, and being introduced to the history of the American civil-rights movement. When Kate graduated from Tot Lot three years later, she had acquired a love of reggae, a flair for the dramatic, and a penchant for talking a good deal tougher than she looked. She was confident, street smart, outspoken, and a bit bossy, and those who met her found it impossible to believe that she had ever been shy or reserved. Less than a year later, during the summer between kindergarten and first grade, Kate taught herself to read and began talking wistfully about the day when she would be old enough to get her own apartment.

Noel, who began her first year in the preschool room at Tot Lot in the fall of 1989, is not at all like her sister. While Kate is moody, demonstrative, and extroverted, Noel is internal and mysterious. While Kate is stubborn and has no difficulty in expressing her opinions, Noel thinks long and hard before opening her mouth. Kate is eager to take charge and always willing to compete. Noel hangs back, and is so uncompetitive that she refuses even to do puzzles if she suspects that someone is egging her on. The teachers describe her as "the perfect child," a quiet, sensitive girl who is willing to give almost any activity a try.

"Noel is such a private person," Peggy says. "When she has a nightmare, she'll come sleep in my bed, but she won't tell me about what she dreamed. Things go on in her head that I'll never know about. But I don't worry about Noel being overlooked. If she really needs something, she asks for it. It's just that she experiences life in an independent way."

As far as how Noel is faring at Tot Lot, Peggy can only guess. Noel doesn't talk about it, and Peggy doesn't have the time to see for herself. This year, for the first time since Kate was born, Peggy is working full-time. Initially this made her nervous: rushing out of her classroom, Kate in tow, to retrieve Noel by 4:15 every day was not her idea of ideal motherhood. She wanted time with her girls, and she hated to rush them. But gradually she began to rationalize.

"When I was working part-time, I'd always try to make a few calls while I was helping Kate build with her Lego blocks," she says. "I felt like I had to clean the house and make dinner by six o'clock because, after all, I was only working part-time, right? Now I don't clean the house every day, and we have take-out food at least once a week. I have an excuse not to be perfect. I feel focused. When I get home, the kids are my priority."

Peggy is wild about Noel's small-group teacher, Marina; she loves her energy, spontaneity, and warmth. Still, Peggy can't keep down a nagging feeling that things aren't quite right at Tot Lot. She feels herself pulling back from Noel's experience, distancing herself from whatever difficulties her youngest might be having at school. Last year, she spent many hours negotiating an ongoing dispute between Margaret and Ben, preschool teachers with radically different styles. The result of all her efforts seems to have been nil: Ben, a teacher whom Peggy had enormous regard for, has left, and Margaret, about whom Peggy has serious doubts, is one of Noel's three morning teachers. She has heard word of difficulties between Margaret and another pre-school teacher and about Margaret's anger, which, it is hinted, is sometimes directed at the kids.

In fact, Margaret is in some ways a better and some ways a worse teacher than Peggy suspects. She is abrupt and unsympathetic at times, but rumors that she has been rough and "inappropriate" with children are overblown. Though her tolerance for misbehavior is lower than it should be, her dedication and creativity have helped several children stretch artistically and intellectually. She is particularly good with curriculum, with putting an activity in perspective and making it a learning experience. Noel, the daughter of educated, middle-class parents, is of perhaps less interest to Margaret than she might be — Margaret is a crusader, and low-key, well-balanced Noel offers her no challenge. Still, Noel is drawn by Margaret's way with fairy tales and by her patient skill with arts-and-crafts projects. The fact is that, while Margaret is unpopular with many parents, far less popular than Marina, she is an important counterpoint to Marina's free-wheeling and sometimes disorganized style. She brings an enormous amount of thought and care to her work, if not always the requisite warmth.

But Peggy and Glen have their doubts. In a school like Tot Lot, with its emphasis on team teaching, leadership is key; Susan, according to Glen and Peggy is no leader. Peggy is doubly frustrated because she doesn't have the time or the will to do anything about what she sees as Susan's laxity.

"Really, at this point, I can't take the time to care about what's going on at Tot Lot," she says late one night, a pile of sewing on her lap. "It may not be ideal, but we aren't looking for perfection for our children. I don't believe that institutions make the child, anyway. Noel always creates her own space where she is happy. As long as she's happy, I'm okay."

Five

INSTEAD OF CHURCH

CAMBRIDGEPORT Children's Center is housed in a squat one-story building wedged tightly into a tiny backyard lot in the Cambridgeport district of Cambridge, Massachusetts, a ramshackle neighborhood in one of the most densely populated cities in the country. Cambridgeport has little in common with Harvard Square, its better-known neighbor to the west. While the square fairly teeters under the weight of its own significance, Cambridgeport has the self-mocking air of the third world about it and a musky, sensual edge that can bring you up short.

Central Square is a favorite haunt of students from the Massachusetts Institute of Technology, who schlepp here in shabby clumps for a blast of sugar and MSG between bouts with computers and cyclotrons. It is also popular with a better-dressed crowd, the drug dealers who emerge from the subway to do business in the alleys behind the cut-rate clothing and furniture stores and fast-food joints that line Massachusetts Avenue. Drunks gather here, too, their faces wrinkled like sun-dried apples, their hands thrust forward in a half-hearted hustle for change. The liquor stores have vast displays of single-slug bottles, peppermint schnapps and Jack Daniels. Cops double-park outside. But there is not much really sinister here. The drunks don't push too hard. The cops spend most of their time sucking doughnut-shop coffee from paper cups. And the drug dealers step aside for broad-hipped, pocketbook-toting grandmothers making their weekly grocery-shopping trips to the Purity Supreme.

The restaurants in Central Square mirror the ethnicity of their clientele: Latin, Portuguese, Haitian, Mandarin, Ethiopian, Caribbean, Indian. Most of the pizza joints are owned by Greeks, and the best place to get falafel, the Middle East Restaurant, hosts reggae and punk bands on Saturday night. Little Joe Cook and the Thrillers have been singing rhythm and blues in the Cantab Lounge for the past fifteen years. A few blocks further down, The Plough and Stars pub has Guinness on draft and shows tapes of British soccer matches on Sunday afternoons.

Below Central Square, Cambridgeport is a jumble of moth-eaten estates, neatly kept row houses, thin-walled apartment buildings, and industrial sprawl splayed across one bank of the Charles River. Early residents of "Old Cambridge" regarded this area as a brazen embarrassment, an eyesore to be tolerated briefly on trips east to Boston. Harvard boys would scurry through "the Port" as quickly as possible, noses held against the stench of manufacture and hard labor, eyes averted from the hungry stares of immigrants.

Cambridgeport's very name is the legacy of an idea gone sour. A bridge linking Cambridge with Boston completed in 1793 suddenly made the swampy parcel of oyster beds and farmland accessible to commercial possibility. Among many ideas was the building of a deep-water port suitable for international trade. The plan, backed by several monied investors, quickly bombed, but the development of Cambridgeport as a commercial link between Boston and the farmlands to the west proceeded briskly and culminated in a big industrial push in the second half of the nineteenth century.

Early industries were mostly small scale, involving, among other things, the making of cigars, rope, cabinets, and leather. Later, more ambitious enterprises such as carriage building and the mass manufacture of soap were made possible by the cheap labor of a growing immigrant population. Later still, the building of a steam railroad opened the area to even more large scale industrialization, inspiring an even greater influx of immigrants. In 1848, just over 2 percent of Cambridgeport residents were reported in census records to have "foreign-sounding names." By 1855, that figure had increased almost tenfold. These newcomers required housing, and the housing of choice became the horizontally divided "triple decker," a low-cost configuration that allowed three families (and assorted boarders) to stack up in some comfort under one (flat) roof.

Industry continued to flood into Cambridgeport until the mid-1920s, when federal quotas sharply curtailed the attraction of the Port to immigrant laborers. There seemed to be no more land to be developed anyway — by any rational standard, Cambridgeport was saturated. But growth did not stop. Instead, whole neighborhoods were yanked down to make way for new and more efficient land use. Apartment houses of four, five, and six stories poked their roofs above the remaining triple deckers. And housing standards slipped disastrously. A 1941 to 1943 Works Progress Administration survey concluded that more than 50 percent of Cambridge residents lived in "substandard" conditions. A couple of federally funded public-housing projects did little to remedy the problem, nor did the construction of new, publicly funded high rises. Industry and the seemingly insatiable land hunger of the Massachusetts Institute of Technology had squeezed just about as much out of Cambridgeport as could be squeezed. In the early 1970s, the expansion of MIT and research-related industries, as well as its proximity to Harvard, had made this lowly working-class community a residential hot spot. The demand for housing became so great that little attention needed to be paid to the maintenance of that housing to attract renters. Prices soared; there was no space to spare. Which explains, at least in part, why Cambridgeport Children's Center ended up in a deserted eighteen-car garage.

The garage had been built in 1929 or 1930, no one recalls for sure, behind a three-story home at 65 Chestnut Street, two blocks north of the Charles River. The house was designed in the late Queen Anne style by J. A. Hasty, a Cambridgeport architect of some note. It is of generous and graceful proportions, a house for the upper middle classes. The garage is a low-slung concrete monolith. To the group of young parents who were scouting it out as space for their fledgling child-care center in the early 1970s, the building was a painful reminder of just how low children had fallen on the city's scale of priorities. One recalls it as a "black hole, a yawning pit."

But it was not without appeal. For one thing, it was available. For another, it had so little going for it that the parents figured it was unlikely that anyone would bother to reclaim it. By this time, the tightly knit group of overextended families had grown tired of play spaces slipping from their grasp. The parents, a motley mix of students, two college professors, a carpenter, a banker, a couple of welfare mothers, a Fuller Brush salesman, one or two psychologists, and others, were on the edge of desperation. Some were women who had abandoned school or a career to raise families and were feeling isolated and trapped. Some were men married to these women. Some were working couples scrambling for a way to keep their children safe and occupied while they worked. And some were single parents who had run out of options.

This was 1973, when more than six million children under the age of six had working mothers. Two years earlier, President Richard Nixon had vetoed a bill passed by Congress authorizing federal dollars to provide day care for the children of poor working mothers. His argument, and the argument of many day care opponents of the time, was that to subsidize day care was to subsidize the demise of the American family. Mothers belonged with their children, and fathers belonged in the workplace, earning money to support their families. No matter that this cherished American ideal had already become an anachronism.

Finding the garage was a huge break for the parents of Tot Lot, whose children had been bounced from one location to another for three years. Tot Lot got its start at the Morse School playground, a jumble of rusty climbing structures stuck into a slab of asphalt that was one of the few open spaces in Cambridgeport. Cooped-up preschoolers swarmed to the Morse on sunny days like locusts to a wheat field, and the city sweetened the deal by giving them access to two of the school's kindergarten rooms for indoor activities all summer. Crammed with as many as forty children, several of them infants in cribs, it was a chaotic, ad hoc setup, but it kept the kids happy and parents sane through sticky New England summers. It occurred to some parents that it might be good to turn this arrangement into a year-round thing for their toddlers and preschoolers. They wanted something less formal than a nursery school but more stable than a playgroup, a program that would be as ethnically and racially diverse as the neighborhood and run not by teachers or administrators but by the parents themselves. Since none of the mothers in the group worked full-time, their concern was not coverage but, as one mother put it, "parental relief and companionship." They also wanted to escape their middle-class isolation, to take a few tentative steps into the ethnicity of their community. And they wanted their children to come with them, as Columbia University historian Sheila Rothman put it, "to educate [their] children to tolerance."

But they needed a place. So they asked; they asked at churches and they asked at schools and they asked at businesses with empty basements. And every time they asked, they were told no. There was some mumbling about insurance costs and liability, but these concerns, the parents thought, were not the real issue. The real issue was tradition. Women who left their children in group care were regarded by many with suspicion, even in liberal Cambridge, with its food co-op and its ban-the-bomb rallies.

"It was like we were trying to do some really terrible thing," a parent recalls. "Somehow, the words 'day care' just drove people crazy."

But, oddly enough, a guy from the Veterans of Foreign Wars seemed to understand. The VFW wasn't exactly the kind of organization the parents imagined would have an interest in promoting group child care. In fact, it was the kind of organization that they imagined would be explicitly opposed to it. But the VFW man agreed to offer them shelter in a building his organization leased from the state. The rent was two hundred dollars a month. The price seemed high, but the city of Cambridge had agreed to foot the bill, so the parents agreed. They were tired of looking.

Cleared of picnic tables and other remnants of summer, the VFW building took on a hollow look. The overall gestalt was incarceration. Cement walls and cement floors refused to brighten with scrubbing. The windows were too high for views. The parents brought in rugs for the floor and a load of toys to make up for the lack of scenery. Anything on wheels like wagons or pull-toys tended to gravitate to one corner because the floor was slanted. But, after a few months, everyone got used to the place, and it became almost comfortable. Then the nice VFW man lost his love of children. He said he wanted the rent paid in cash; the parents insisted on paying by check. The VFW man began to nag and then to threaten. And then one chilly December morning, the thirteen children of Tot Lot plodded through the rotting leaves and fallen branches to their hangout, only to find it locked with a lock for which the parents had no key. Furious, but helpless, the parents wrote a letter to the city. The city wrote back that the building in question was leased to the VFW for one dollar a year, in exchange for which the veterans had agreed to make it available to local civic organizations at no cost. In other words, they were improperly charged; the nice VFW man was ripping them off.

By then it was March, and the parents had already moved their children into the only other available space they could find in their end of the city: the bathhouse at Magazine Beach. Like most public bathhouses, the facility had two changing rooms, one wide-open space for men, one room full of cubicles for women. Tot Lot settled in on the men's side. It was dimly lit, unheated, smelly, and spare, but it was free, and there was no shortage of showers or toilets.

When summer came, the bathhouse reverted back to its intended use, and Tot Lot returned, with some relief, to the Morse School kindergarten classrooms. The parents agreed that another winter on Magazine Beach was out of the question, but they had no idea where else to go. The original cadre of six families was by now exhausted, worn down not only by the constant search for space but from pressure applied by some members of the community to change the character of their program. Gradually, they found themselves thrown into battles they otherwise would have avoided. Suddenly, day care had become a hot political issue.

Every decade or so since 1909, the White House has hosted a Conference on Children and Youth. Until 1970, the conference consisted of finding ways to make it easier for mothers to stay home. This, after all, was considered the natural way of things, the American way, and provided the rationale for such programs as Aid to Families with Dependent Children, which paid single mothers to stay home and care for their own kids. But in 1970, things changed. Families, it was acknowledged, weren't so traditional any more, not only single but married mothers were working, and even children of two-parent families were in need of quality care. The conference ended with a consensus that the federal government should support a network of day care facilities, a consensus that resulted in the Child Development Bill of 1971, vetoed by President Nixon, who deemed it unpatriotic.

But in Cambridge the majority of voters went wild in their support of child care. They passed (by no less than a two-to-one margin) a referendum mandating free, twenty-four-hour, community-controlled child care for all residents. Not surprisingly, the money to back up this utopian notion was not forthcoming, and the referendum faded into well-meant oblivion before anyone was forced to take it too seriously. Nonetheless, day care had become, if not the issue of the moment, an issue to be reckoned with. And in noisy, contentious Cambridge, that was saying a lot.

"Just everyone was trying to break into that little Tot Lot group," recalls a woman whose daughter was to be one of the gate-crashers. "You have to understand things in the context of the time. At the time, everyone needed child care. And there was almost none to be had."

This new wave of parents envisioned Tot Lot as a focus of community action and solidarity. They considered child care not a nicety, but a societal imperative, key both to social integration and to the women's liberation movement. Without day care, it was reasoned, children would continue to be segregated, and women would be forever bound by what narrow thinkers viewed as their biological destiny. Group care seemed the only ethical option. "We believed," one father says, "that kids were better off in day care than they were at home."

ANSTI Benfield was one of those believers. Ansti is something of a legend in Cambridgeport. The legend is built around her efforts to foil the Inner Belt, a federally backed plan to circle a strip of eight-lane highway around Boston's downtown core. The Belt was meant to make it easier for suburban commuters to get to work, but it would also have sliced through dozens of neighborhoods in Roxbury, the Fenway, Brookline, Somerville, Charlestown, and Cambridge and displaced thousands of people. The loop of highway, Ansti says, was planned to cut straight through her living room. Ansti is modest about her contributions to the protest effort, denying more than a cameo role, but those in the know remember otherwise. As evidence, they point to a mural painted larger than life across the back wall of the Cambridgeport Stop and Shop supermarket. The mural, created by Cambridge artist Bernard LaCasse, depicts an angry crowd of residents and businesspeople shaking their fists at a bulldozer. Though she denies it, most people close to the event insist that the woman at the head of the mob, nose to bucket with the bulldozer, is Ansti Benfield.

The fight to kill the Belt ended in 1971, when Governor Francis Sargent declared a moratorium on all new highway construction in metropolitan Boston. Ansti had three small children and a job at the time. Her husband, Mike, was a bank teller, and his wages were insufficient to support the family, but that, Ansti says, was really beside the point. She has always worked, she says, and always will. Ansti and Mike raised their first two children with the help of friends, with whom Ansti rotated babysitting duty until the kids were old enough for school. But when her youngest son was born, she looked around for a more reliable arrangement. She'd heard about Tot Lot's search for space, and the Benfield home, a rambling three-family spread over a large chunk of property at 140 Chestnut Street, was just the ticket. "It seemed like a fun idea to me," Ansti says.

It took four months of scrubbing, scraping, and fixing to bring the first floor of Ansti's apartment up to city health and safety codes. The parents did all the work themselves and held bake sales to pay for the renovation materials. When they were finally finished, the place was so clean the kids could eat granola off the kitchen floor.

But Ansti hadn't figured on the fire department. No one had. Everyone knew there were kids in unlicensed family day care homes all over the city — and the fire department never bothered to close those places down. Tot Lot was trying so hard to play by the rules. It didn't seem fair. But to the Cambridge Fire Department, Tot Lot was nothing more than a headlong affront to common sense, a firetrap with good intentions, but a firetrap nonetheless.

Ansti says there were several violations but recalls as critical the lack of a fire barrier between the furnace room in the basement and the play area in the living room. This was not altogether surprising — how many people have a fire wall between the basement and first floor of their homes? It was clear that the chief assumed that Ansti and her friends, upon being confronted with this obstacle, would stop playing school and take the kids home where they belonged. But the parents had no such intentions. They spent the weekend packing the basement ceiling with asbestos mud ("that was before we knew about asbestos and cancer") and called the fire chief in to take another look.

"Well, you could tell the minute he walked in that he'd be damned if he'd license a day care center," Ansti says. "He said he had eight kids himself, and he wouldn't dream of having them in a center. He said mothers were meant to stay at home with their kids. He also said that, since there was a kitchen in the house, he couldn't license the place anyway. And then he left."

The parents convened at once to decide what to do about this latest setback. This being Cambridge, they settled on a philosophical tack. The question was, "What is a kitchen?" The answer, according to the Cambridge Department of Buildings and Grounds: any room with a stove. The solution: get rid of the stove, and the kitchen, too, would evaporate. The stove was unceremoniously unplugged and hauled to a second-story alcove. The fire department was summoned for a third look.

"The fire chief had a look of sheer obstinacy," Ansti says. "He simply wouldn't sign the paper. You could tell he wondered where the stove was, but he was too stubborn to ask. He just stood there and stared at us. Finally one father stepped forward and said, 'Chief, I don't know whether you remember that I took your daughter to the senior prom back at Rindge High?' This man was a lifetime Cambridgeport resident, a working-class guy. And the fire chief realized immediately that the guy was Catholic, I mean, he would never let anyone but a Catholic take his daughter to the prom, right? I guess he figured if a Catholic guy was in on this, it had to be okay. So he signed the paper. But he also came back every two weeks for the next two months, looking for that stove." In January 1972, Tot Lot became the first licensed day care center in Cambridgeport.

The Benfields cooked dinner on the second floor of their home for the next three years. Ansti recalls that time as "like having a birthday party in your home five days a week," and she has the Super 8 movies to prove it. From the looks of it, Tot Lot was the kind of party where kids get overtired and smear ice cream and cake on the walls and dump the cat in the toilet. There was not a lot of structure. The teacher, a newly minted college graduate of the late flower child genre, was clearly a kind and gentle fellow. He had free-flowing brown hair and long, white fingers that looked ready to strum out a rousing rendition of "This Land Is Your Land" or "Puff the Magic Dragon" at the least provocation. He had never taught before, but he took the job because he liked kids and because he thought it would be a good experience, though for what he wasn't sure. At any rate, the idea behind the place was not so much to teach the kids as to allow them to learn from each other. And to have a good time. In the home movies, at least, that mission seemed to have been well accomplished. There is much frolicking in the backyard and playing around with the family dog and making angels in the snow and running around with few or no clothes on. Meanwhile, mothers in Carnaby Street hair, black turtlenecks, and bell-bottom jeans smile weakly at the camera as they pass juice and cookies in the crowded nonkitchen.

In exchange for all this fun and frolic, parents contributed five dollars and two hours of their time per child per week. Since there were no supplies to speak of, they also hauled in toys, bottles, bikes, and diapers. There was no set curriculum, not even a daily game plan. "There was never any issue made over how the place should be run," Ansti says. "It just ran."

But not forever. In June of 1975, three months before their youngest child started kindergarten, the Benfields sold their home. Tot Lot was once again in search of a place.

The teen center on the corner of Henry and Brookline streets was the only place they could find on short notice, and notice was always short. It was just a basement, really, the bottom of a two-story office building owned but no longer used by the Polaroid Corporation. It was dank and cavernous. Sound bounced off the walls like a squash ball. The only bathroom was on the second floor. But it was available, and it was free, and, at that time, that was enough.

The parents made the best of things. They broke the space up with room dividers and brightened it with storage shelves on wheels painted in cheerful primary colors. All of the furniture and equipment was portable. One parent describes it as "Transformer furniture." It was portable because it had to disappear at one o'clock each day, when the space reverted to its former incarnation as a teen center.

"We had to hide an entire day care center every day so the teens could come in and not feel like there had been babies in the place," a parent recalls. "Polaroid thought that the teens would be insulted if they knew that little kids had been hanging out in their space."

So the toddlers messed around merrily all morning, only to be hustled through lunch so that there would be time to pull down the dividers and pack up the preschool stuff before the teens arrived. It was exhausting for parents and for the new teacher, Sally Benbasett. Sally was used to difficulties, but this was a circus.

An alcoholic janitor opened the doors of the teen center every morning when Sally arrived. "I'd get one whiff of his breath and practically pass out," she says. "And the room was so big, it echoed. But it was a neighborhood school, and the parents were totally committed. In the name of those children, a whole social network evolved. It was like instead of church."

But it was a church that closed its doors after lunch. By this time, most of the parents were working and needed full-time care for their children. They needed a permanent, dedicated space. Once again, they began to search. This time, they had a lead: an old friend of Sally's from her Washington days (they had belonged to the same feminist health collective), had moved with her husband into a beautiful house at 65 Chestnut Street. The one problem with the place was an ugly cement structure that nearly filled the backyard. No one was sure what the building had been constructed for, but it was rumored that it had once been a repair shop for Model T Fords and that it had held as many as eighteen cars at a go.

Those rumors turned out to be false. In fact, the garage had been erected by a former owner, a dentist with a great love of automobiles and a generous spirit, who allowed neighbors to store their cars there in the winter. A neighbor recalls the dentist throwing a party in the garage, complete with a dance band, to celebrate its completion. But when the dentist moved out, 65 Chestnut Street was sold to people who loved cars a lot less. The garage became a warehouse for junkers, all of which were eventually removed by a city tow truck after the garage was condemned as a safety hazard. By the time Sally's friend moved in, the garage was nothing more than a hulking shell, an enormous cement garbage can. The new owners had been wondering what to do with it when Sally called.

Turning a filthy condemned garage into a day care center was the kind of hopeless task that the Tot Lot parents thrived on. They toured the spooky space with flashlights, as though it were an underground archaeological site. They checked out the ancient automobile turnstile embedded in the dirt floor. They waded through the several feet of black goo in the basement. They gravely noted that there were no windows or walls or even a ceiling to speak of. And then they rolled up their sleeves and did what people in Cambridge do: they wrote a grant proposal. The proposal went to a number of local foundations and businesses. They got a thousand dollars in long-term loans, with a promise of two large grants to come, more than enough to begin renovations.

But there were still the neighbors to contend with. In particular, there were two music critics who lived next door, young guys who spent a lot of late nights listening to rock and roll and writing about it for *The Real Paper*, a progressive alternative newspaper. These guys didn't have kids, and they didn't want other people's kids waking them up before noon. They were also afraid that the kids might scare their dogs. So they passed around a petition demanding that day care centers be banned from residential neighborhoods. A couple of other *Real Paper* staffers and a few other neighbors got behind the idea, but it didn't go too far. The Cambridge City Council refused to back it, and Tot Lot was approved by the zoning board. Sally's friends agreed to a ten-year lease of the garage in exchange for renovations, one dollar a month, and free day care for their own kids.

Parents recall the building of Tot Lot as an intense, almost religious experience. Work went on twenty-four hours a day, in shifts. One of the parents, a physics professor, served as informal foreman, posting lists of jobs on the bare concrete walls. People contributed when and where they could, dropping their kids off at friends' houses or bringing them along to nod off to sleep on paint-stained drop cloths.

"Working there seemed like a life-style choice rather than just building a place to put kids," recalls one mother. "We were building a community."

One by one, the jobs got done. Parents hauled three feet of mud from the basement bucket by bucket. They pulled a stump out of the yard area with ropes. They bashed window holes in the cinder-block walls with sledgehammers. They didn't really know what they were doing, but, somehow, they did it. On September 4, 1975, Tot Lot was opened for business. To commemorate the occasion, a group of parents wrote a song, "The Talking Migrant Tot Lot Blues" (with thanks to Woody Guthrie), detailing the center's fateful history. The last verse goes:

> The Cambridgeport Children's Center,
> A dream come true,
> But its long-term survival depends on me and you . . .
> For if we don't let frustration get us down,
> And if we do let the kids' joy keep us up
> And give each other the help we need,
> Then community day care will have to succeed.

Six

WATER PLAY

November

MONDAY is sunny, with a slight morning chill left over from the previous week of drizzle and downpour. The teachers are grateful for the break in the weather, relieved that the day's field trip won't end up like the last one, with the kids huddled under a couple of apple trees in that orchard near Gloucester, waiting in vain for a pelting rainstorm to let up. Molly had somehow forgotten to bring David's pacifier, and he howled his lungs out on the bus ride home, which took over an hour, and the kids got hardly any apples because the orchard manager had confined them to gathering the windfalls from a single tree. All in all, not a stellar experience.

Today's outing to the New England Aquarium on Boston Harbor has been craftily choreographed to preclude such disasters. For one thing, the weatherman has all but guaranteed clear skies. For another, the toddlers are not coming, thereby eliminating the need for pacifiers. And the preschoolers have been prepped for the day with a series of talks and activities designed to illuminate them on all things aquatic. The day before, they had spent the afternoon knee-deep in old *National Geographics*, searching out and excising photos of fish.

But as the morning wears on and several students have yet

to arrive, the teachers realize once again that there is one variable they can't control for: the parents. Already the day's schedule, so carefully planned around nap- and snacktimes, has been shot to hell, and the kids are beginning to sense it. Peter has served his first "time-out" of the day, for spitting, and is on the verge of earning a second. Marcel, Dylan, and Mike wrestle wildly, stopping just short of hurting each other. Ruth mugs and pouts and lectures, pounding her feet and raising her voice to the brink of a tantrum. The others, stomping and snorting and sweating in their winter jackets, are hungry to get loose. Even Noel toys with the edge of mischief, circling the wrestling boys with a look of quiet conspiracy. The teachers, Marina, Linda, and Margaret, raise ironic eyebrows at the clock. It's 9:15, a full thirty minutes beyond the absolute limit they'd given parents to get their kids in by today. Once again, the parents haven't taken them seriously. The teachers take one last look around the room, which by now is near chaos, and make the painful decision to head for the bus stop. The latecomers will have to stay behind with the toddlers. It's a shame, Margaret says, that the kids always end up paying the price for their parents' laxness.

The preschool room unloads onto the sidewalk. The teachers organize the kids into pairs and hustle them down the near-empty streets with the vigilance of secret-service agents maneuvering a string of dignitaries through a crowd of suspected terrorists. The preschoolers walk hand in hand, eyes fixed forward, ears braced for Marina's loudly shouted warnings against dawdling, against fighting, against daydreaming in traffic. There is only one street to cross, but Cambridge drivers are notorious for their impatience, and there is no telling what one of them might do when confronted with a horde of laggardly four-year-olds. It takes ten minutes to get to the bus stop outside the Laundromat.

The kids peek inside the Laundromat windows and wave knowingly at the early-morning crowd shoving their sheets and underwear into the machines. (The Laundromat was an earlier field trip, deemed successful by one parent because "it taught my kid once and for all that clothes don't clean themselves.") The teachers keep their eyes peeled for the bus. It's colder than it looks, and the children pull their hoods tight and stamp their feet for warmth. The bus doesn't come, and the foot stamping escalates. Peter entertains himself by alternately kicking the Laundromat door and engaging in not-quite-mock kick-boxing with Quy. Peter got special permission to skip his morning program to come on today's trip, but now the teachers wonder if that was such a great idea. He seems remarkably skilled, almost balletic, taking a quick poke at the air a few inches above Quy's head with his foot, then spinning to avoid retaliation. Mike watches Peter wistfully, takes a few clumsy kicks himself, and then starts to whine, writhing in Linda's iron grasp. Margaret, looking formidable in a great forest green poncho, glares down the middle of Pearl Street, silently commanding the bus to honor its schedule.

The bus is nearly half an hour late, but the driver makes no apologies. He screeches to a stop and swings open the doors just as Monica, jacket unzipped and flapping, comes tearing around the corner from Tot Lot. Monica's mom comes, too, wearing her usual slippers and thin housedress and carrying Monica's younger brother Carlos tucked like a football under her bare arm. She slides Carlos to the pavement and hoists Monica up toward the bus doors and Marina's outstretched arms. She stuffs a crumpled dollar bill into Marina's hand and asks her to buy the girl something to eat — she didn't have time to pack a lunch.

Marina and Linda exchange exasperated glances. The children were required to be at school an hour ago, with a brown-bag lunch. What kind of lunch can you buy in downtown Boston for a dollar? Sometimes they wonder just what these parents are thinking about or if they're thinking at all. Monica's mother has no excuse; she's not single, poor, or overburdened. Monica and her brother are in subsidized day care slots, they get vouchers from the Department of Social Services, but it's rumored that they are technically ineligible for public support. There's talk that the family owns property, a house in Boston, and is playing fast and loose with DSS, pretending to be poorer than they are in order to get cheap day care for their children. And no one is even certain that Monica's mother spends much time working or going to school. She sometimes comes to Tot Lot at noon to pick up her youngest, Carlos, leaving Monica behind. It sometimes appears that Monica's parents are using Tot Lot casually, as a state-subsidized baby-sitting service. The teachers do not believe it is their job to police the parents, but if people are going to exploit the system, they should at least try to play it cool and follow the center's rules. (In fact, the school is technically required to report suspected infractions to the Department of Social Services, but Susan never does, for fear of losing children in need.)

The bus grinds to a start, sending Monica and a few other kids flying and the teachers scurrying to find them seats. In the confusion, Peter is pushed down next to Mike. The boys square off, look each other up and down, and then, as if on cue, break into a song, the refrain of which revolves around getting "hit in the butt with a two-ton truck." The teachers, thankful that the boys are not pummeling each other senseless, ignore the glares of offended passengers. It's only five minutes to Central Square and the subway.

The bus pulls into Central Square and dumps its cargo at the head of the stairway leading down into the Central Square "T" stop. The children hop down the steps, through the gate, and into the waiting Red Line car. The train is packed, forcing the kids to stand and sway in the aisles and giving them ample opportunity to collide with each other. They tumble and ricochet like a circus of midgets, setting off a ripple of smiles through the crush. Dylan seizes the moment, breaking into a rousing rendition of "Itsy-Bitsy Spider." Monica, Quy, and Marcel join in, and the straphangers crack up. Peter, nose pressed to a window, sings quietly to himself.

The Red Line squeals to a stop at Park Street, and there's a change of trains. The teachers line the children up against the wall for a head count; then, satisfied that no one is lost, they station themselves strategically between the children, the other passengers, and the tracks. An elderly drunk, toothless and unshaven and wearing a yellow slicker and dark blue fisherman's cap, manages to find a gap in their vigilance. He brandishes a pint of Jim Beam in Dylan's face and then turns to lecture Noel and Jacob on the dirtiness of politics and the perils of marriage. He says that Douglas MacArthur was the last real American and that it's worthless to marry because your wife will only throw you out the minute you take a drink. The children stand mesmerized, hovering between disbelief and respect. They sense that there is something righteous about this man, an adult who is willing to take children into his confidence. Margaret, suddenly noticing what's going on, smiles politely and says nothing as she gently nudges the children toward the opposite end of the platform. Just as the train pulls in, Dylan and Noel step forward and shake the toothless man's hand.

Government Center Station is nearly empty, with just a sprinkling of late commuters and a man dressed in skimpy summer pastels hammering out Caribbean rhythms on a steel drum. The children gather around while the drummer explains how his instrument works and then taps out a note-perfect "Twinkle, Twinkle, Little Star." Luke grins and throws his feet into a high-gear break-dance routine. Marcel and Dylan join in, and then Mike, wiggling his rear suggestively as if to compensate for the slowness of his feet. The roar of the Blue Line train brings them up short, drowns out the drum. Sobered by the noise, the children board the car with reluctance, as if leaving the highlight of their day.

The group emerges onto the platform at Aquarium Station and into a claustrophobic's nightmare. The tunnel leading to Aquarium Station was dug deep under Boston Harbor, so deep that an official of the Massachusetts Bay Transit Authority described it as "being situated somewhere between the dirt under Boston Harbor and the earth's mantle." The escalator leading out of this subterranean chamber is impossibly long and so narrow that it can accommodate only one body at a time. The teachers groan: the children will have to make the long journey into daylight alone. There's no telling what some of these kids might do, given all that time and all those moving stairs, but the possibilities are too terrifying to contemplate for long. Mustering courage, Margaret rides the escalator to the top and then waits, poised, while Marina hoists each child up under the arms and deposits him or her on an unfolding step. The children, rising to the top like bubbles, giggle and play patty cake with the handrail. Dylan wiggles his behind at Marcel, who wiggles his butt at Noel, who does not wiggle but looks amused. Peter is sent up last, wedged on a step between Linda and a parent volunteer. Linda grasps his hand so tightly that his fingertips turn blue.

After such a journey, the aquarium is anticlimactic. An imposing structure set back from the street by a large plaza punctuated by pretzel vendors, it seems, from its exterior, to be without appeal. There are no spinning globes, no balloons, no neon, nothing to catch a weary eye. The children drop, exhausted, onto concrete benches while Marina dashes into the building to buy tickets, and Margaret and Linda dole out the traditional field-trip snack of slightly squashed slices of raisin bread. The children stuff the bread down and ask for more. Marina returns with the tickets and the sad news that the dolphin show has been canceled for the day. Seems that one of the dolphins is ailing. Margaret looks crestfallen, and the children, who until that moment hadn't given the dolphin show much thought, sigh with disappointment. Then, tickets in hand, they push through the glass doors and into the watery gloom.

The New England Aquarium is built like a nautilus, with exhibits set in galleries on a walkway spiraling around a 187,000-gallon "Giant Ocean Tank," or GOT, as the volunteer guides call it. Today, the place is crammed with school groups. Margaret, Linda, and Marina quickly agree on a game plan. It's clear that the kids won't last through an exhaustive tour of the place; a Cook's tour will have to do. They settle on a goal-oriented strategy. They'll make brief stops at the electric eel tank and the hands-on exhibit, but, basically, everyone will proceed promptly to the top of the spiral and a bird's-eye view of the GOT.

The plan falls apart immediately. The children simply refuse to rush. Peter, in particular, is fascinated. He stops at every exhibit, pressing his nose to the glass of each tank, sometimes giving the cold glass a lick. At the hands-on table, he cradles starfish and sea urchins like melting snowflakes, holding them so gently that a museum volunteer commends him on his technique. Peter seems truly enchanted by the cool, dark, mystery of the place. He is calm and wholly absorbed. The teachers smile privately to each other, nod knowing heads. Perhaps bringing Peter wasn't such a bad idea at all.

An hour later, the group straggles to the lip of the Giant

Ocean Tank, where the children strain to get a glimpse of the sharks, stingrays, and other aquatic monsters paddling languidly below. Peter demands that one teacher after another give him a boost above eye level of the guard rail. He comments on the flatness of the stingrays and on the surprisingly small size of the sharks. He thought they would be as big as a house, or a car anyway. He wonders out loud if one particularly sour-looking creature, circling slowly after 535-pound Myrtle the Turtle, would like to eat him. And then Jacob lets go with a howl. The other kids laugh and then blanch as it becomes clear that Jacob is not merely providing sound effects. Jacob rolls on the floor in agony. Mike rolls with him, his teeth sunk deep into the skin of Jacob's stomach.

It takes time for all this to register with the teachers, each of whom is holding at least one child. It takes long seconds for them to drop the kids to the floor and rush to Jacob's aid. They peel Mike off and shove him aside and then yank up Jacob's polo shirt. There are four bloody teeth marks on his belly. Marina gasps. The teachers huddle, considering their course of action. Is this like an animal bite? Are they obligated to report it to the Department of Social Services? What about AIDS? The school is not allowed to demand AIDS tests of the kids, nor would the teachers request them, but at this moment they wished they had. How do they protect Jacob? As Margaret rushes to a pay phone to call Susan for answers, Linda holds the other kids at bay while Marina chastises Mike in her megaphone voice. Marina dotes on Jacob, an almost laughably cute moppet with puppy-dog pudge and a wide-open face framed by floppy carrot-colored ringlets. Marina believes Jacob and she are soul mates, bonded by their hair color. She scolds Mike in a voice made scary with anger. Mike runs to hide his face in a dark corner. He kick-boxes with his shadow.

The next day, in circle time, the teachers ask the children what they remember most vividly about the trip. Samantha says the penguins. Quy says the sharks. Ruth says the giant turtle. Dylan says the sharks. Luke says the sharks. Jacob says the sharks. Mike says biting Jacob. Later that day, Mike tries to bite Jacob again — twice.

The day before was not the first time Mike had taken a bite out of a classmate, though it was the first time he drew blood. The previous year, when he was still in the toddler group, he bit so many children so many times that a social worker was called in to help deal with the problem. The social worker talked to Mike once a week and to his mother, Elizabeth.

But Mike is no longer a toddler, and the preschool teachers had hoped that many months of weekly talks with therapists had cured him of the need for this particular brand of oral expression. Clearly, they hadn't. The question is, what to do about it? The AIDS worry is really a red herring; they have no real reason to believe that Mike has AIDS and, besides, the teachers are well aware that AIDS is not so easy to transmit. Nor had Mike done any real damage to Jacob. But Mike's hostility toward other kids is disruptive and, at times, a little scary. Tot Lot is not licensed to deal with severely troubled kids; the teachers are not trained in special education or psychology. Today, during a lunch meeting, everyone agrees that Mike would do better in a special day care program, one that would offer closer supervision and therapy. Still, the teachers are reluctant to recommend that Mike be transferred. To pass Mike along would be to admit to yet another defeat, like Zack.

Mike's case, the teachers agree, is not without hope. Elizabeth seems well adjusted and eager to make things work. She makes efforts to cooperate, meeting (albeit erratically) with social workers and counselors and even coming into Tot Lot to help Susan with the bookkeeping. She is outspoken and feisty. But Elizabeth has at least one weakness that keeps setting Mike back: Mike's father, Jack. Jack has an alcohol problem and difficulty controlling his temper, and every time he spends the night with Elizabeth, Mike comes to school freaked out. And on at least one occasion, Elizabeth says, Mike has seen Jack take a bite out of her.

Molly is not comfortable with this discussion of Mike's family. She is an instinctive behavioralist, preferring to focus on the problem at hand rather than digging into a child's home life. The key to dealing with Mike, she says, is to avoid words like "angry" or "mad," words he associates with the violent behavior he's lived with all his life. Mike sees adults reacting to frustration with violence, so he reacts in kind. Mike, she says, has never felt really safe in his life.

The other teachers tentatively agree to wait and see if the biting persists before taking any further action. Still, they are skeptical. They have little sympathy for Elizabeth, who, they believe, is putting her need for a man before her feelings for her child. Says Linda, "I care a lot about Mike, but at this point I'm more worried about the safety of the other kids. Let's face it, the boy is out of control."

Elizabeth likes to think of her son as a "boy's boy," a tough little tyke who can stick up for himself. He's a fireplug of a kid, a real Buster Brown, with sandy brown hair, expressive brown eyes, and what looks like a beer belly. Mike is partial to underpants printed with superhero figures, and Elizabeth is happy to oblige him. She also bought him a pint-sized leather bomber jacket.

Mike is a follower rather than a leader, a kid who picks fights but doesn't know what to do after he starts them. Elizabeth says he is like his father in that he basically means well but is susceptible to bad influences.

Elizabeth is twenty-three years old. She grew up in Cambridgeport, has lived there all of her life, and is proud to call herself a "townie." She is suspicious of newcomers, especially university types. She says she knows people like that at Tot Lot, and they make her feel uncomfortable. Glen Barth and his wife, Peggy, are like that, she says, the type who think they run the place. Elizabeth concedes that Glen Barth lets everyone have a say at general meetings, lets everybody talk, but that doesn't mean he's listening. She thinks that he has his mind made up beforehand and that, usually, things go the way he wants them to, no matter what anyone else thinks. Now that she helps do the books, Elizabeth knows which parents are private payers and which, as she is, have their children's day care subsidized by the Department of Social Services. She says the private payers, the people with money, have most of the control at Tot Lot. They make the rules, some of which she doesn't agree with. For example, there's the one about not allowing children to bring sweets to school. Elizabeth thinks that one's really dumb. Once she packed carrots in Mike's lunchbox, and he refused to eat them. That night, he told her, "You know, Mom, I'm not a rabbit." She thought that was hysterical — Mike sure got that one right.

CAMBRIDGEPORT Children's Center takes great pride in its multicultural heritage and intentions and its wide range of kids. Multiculturalism and diversity are what attract many middle-class parents here, parents like the Thompson Barths, who might otherwise have looked elsewhere, and it has proved to be of no little help in fundraising efforts. The families of Tot Lot take multicultural education very seriously. It is a frequent theme in general meetings, where, for example, parents mull over the possibility of forming "sister center" relationships with day care centers in developing countries during potluck dinners of ethnic foods. And the teachers encourage children to mingle, both in and out of school.

Encouraging children of all races, ethnic backgrounds, and socioeconomic levels to get to know and appreciate each other as people rather than as representatives of alien cultures is a dream goal of day care planners. Few child-care centers achieve it, and many that have have failed to maintain it. Budget cuts have forced many centers to drop subsidized slots, and soaring costs have caused some centers to raise their prices beyond the reach of even the middle classes. In Massachusetts and many other states, this has resulted in a two-tier day care system, a system in which both the affluent, who can pay for quality care, and the poor, who have access to state-subsidized care, come out on top. The working class ends up making due with whatever level of care they can afford, which is often fairly low.

Historically, Tot Lot attracted families from all income levels, but this has changed. The school's sliding-scale tuition plan has become fixed; Tot Lot can no longer afford to subsidize working-class families. (One working-class family did use the center briefly this year but was forced to drop out when the mother lost her job as a truck loader.) As a result, Tot Lot is itself a two-tier school, attracting both poor and affluent families. And this leads to clashes. Inevitably, as Elizabeth observes, the wealthier, better-educated families dominate the decision making, often to the great frustration of members of the less well off faction. And despite a great deal of rhetoric to the contrary, most of the children of Tot Lot do not socialize with classmates of different socioeconomic circumstances outside of school — the gap between the educated middle class and the poor is just too wide.

ELIZABETH and Mike and Mike's baby brother, Benjamin, live in a two-bedroom apartment on the thirteenth floor of a high rise overlooking the Charles River. It's a nice place, spacious and clean and safe, and Elizabeth's rent is subsidized by the state. Still, Elizabeth's not crazy about the arrangement. She prefers to live where the neighbors give you the time of day, and here, she says, most people keep to themselves. When you walk outside, there's nothing to look at but a gas station and Memorial Drive and the river. She's not at all sure she'll be able to stay here much longer anyway, because she's heard the rent is about to climb beyond the means of her budget. She says that will be hard on Mike because he's already had four changes of address in fewer than four years.

Elizabeth has worked in several jobs, as a secretary and as a travel agent and as an electronics technician for Digital Equipment Corporation. But these days she collects welfare. She's not comfortable with this; she likes to think of herself as an independent person, but she has no real alternative. Benjamin, like his brother, was two months premature, born before his lungs could fully mature and with a higher than average risk of sudden infant death syndrome. Elizabeth has to monitor his breathing, which makes it pretty much impossible for her to return to work. If the monitor goes off, she has only seconds to respond, though so far there have been only false alarms. This keeps her on edge, of course, and makes her patience for Mike's antics even slighter.

Benjamin is two months old now, and he eats well and is growing quickly. Still, Elizabeth is undecided about whether she'll be ready to return to work the following month, in time to get her old job back. Digital gave her six weeks of paid maternity leave after Mike was born, but she stayed home with him for nine months. She has her doubts about day care. Mike was a calm, contented infant, she says, until he entered a center.

Tot Lot is Mike's third day care center. It was in the second center, Elizabeth says, that Mike learned to bite. She says he picked up the habit from the other kids. It got so bad that she pulled Mike out of that center and stayed home with him for a while. He seemed to calm down and focus with her, but he also missed being with friends. So she enrolled him in Tot Lot. Tot Lot, Elizabeth says, is a trade-off. She likes some of the teachers, especially Molly, but she thinks that spending whole days there drives Mike crazy. Elizabeth says she is not altogether certain that day care is the best thing for her children. On the other hand, she wouldn't know what to do with Mike all day if she had him home.

Elizabeth herself attended Head Start as a preschooler, not because her mother worked — she didn't until Elizabeth entered kindergarten — but because her father had abandoned them, qualifying the family as disadvantaged and in need of remediation. At the time, Head Start was not intended as day care for working families; in fact, it offered little full-time care. It was an enrichment program, a way of giving poor children a developmental leg up before they entered the relative rigors of kindergarten. It seemed to have the desired effect on Elizabeth because she recalls doing quite well in elementary and high school. She graduated at seventeen and went on to take a secretarial course at Bunker Hill Community College in Boston. It was while attending college there and working part-time as a clerk typist for the Department of Transportation, that she met Jack, a twenty-seven-year-old high school dropout with no visible means of support. By then Elizabeth was bored with school and disillusioned with the idea of becoming a secretary, which she decided was akin to being "a glorified maid." Jack took her away from all that. He was different, more exciting, than her steady high school boyfriend, a Catholic boy who played football, made good grades, and had left Cambridge to attend college in California. Jack was smooth, worldly. He always had enough money to pop for beer and wine coolers and show her and her friends a good time. He played pool and had gallant manners and reminded Elizabeth of

James Dean. He studied auto mechanics at ITT Tech and knew everything about cars. Best of all, Elizabeth's mother hated him. She thought he drank too much, like Elizabeth's father, and that he would amount to nothing but trouble.

"I didn't see it," Elizabeth says. "I was only eighteen. So I moved out of my mother's house and in with my girlfriend and then in with Jack. Then I got pregnant."

Elizabeth found her own apartment and looked forward to having a baby, something, she says, that would be "all mine." And then the pregnancy got difficult, and Elizabeth had to quit her job, and Jack had to quit night school to take care of her. Jack tired quickly of sitting around the house and started hanging out with a crowd of heavy drug and alcohol users. This frightened and angered Elizabeth. She moved back in with her mother and refused to live with Jack until he got sober. Jack promised to keep off booze, got a truck-driving license, and a job. Elizabeth took him back and, after a year and a half, in August 1988, she and Jack were married. And then Jack had an accident and threw out his back and couldn't work anymore. Elizabeth was still working at Digital at the time, pulling in decent money, and that seemed to make Jack feel small. He started drinking again and getting abusive with Elizabeth, and, just before Christmas, she told him to get out. It was just about that time that she discovered she was pregnant again. This pregnancy was even more difficult than the first, and by spring Elizabeth was forced to leave her job in yet another attempt to ward off premature labor. It helped, but not a lot: she was just seven months pregnant when Benjamin was born.

Elizabeth blames much of Mike's aggression on his prematture birth. She says experts at the hospital warned her that prematurity causes some children to have short fuses and shorter attention spans. (This is only partially true. Although premature infants are sometimes more jittery at birth, they are no more likely than full-term infants to grow into aggressive toddlers and preschoolers.) Elizabeth expects Benjamin will have similar symptoms. But she is not naive; she knows that things are rough at home and that what Mike has seen and heard has affected his behavior.

"Mike remembers every detail of our fights," she says. "He remembers Jack hitting me and making me bleed, and me hitting Jack and making him bleed. Sometimes I think he believes that the fights are his fault."

Elizabeth is not unconcerned about Mike's outbursts at school, but she has trouble keeping appointments with social workers and teachers, and she gets tired of them making a big deal about everything. She also suspects that some of the teachers at Tot Lot are prejudiced against her son. One day when she was going over the books in Susan's office, she overheard Margaret refer to Mike as being a "basket case today." That made Elizabeth mad. She worries that Mike's bad opinion of himself might stem, at least in part, from such thoughtless negativity.

"When they called me to tell me that Mike had bit Jacob, they said I was lucky that Jacob's parents were so mellow," she says. "Well, I thought that was strange. What does a parent being mellow have to do with it? I mean, I know biting is terrible, but kids bite all the time. And the teachers weren't very discreet — just about every parent in the school knew that Mike was the biter, and I don't think that's so great for his self-esteem."

The teachers at Tot Lot are, in fact, as discreet as they can be, given the need to protect the other children as well as Mike's privacy. While they didn't volunteer the fact that Mike had bitten Jacob, they didn't deny it when parents asked. Most parents took it in stride, but some couldn't help being cautious, steering their children away from Mike when they dropped them off in the morning. Mike is a live wire, and everybody knows it, and it is true, as Elizabeth suggests, that he's beginning to regard himself as a problem and act accordingly, becoming more outrageous by the day. It is also true that Mike keeps bad company, but what Elizabeth has trouble acknowledging is that he's not keeping that company at school.

SUSAN Evans has managed the home-based special-needs program for the Cambridge Public Schools for fourteen years now. She has degrees in social work and psychology, speaks four lan-

guages, and has worked in three different countries. Here, she
and her staff work out of an office in the back of an elementary
school, in what is basically one big room with a couple of ply-
wood walls stuck up as an afterthought. Susan's worktable is a
rubble of folders and forms, with a phone pulled over from
across the room. The phone cord tends to trip people. There are
toys scattered everywhere.

A large part of Susan's job is to send counselors to the
homes of preschool children in trouble. Susan says meeting with
people in their homes is often the only way to get to the bottom
of things. Parents of troubled children often don't feel comfortable confiding in teachers, and teachers are rarely in a position
to get really involved with parents who do. Besides, the view
from the classroom can be misleading. Sometimes a kid acts out
in school, and social workers push his parents into marriage
counseling, his father into Alcoholics Anonymous, and the child
into play therapy when, in fact, what's really needed is a way to
get the mother to Stop and Shop to buy food for breakfast. A
home visitor can pick up on things like that fairly quickly. On
the other hand, sometimes a kid acts out because he goes home
every night to a screaming sibling and a mother whacked out on
crack. Home visitors can pick up on that, too, but they can't do
anything about it unless the child shows serious signs of being
endangered, and then they call the Department of Social Services.

"We have no legal clout," Susan says. "All we can do is
help maintain the child at school so that he's fairly safe and hope
that the situation at home changes. When we call in DSS, you
get this multiagency situation, which can get very confusing. I've
seen parents sitting at a table with five or six agencies, three
people from each agency, and it seems so weighty. I don't know
how that family can survive."

Susan says that Cambridgeport Children's Center is better
than average when it comes to letting parents know that their
kids are having difficulties. "Day care centers can't tell parents
'shape up and parent better,' " she says. "They have a financial
relationship with these people; the parents are, in a sense, the
clients. And some parents will get defensive and demand to

know a teacher's qualifications to make such a judgment, the 'who are you to tell me' kind of stuff that can really be intimidating. As a result, it's common for day care staff to avoid talking about problems with parents."

Susan Evans has been involved with Elizabeth and Mike for two years now. At Tot Lot, she says, the boy's every move is monitored by adults, who are rightfully concerned for his safety and that of the other children. But Mike has learned to play into this concern and to demand that adults set limits rather than learning to set his own. The teachers have developed a hair trigger with Mike, jumping on him the minute he starts to act out. As a result, he has almost no self-control. This is nobody's fault: in day care the needs of the individual have to be balanced against the needs of the group, and Mike's needs are already tilting the balance at Tot Lot.

Molly has a lot of respect for Susan Evans, but she sees things a little differently. Mike is one of her favorite kids. She sees something in him, an openness, an almost desperate eagerness to be liked, that touches her deeply. And she empathizes with Elizabeth. Unlike the other teachers, she understands completely why Elizabeth can't bring herself to leave Jack. Molly was there once herself.

"I remember being a single parent right out of high school, and all I wanted to do was boogie," she says. "You want to boogie, and you want to be taken care of. We're talking about kids with kids here, and when their husbands leave, they are kids left alone to handle everything themselves. Who takes care of Elizabeth?"

MOLLY'S ex-husband, Larry, abused her repeatedly, but she couldn't bring herself to leave him. Without Larry, she had no future, or at least that's the way she saw it at the time. Larry Fontaine was the older brother of one of Molly's best friends. He was handsome, popular, and athletic. He was also a celebrity, the son of Frank Fontaine, the actor best known for his role as Crazy Guggenheimer on the Jackie Gleason Show. Molly met Larry at the height of his father's fame, years before the old man was indicted for tax evasion. She has family snapshots in her scrapbook. Larry is about twenty in the photos, blonde and dashing in a suit and tie. Molly is eighteen, with bleached blonde hair and a perky smile, a dead ringer for Donna Reed. She sits next to her husband holding a beaming, red-cheeked Patrick on her lap. They look the ideal young family, but, of course, they are not. Theirs was a shotgun marriage, a marriage that neither Molly nor Larry wanted or was ready for.

"I had no problem dealing with the baby," Molly says. "I'd been changing diapers since I was ten. But the thought of sleeping with this guy every day of the week for the rest of my life, that was scary. I was too young for such an invasion of privacy. No one asked me if I wanted to get married. But the fact was, we were Catholic. What choice did we have?"

The marriage lasted just over a year. Larry's parting words were "I'm looking for more fruitful ground," meaning, Molly says, that he wanted to screw around. Patrick was fourteen months old at the time. Neither he nor Molly has set eyes on Larry since.

Molly was left with no money and no connections and with no option but to move in with her parents. It was not a happy scene. Molly's confidence, always shaky, hit bottom, and she slipped further and further into depression. She has never been a particularly religious person, but she found solace in the church, the only place where someone actually listened to her without judging her. A priest convinced her to leave her mother's house.

"He told me that Patrick and I were a family now and that I had to get out of my parents' house and make a home for myself and my son," Molly says. "I thought that was a very liberal suggestion, coming from a priest, and I took it."

Molly moved to an apartment in South Medford and went out to look for work. She was neither surprised nor particularly disgruntled when no one would hire her.

"I applied for a job with an electric company," she says. "I passed their tests. But they said they couldn't hire me because I had a son and that he might get sick and that I'd have to miss work to take care of him. At the time, I understood their reasoning — I figured they had a business to run and they couldn't let a sick kid get in the way of running it."

Eventually she got a job as a receptionist for the Massachusetts Council on Crime and Correction. She didn't like it much, but it paid most of the bills. She also volunteered as a typist for a prisoners' rights organization, which provided her with child care in exchange for her services. It was there that she met Steve. Steve had recently completed an eleven-year sentence at Leavenworth for transporting a stolen car across a state line. Steve said he was only seventeen years old at the time of the heist and dumb enough to take the rap for a ring of older, more experienced car thieves. Molly believed him. Steve didn't seem like the criminal type. He was gentle and soft-spoken and had a steady job at a fried-chicken joint downtown. He seemed to like Patrick.

Steve and Molly started dating, and after a few months, they were engaged. Molly felt lucky; she figured she'd licked her loneliness problem and found Patrick the father he'd never had. Then she woke up one night to find her apartment surrounded by police pointing shotguns at her bedroom window.

"There were FBI there, too," Molly says flatly. That's because Steve had robbed a bank, a federal crime.

Steve was sentenced to eighteen to twenty years for bank robbery, and Molly and Patrick were evicted. The landlord said he hated to do it but that he didn't think his weak heart could take that much excitement.

Molly packed up Patrick and moved to Cambridgeport, where she had a friend with an empty room and a sympathetic ear. It was then, Molly says, that everything changed. Molly became close friends with a political activist who found her an apartment in a rent-controlled building and got her working as a tenant organizer.

"Molly's politics come from the heart," the friend says. "In Cambridge, her exposure to so many movements, to the feminist movement, to the tenants' rights movement, to the day care movement, just encouraged what was already in her to come out. She's a loving, caring person and totally natural. She's exactly the kind of person people want to take care of their kids."

Molly swore off secretarial work ("I was sick of being pushed around by white men"), went back on welfare, and made money on the side caring for two infants and a kindergartner in her apartment. When a fourth mother requested her services, Molly said she couldn't handle more than two infants on her own but suggested the families get together and organize a playgroup, with one parent rotating in every day to help her with the kids. The other parents agreed to the plan, and Molly was launched as a teacher of infants and toddlers. Molly loved it but, after six years, found herself working full-time and still not earning enough to get off welfare. She decided it was time for a move. KLH seemed like the best bet.

KLH Research and Development, a Cambridge-based company that specialized in the design and manufacture of high-fidelity sound equipment, had always prided itself on its ability to change with the times. The company's progressive labor policies had earned it a citation from the U.S. Chambers of Commerce for hiring and training the "hard-core unemployed." But when Henry Morgan was hired on as a manager at the company in 1963, he was shocked to discover how terribly difficult it was for many of the firm's assembly-plant workers to find child care. Some employees confessed that their children slept in the homes of relatives and friends several nights a week. One couple even shipped their kids off to Alabama to live with grandparents. Morgan had five kids himself, and he couldn't imagine having to send them away. He investigated and found to his alarm that there was no day care program in Cambridge. He asked his wife, Gwen Morgan, to research the cost of setting up an on-site day care center at KLH.

"This was 1963, and in those days workers didn't tell other people they had kids at all, let alone that they were having trouble finding day care for them," says Gwen Morgan, who has since gone on to be the state's best-known child-care educator and advocate.

Morgan wrote to the newly created federal Office of Economic Opportunity (OEO) and asked for a grant to help KLH hire and train sixty welfare mothers from Boston and to set up a child-care center for the children of both these women and of other parents who worked at the plant. The idea was to split the bill three ways, with KLH, parents, and the government each chipping in a third. OEO turned her down flat.

"OEO said they couldn't support us because if we hired these women and paid them a fair wage, they would cease to be poor and cease to be qualified for government support," she says. "I thought to myself, 'oh, that kind of war on poverty, the kind that makes sure that people who are poor stay poor.' That's not my definition of economic opportunity."

It took several years, but Morgan was finally able to obtain federal support for the program, which opened its doors to KLH employees in 1968. KLH Research and Development went out of business in the early 1970s, but the day care center survived. It was going full force when Molly signed on as a teacher there in 1981. She took the job partly because KLH catered to the poor but also because it offered full health insurance coverage for both herself and for Patrick. Molly didn't worry much about money, but she worried a lot about medical bills. The fact that rich people could afford better health care for their children than could poor people was a source of constant amazement and indignation to her — the inherent unfairness of it still makes her fume.

Molly lasted just a year at KLH, which at the time accepted only older children. She missed the intimacy and challenge of working with infants and toddlers, who she commonly refers to as "fascinating people." She also worried that good infant care had become so scarce that many families were turning to un-qualified caregivers to provide it, and she felt a deep need to help remedy that problem.

"I think it's terrifying for women to go back to work and leave their infants," she says. "It's terribly stressful. I'm not convinced that group care is the best thing for very young children, but given that it's a necessity, only the most qualified people should be involved with it, and I believe I do my best work with infants and young toddlers. I believe I can have a positive impact on their lives."

Seven

OUT OF THE CLOSET

DAY care in this country has traditionally been associated not with the care and nurture of children who are otherwise well taken care of but with the idea of providing a sort of safety net for the disenfranchised, those families who are too sick or too poor or too ignorant to provide for themselves. As developed in the early nineteenth century, day care was largely envisioned as a charitable response to the needs of a burgeoning immigrant population and to the industrialization that took what were generally described as "foreign" mothers away from the home and into the factory. With extended families left behind in the old country, many of these parents were on their own — with no loving grandmother, cousin, or aunt to mind the children while they worked. So children ran the streets or huddled around heating stoves in locked apartments, waiting for their parents to return home. Some children, it is written, were tied to bedposts to keep them from running wild. It was a pathetic scenario, one from which moral imperatives could be clearly drawn. There was no ambiguity here — these children were in need of help.

Early support for day nurseries was justified not only on humanitarian but on fiscal grounds. Through much of the nineteenth and well into the twentieth century, day care was looked upon as a relatively economical alternative to institutionalization. It was not uncommon for slum dwellers to free themselves up for work by committing their children to orphanages — better an orphan than a starveling. Hence, day nurseries were seen as a means of preserving families that otherwise would be destroyed, as a way of reducing trauma in an otherwise extremely troubled home.

The Boston Infant School, which dates from 1828, is thought to have been the country's first day care center. In its constitution, trustees of the school explained their efforts as follows: "The children would be removed from the unhappy association of want and vice, and be placed under better influences. . . ." Later, day nurseries would become a favorite philanthropy of service institutions, particularly those headed by wealthy society matrons. These women, often the wives of successful industrialists, supervised the day-nursery staff, organized and chaired fund-raisers, and attended board meetings. They were not without critics. Some argued that the wealthy supported the day-nursery service in part to free poor women up to become low-paid domestics or workers in their homes and factories. In any case, the day nursery rarely offered more than custodial care, its main concern being hygiene (which included a thorough daily scrubbing at the hands of the matron or nurse) and a stern introduction to the rough points of proper grammar and etiquette. The day nursery was first and foremost a place to tidy up and socialize the children of immigrants.

At the turn of the century, yet another wave of European immigration, coupled with a steady influx of rural Americans, crowded city tenement neighborhoods and caused labor surpluses, pushing salaries down and forcing mothers into the workplace in record numbers to augment the meager earnings of their husbands (if they had them). Industry responded not by discriminating against women workers, as expected, but by making a direct bid for them. Women, after all, considered themselves lucky to have jobs of any kind and were less likely than men to squabble over low wages and long hours. They were easy prey for industrialists, some of whom went so far as to take the eerily futuristic and seemingly humane step of offering on-site child care. The thinking behind these on-site facilities, of course, was more mercantile than altruistic. Industry nurseries were generally dank, ill-equipped places poorly run by uneducated women who knew little and cared less about their tiny charges. These centers were regarded as little better than baby dungeons by child advocates of the time, who vigorously opposed them and applauded their demise in the early 1920s.

By this time, the number of independent day nurseries (most of them funded by charitable organizations and modest tuition fees) had ballooned to more than six hundred. Like the French crèches they were modeled after, day nurseries focused on bodily upkeep and moral uplifting, their purpose being to rescue children from unhappy and often dangerous homes. (In France, this was meant quite literally, as the crèche system was established in direct response to the high death rate of the children of factory workers.) Often these nurseries had neither the time nor the resources nor the wherewithal to offer education or enrichment. The following situation was described by a social scientist as "only too typical of a day nursery run by those who lacked both vision and funds."

> A day nursery was supported by a church known over a large section for its humanitarian and social welfare work. It was housed in the church basement where no sunlight ever came, with no furniture but church settees, chairs and tables. The children were in charge [sic] of an ignorant woman who was given the position as an act of charity and against whom charges of cruelty to the children were preferred. There was no medical supervision, no provision for cleanliness or rest, no opportunity for outdoor play or fresh air, no playthings but a broken, torn assortment of second-hand toys. And yet all efforts to have these conditions corrected met with this response from the church supervisor: "We cannot afford to do more and what would these working mothers do without us? They are grateful for this." (Whipple 1929, 96)

The day nursery had become something of an embarrassment, and public sympathy for the institution was on the decline. While it was quite clear that the mothers using the nurseries had, because of one misfortune or another, no choice but to work, there was a prevailing belief that the day nursery, by its very existence, was encouraging mothers to abandon their children. Day-nursery admission requirements that excluded all but the most desperate families, defined as "destitute widows" or "women with a sick husband," served to stigmatize further not only the day nurseries but the working mothers and the children who used them. Working mothers had become, almost by definition, contemptible or pathetic or both.

This image was enriched by what became known as the "cult of motherhood," the elevation of mothering from just one more domestic chore to the essence of feminine virtue. Common wisdom had it that no woman was complete unless she had a child and no child was complete without its mother nurturing and supervising its every gurgle and burp. In the early 1900s, the child-study movement lent "scientific" credence to the notion that children were in need of almost constant attention from their mothers, and the very idea of surrogate care was pronounced repugnant. The first White House Conference on Children and Youth, held in 1909, declared life at home with mom to be "the highest and finest product of civilization" and urged that children be cared for in their own homes whenever possible. Never mind that the home was sometimes shabby and unsafe and the mother was depressed, unable to cope, or even cruel. Home was where the heart was, and children were the heart of the home.

In its Children's Charter, the conference recommended that rather than fund day nurseries, which separated children from their mothers, states provide funds directly to mothers to encourage them to stay home with their children. By 1919, the idea had caught on: thirty-nine state governments were paying single stay-at-home mothers stipends ranging from two to four dollars a week for the first child. (Stipends were not available to married women, even if their husbands were unemployed or absent.) Social workers advised single mothers to quit their jobs, take their children out of day nurseries, and make due with the pension. And many mothers did remove their children from the nurseries, though not necessarily to stay home. Unable to support a family on the paltry sum, many women found themselves sneaking back to the factory and leaving junior and sis with a neighbor, an older sibling, or alone.

Ironically, the decline of public support for the day nursery was paralleled by a growing awareness and interest in the education and nurture of young children. This education was increasingly likely to take place not at home but in the nursery school. In England, where it originated as the so-called "infant school," nursery school was designed as a philanthropic institution, a partial substitute for rather than a supplement to home care. Nursery schools in this country, by contrast, were generally privately funded and functioned to provide enrichment opportunities for the children of the middle class, which regarded them as a way to give their children a head start in education and a leg up on the status quo. Rooted in, among other things, the philosophy of Friedrich Froebel, who considered childhood not a period of depravity (as did earlier and even later thinkers) but the "uncorrupted embodiment of God's reason," nursery schools were not conceived for the benefit of the family per se but for the benefit of the child.

There were few public nursery schools in America, and the private ones were costly and exclusive. Nursery schools were, as an institution, decidedly not intended for the relief of working mothers, who, at any rate, could hardly afford them. (One notable exception to this was the Ruggles Street Nursery School, set up in Boston in 1922 with the explicit purpose of serving families from a broad range of socioeconomic backgrounds.) In general, the day nursery was looked upon with contempt by nursery school advocates, who, concerned that the day nursery would muddy public understanding of the nursery school concept as an elite and sophisticated institution of learning, did much to undermine its support.

By the end of the 1920s, the day nursery had become a marginal and much maligned last resort for families who had no choice but to submit themselves to the onerous designation of "pathological." No mother with the means to avoid it would subject her child to such a stigmatizing experience. The acceptable child-care choice was a nanny, perhaps in combination with nursery school, a choice out of reach of the poor and working classes, but one that helped to buffer more affluent women from the indignation of the disapproving. (Perhaps it is not so surprising that social critics of the time did not address the nanny issue, a uniquely upper- and upper-middle-class phenomenon.)

Day care as an institution got a temporary reprieve in 1933, not because new research showed it to be good, bad, or otherwise for kids, but largely because the economy had gone bust and a good number of teachers, among others, were in need of jobs. President Roosevelt decided day nurseries were fair places to employ people and provided federal funds for them through the Works Progress Administration. At its height, the WPA program hosted 40,000 children and employed 3,775 teachers, the vast majority of whom had never taught preschool-age children before, and a large minority of whom had never taught anyone before.

Not surprisingly, what little public interest there was in day care waned as WPA money dried up; the nurseries were closed, and the teachers, nurses, clerks, janitors, and cooks who worked in them found other jobs. Though short-lived, however, the WPA effort was a ground-breaking one — it was the first time the federal government had seen fit to support the care and education of preschoolers. It also served to spark public consciousness of the value of early education. But the WPA program was designed specifically for the underprivileged and, as such, did little to change public opinion about the status of the working mother. For that, there was World War II.

Public concern over the consequences of day care on children and families all but evaporated in the rush to feed the war machine. The exodus of America's male work force to foreign shores caused a massive march of women into the factories, magically changing the working mother from "pathetic wench" to "patriot." The Community Facilities Act (commonly known as the Lanham Act), passed by Congress in 1942, provided funds for day care, as did a number of industries that relied on women workers. Suddenly, centers were popping up all over the country. By 1945, more than a million and a half children were being left in the hands of day care workers while their mothers went off to rivet airplane bellies or pack parachutes. There were no quality standards, and many of the centers were disorganized, poorly run, underequipped, and understaffed. But others were exceptional. The Kaiser Child Service Centers, for example, set a standard of care that has yet to be duplicated on a large scale.

Kaiser Shipbuilding Corporation of Portland, Oregon, set up its centers not in dank basements or echoing warehouses but in spanking new buildings built specifically for the purpose, with large banks of windows, pastel-tinted walls, and specially designed children's bathtubs. There were plenty of toys and rolling lawns planted with trees and shrubs. The teachers were well schooled in both early education and child development and were willing, for the sake of the war effort, to work long and hard. The centers were open around the clock, six days a week, and the staff prided itself on being helpful and supportive to the entire family. Almost everything was taken care of, from grocery shopping to caring for sick children to cooking take-out dinners. If parents wanted to catch a movie or go Christmas shopping at night, the staff was more than willing to baby-sit. It was day care without strings, without guilt. It was day care that worked extremely well.

The hope of educators who participated in the Kaiser experiment, the hope that kept many of them going through twelve-hour days and endless nights, was that their center would serve as a model for other centers after the war. Wrote James L. Hymes, a professor of early childhood education and director of the Kaiser centers:

> Perhaps most buoying is the hope each teacher has that here in Portland ground is being broken for a vast postwar development in nursery education. There is the vision that perhaps the Kaiser answer to a wartime problem can show the way to a country's answer to similar peacetime needs. . . . It may be, these teachers hope, that here is the forerunner of other Centers equally geared to aid families and children.

This hope was not realized. In fact, after the war, the benefits of day care, to children and to families, went largely unacknowledged or were dismissed. Day care for young children was once again deemed a necessary evil, one to be promoted only during times of extreme crises, such as wartime or periods of unemployment. The shipyards closed, and the Kaiser Child Service Centers closed with them, as did most of the centers organized under the Lanham Act. And the nation heaved a collective sigh of relief knowing that children were safely back home with mother.

They weren't, of course. By 1950, a full seven years before "Leave It to Beaver" was to swaddle prime time in the comforting images of life at home with mom, nearly two million mothers of children under age six were in the work force. By the middle of the next decade, more than one in four mothers of preschoolers were working or looking for work. The sheer volume of working mothers did nothing to sway prevailing public opinion away from the idea that mothers of young children really ought not to work outside the home. In 1963, for instance, the year "Leave It to Beaver" went off the air, the Children's Bureau found that:

> The child who needs day care has a family problem which makes it impossible for his parents to fulfill their parental responsibilities without supplementary help.

And for those millions of working families who didn't believe they had a problem, an alternative guilt trip was proffered: the generally accepted but fully unsupported belief that day care, per se, was dangerous. The origin of this notion is unclear but is often traced to a misinterpretation of the work of John Bowlby, a noted British physician and child psychologist.

Bowlby was no fan of day care. In his report "Maternal Care and Mental Health," first published in 1951, he wrote:

> As regards health, day nurseries are known to have high rates of infectious illness and are believed to have an adverse effect on the children's emotional growth. As regards production, there is little net gain in woman power, since for every 100 mothers employed 50 workers are necessary to care for the babies and, as every industrialist knows, mothers of young children are unsatisfactory employees and often absent on account of minor illnesses at home. For these reasons day care as means of helping the husbandless mother should

be restricted to children over three who are able to adapt to nursery school.

In this report, Bowlby also described a condition called "maternal deprivation," in which children separated from their mothers suffer mental and physical retardation. The fact that the children in Bowlby's study had been wrenched permanently from their mothers because of catastrophe or neglect, and that many of them were in orphanages and foster homes of questionable repute, was overlooked or ignored by many social scientists in their rush to generalize Bowlby's conclusions to bolster condemnations of day care.

Bowlby's research, albeit misinterpreted, added "scientific" legitimacy to the prevailing notion that mothers belonged at home with their children. To think or, in particular, to act otherwise was deemed somehow unnatural. In the sixties and early seventies, experts in early childhood, from Benjamin Spock to Berry Brazelton to Burton White, would argue that no mother should, as Spock put it, "pay other people to do a poorer job of bringing up her children" and urged mothers to delay their return to work as long as possible. The fact that most mothers had little control over whether or when they returned to work did not decrease the guilt heaped on them for doing so. Most early childhood experts of the time regarded child care the way that Victorians regarded sex — as a need to be denied until it somehow went away.

These days, the question of whether infants and young children can successfully tolerate extensive daily separations from their mothers continues to be the subject of hot debate among researchers, politicians, and parents. The current literature is replete with arguments on both sides. Some experts contend that babies in child care show a less secure bond with their mothers than do babies raised by mothers at home and that these infants, on average, grow up to be more aggressive and undisciplined schoolchildren. Others argue that there is no evidence that day care per se weakens the bond between mother and child and that what some may interpret as aggressiveness could as easily be interpreted as increased independence and assertiveness. Of course, no one is sure of any of this. Child care, especially for infants, is an ongoing social experiment, the outcome of which is yet to be determined. It's really not possible to compare children in day care with children who stay home with their mothers all day because every day care center is different, every home situation is different, every child is different, and every family has a different reason for doing what it does. It can be safely said, though, that the type of care is probably less important than the quality of care, especially at the extremes: bad day care is not good for children, but there is no evidence that good day care is bad, and there is plenty of evidence that very good care in a center is preferable to very bad care at home. Many Americans have yet to come to grips with this, partially because we are reluctant to pay for an alternative, of course, but also because so many of us harbor a cherished utopian vision of family life, a vision that lets us deny that so many of our children — the majority, in fact — are no longer at home all day every day with mom. We are the last industrialized nation to cling to this cherished myth, a myth for which our children are paying mightily.

Eight

SEX AND VIOLENCE

LINDA de Lissovoy doesn't think of herself as a social services sort of person. She created her own major at Penn State, taking courses in religion, film, English literature, and community studies, and only later, after earning a B.A., reluctantly returned to college to pick up a teaching certificate. Linda says she prefers poetry to people and that deep down inside she's a misanthrope. That may be true. But it is also true that people, particularly children, are frequently what's on her mind.

Linda works as a licenser for the Massachusetts Office for Children. Technically, her job is to inspect and license day care centers in Cambridge and four other communities in greater Boston, but Linda does not dwell on technicalities. Usually she gets more involved with the centers and the people who use them than her job description dictates, a good deal more involved, one would think, than a misanthrope would choose to be.

Linda started out years before as a day care teacher and went on to direct a day care center of her own, a small family-oriented place with the kind of sixties values she still espouses. But Linda needed to do more, and the job at OFC offered her the opportunity to reach out to thousands of children at dozens of centers. She has been at it for ten years now, far longer than most, and she says she thinks she's had just about enough of the job. A recent trip to Sweden, and a casual tour of day care centers there, has, she says, pushed her to the brink of tolerance for the American child-care system.

"In Sweden," she says, "there is a recognition that we all start out as children. This is not true in America."

Linda says that, in Sweden, there seemed to be day care centers on every corner and that the centers were so well equipped and skillfully organized that the sight of them would send shivers of envy up the spines of American day care workers.

"Children in American day care centers get macaroni and cheese for lunch, if they're lucky," she says. "In Sweden, they get smorgasbord."

Linda says this while sitting behind a gray metal desk in the Waltham field office of OFC's licensing division. She is a compact woman of forty, with a preference for colorful, loose-fitting clothes and sensible shoes. She wears no makeup and her hair, cut to a medium length in a casual, low-maintenance style, is lightly flecked with gray. Photographs of children she taught as a day care teacher peer out from among the notices plastering the bulletin board above her desk. Her radio is tuned to bluegrass, a fiddle player she knows and likes. She keeps the music going all day for comfort.

Linda's office feels large because the women who once sat at the other two desks no longer work there. Budget cuts have made it impossible to hire replacements. In fact, the budget for OFC's licensing division has shrunk steadily in the last couple of years, resulting in a 16 percent job-vacancy rate across the agency. Meanwhile, the number of out-of-home day care facilities in the state has burgeoned to nearly fifteen thousand. As a result, Linda's job, and the job of all licensers, has grown close to impossible, with each licenser being responsible for ninety-five to one hundred day care centers. But Linda says it's not as bad as it was.

"This agency used to be run as though out of a corner of somebody's kitchen," she says. "When I started here, I was in charge of one hundred and ten day care centers, some of which hadn't been inspected in four years. Then, five years ago, we were down to twelve licensers for the entire state, each of whom was responsible for as many as one hundred and eighty-five centers. There was only one licensing supervisor for the state. There was next to no money, and there was constant squabbling over the few pennies that were available. We were given the impression that what we did here didn't matter. Basically, we were thought of as the people who went around making sure day care centers had enough crayons."

That was in 1984. By then, Linda had been working as a licenser long enough to have developed a pretty keen sense of what made a center a good or a bad place for children to be. She could go into a school, chat with the director, talk to the teachers, observe the children, and make a fairly accurate appraisal of the quality of the care, an assessment that might well have little to do with the regulations that she was required to check off on the long list the OFC provided. Like all licensers, Linda found violations at just about every center she visited, some of them little things, some of them not so little. Most of the time she would work with the center director and staff to correct these deficits rather than rush to close the place down. She saw her job as that of a partner, not that of a policewoman. The very fact that a center was licensed or was seeking a license rather than operating illegally was considered a good sign. (No one knows how many day care providers are operating illegally in the state, but given the number of legal spots versus the number of working families, it is assumed to be large.)

But there was one center under her supervision, the Fells Acres School in Malden, in which Linda could not bring herself to see her role as collaborative. Fells Acres set her sensibilities distinctly on edge, so much so that, despite her overwhelming caseload, she found herself returning to this center again and again.

The Fells Acres School, set in a white clapboard-covered home in a well-kept section of a tidy middle- and working-class suburb, had been run for eighteen years by Violet Amirault, a fifty-nine-year-old woman given to wearing pearls and commonly described as "grandmotherly." Violet's daughter, Cheryl Amirault LeFave, was a teacher at Fells Acres, and Violet's son,

Gerald, worked there as a cook and bus driver. Linda recalls that Cheryl would sometimes dress inappropriately in low-cut dresses and heels, "like a madam," and that the place was almost unnaturally clean, as though constantly vacuumed by a compulsive housekeeper. Most unsettling, though, was that whenever Linda came to check on the school, the children would cluster around her and cling to her as if for their lives.

"You have to use your intuition as well as your intellect when you look at a center, and while I couldn't put my finger on just what was going on, I knew that I loathed the people who worked at that school," she says. "These were extremely powerful, magnetic types, and they were also somehow very threatening. They frightened me."

One day, Linda arrived at Fells Acres, knocked on the door, and was literally thrown out by the Amiraults. Shaken, she returned to her car, drove back to her office, and called her supervisor, who told her to make note of the incident and take care not to return to the school alone. It is uncommon, but not unheard of, for a licenser to be attacked by an irate day care center director or teacher, and her boss's first concern was keeping Linda safe. The irony that an educated and fully capable adult was warned off an establishment patronized by three-, four-, and five-year-olds seemed, at the time, to escape everyone except Linda. She returned to Fells Acres four times after that, each time bringing another licenser with her. Every visit produced evidence of violations aplenty, and though the Amiraults assured her that they would be dealt with immediately, Linda was not satisfied. Finally she convinced her supervisor to visit the place with her, but he, while acknowledging that Fells Acres had a bad smell about it, could find no reason to conduct a formal investigation.

Frustrated, Linda decided to take the only independent action she could. When parents called the Office for Children to ask for a list of day care centers in the Malden area, she sent them a photocopy on which Fells Acres did not appear. This was not official procedure. In fact, Linda was clearly exceeding her authority. At the time, parents had no formal way of learning which centers were in violation of regulations, regardless of the seriousness of those violations, and OFC was vague on whether such information should be given out by licensers, even when parents explicitly asked for it.

"As in any state agency, the people who work at OFC are afraid to say what they think," Linda says. "The tendency is to avoid taking a stand. When a restaurant violates health codes, the board of health publishes that violation in the papers. But we are not allowed to do the same with day care centers. All this tight-lippedness is not good for children; in fact, it is tragic for children."

By August of 1984, Linda was frantic. She was certain there was something terribly wrong going on at Fells Acres, but she still had no solid evidence to support that belief. She left on vacation to attend a Shakespeare festival in Oregon with a feeling of dread. When she returned, Fells Acres was closed, its license temporarily suspended by OFC. The agency had investigated a Department of Social Services suspicion of child abuse at the center and concluded that the allegation had substance. On September 6, Gerald Amirault was arrested, charged with rape and indecent assault. The response to his arrest and, more particularly, to the school's closing, was immediate: most parents vehemently opposed it.

"The center had been there for eighteen years," Linda says. "It was a neighborhood institution, run by a nice old woman and her son and daughter. The parents needed it. They were totally against our closing it."

On September 7, the day after Gerald's arrest, the parents applied for an injunction to reopen the school. When that failed, Violet Amirault countersued to remove OFC's emergency suspension ruling and to prevent state officials from notifying parents of the cause of the suspension. The parents were firmly behind her. They still didn't know why the center had been closed, but they had heard rumors and they didn't believe them. Besides, they had jobs to go to.

"No one can tell us how long the school will be closed," the mother of a preschooler told the *Boston Globe* at the time. "We working parents are dependent on the place."

Linda recalls her agency working tirelessly to "keep the godforsaken place closed" long enough for the investigation to get under way. Through constant resistance to the mounting pressure of parents, OFC managed to prevent the center's reopening long enough for the Malden police to discover twenty-nine photographs of children in various states of compromise. That done, the story came tumbling out, with one child after another coming forward with horrifying accounts of sexual and physical abuse. Even then, many parents refused to believe the stories and continued to defend the place.

"There is a defense mechanism that goes off when people hear about little children as victims," Linda says. "We live in a culture of denial; we want to believe it's an okay world."

Linda remembers one OFC hearing in which a father stood up and said that abuse couldn't have taken place at Fells Acres without his knowledge because he was at the center "all the time."

"When he was asked what he meant by 'all the time,' he said, 'I'm there every day at six p.m.,' " Linda scoffs. "The fact is, aside from attending Cheryl Amirault's wedding, there was absolutely no parent involvement at that center. That in itself is a very bad sign."

In July 1986, Gerald Amirault was found guilty of eight rapes and seven indecent assaults on children at the center. Almost exactly one year later, his mother and sister were found guilty of rape, indecent assault, and battery. All three received jail sentences. The center was never reopened.

Linda can't help blaming herself for what happened at Fells Acres. She knows she was not responsible, that she tried her best, but, somehow, she feels she could have done more. The very mention of the school makes her eyes mist over and her fists clench in frustration.

"It took sex and violence for the legislature to think that maybe it should fund this agency," she says, referring to OFC. "A little sex and violence works every time."

After Fells Acres and an incident at another Boston area day care center, in which a five-year-old girl was crushed to death by a tumbling bookcase, the Office for Children appropriated funds to double the number of day care licensers to a total of twenty-four. Although each licenser was responsible for roughly eighty-four centers, far more than the fifty to fifty-five federal guidelines recommend, things were clearly improving. OFC appointed a new director who seemed to care deeply about quality issues and who said she was committed to making the agency accountable. The number of reports of child abuse began to slip to where, in 1988, there were no publicized cases of physical or sexual abuse in any day care center in the state. That was also the year OFC's budget was frozen. The number of licensers at OFC has been dropping ever since.

IT was in the fall of 1985 that Linda was reassigned to the Cambridge beat. Tot Lot had changed considerably from the early days when parents seemed to spend almost as much time there as they did at their jobs. Tot Lot remained a hub of community action — progressive political groups continued to hold fundraising dances there, for instance. These were legendary parties, some attended by a local motorcycle gang, whose members would double-park their hogs in the street, swagger in, and, between sets, sit tame as lapdogs at the tiny tables and chairs, taking dainty swigs of soda and punch and admiring the collages pasted on the walls and the papier-mâché mobiles dangling from the ceiling. Tot Lot was neutral ground, a place where everyone in the neighborhood felt welcome. But the emotional energy that had led to the creation of the day care center had waned. The requirement that parents spend four hours a week assisting teachers at the school, a policy long disputed by both parents and teachers, had finally been dropped. Most parents were working full-time by then and had no time to drop by for casual visits, let alone spend entire mornings preparing snacks and scraping finger paint off tables. By 1985, Tot Lot was considered by many families as a service to be used rather than as an organization to be part of. There was still plenty of spirit, plenty of good intentions, but there was less time to back it up with action.

"Once the parent teaching was gone, there was a fundamental change," recalls Sally Benbasett, who left her job as Tot Lot teacher in 1978 and whose two children attended the school after she left. "People stopped hanging out; they just dropped off their kids and went to work. We didn't really get to know each other or each other's kids. We didn't really know what went on at the center day to day. All we knew was that we were paying a lot of money to have our kids taken care of while we worked." And, Sally says, for the first time parents started to refer to the staff as "those teachers."

Lisa Suyemoto was one of those teachers. A recent graduate in child development from Tufts University, Lisa had chosen to teach at Tot Lot over a number of other preschools because of the diversity of its clientele and the freedom it gave its staff to innovate. When she took the job, in June 1985, she had no idea what she was walking into.

"The director at the time was very tight-lipped about things," Lisa says. "I did know that there were some very troubled children there, but I didn't know what kind of problems they had or to what degree."

Lisa worried that focusing so much time and energy on the troubled youngsters was preventing her and the other preschool teacher from paying much attention to the less demanding children. This is a common dilemma in day care, and in elementary schools, where teachers are often warned to "watch out for the quiet little girl in the back of the room." Unfortunately, teachers are frequently so involved in putting out fires set by the more rowdy kids that the quiet little girls are overlooked until they start quiet little fires of their own.

To remedy this, the teachers kept a record, noting the time they spent with each child and making sure that everyone got attention. Still, they couldn't help putting the lion's share of their energy into the problem kids, and they wondered why the state's social service agencies weren't working harder to help them out. If anything, Lisa says, the Office for Children and the Department of Social Services were making things worse.

"We had no support," Lisa says. "One time I called the Department of Social Services to report that one of my children had been burned by his parents. Not only had he been burned repeatedly and over large areas of his body, but he had been locked in the bathroom and left there all night. So I and a couple of other teachers reported this to DSS, and the next day I called to see what had happened. DSS said they had called the house but that no one had answered the phone. They said there was nothing more that they could do." Meanwhile, the burned child continued to attend Tot Lot.

The director had great difficulty managing people and dealing with conflict, so much difficulty, in fact, that when things got rough, she would leave, sometimes for hours or even days at a time. And at Tot Lot, things were frequently a lot rougher than many people cared to admit. The place was slipping from comfortably funky into a state of physical and psychic disrepair. There were money problems and staff problems and parent problems and even physical-plant problems. (Susan recalls that when she first arrived at Tot Lot, there was a ring of barbed wire surrounding a skylight on the roof play deck and that one of the climbing structures was falling apart.) The Child Care Resource Center, the Cambridge-based day care reference and referral agency, had crossed Tot Lot off its referral list.

"It was terrible," says Linda de Lissovoy, recalling her first visit to Tot Lot in 1985. "The director was hysterical all the time. She had no idea of how to work with parents. And after my first couple of visits, she became incredibly defensive. I'd walk in the door, and she'd say, 'Stop right there, I'm calling a lawyer.' "

But the director's behavior was not simple paranoia. By the time Linda came on the scene, Tot Lot was being subjected to a level of scrutiny that bordered on harassment. DSS and the Office for Children descended on the center at the least provocation. A particularly telling incident was when a parent called DSS to complain that a teacher had scratched her child. DSS wasted no time in checking out the charge: the agency dispatched an inspector immediately to determine whether the teacher's fingernails were in need of a trim. This is the same agency, the teacher points out, that could not find its way into the home of a child who showed clear signs of being burned repeatedly.

The Office for Children's newfound interest in Tot Lot stemmed, in part, from an event that took place at the center shortly after the Fells Acres case had hit the newspapers the year before. The Fells Acres affair sparked a spasm of highly publicized searching into the suddenly perceived erosion of the state's child-care system and prompted a new consideration of the many rhetorical questions concerning the validity of day care as an institution. The fact that most child abuse is committed by relatives and family friends in children's own homes did nothing to quell the outcry. The home, after all, is sacrosanct, its invasion an aberration of the democratic system. But day care centers are something else again, and no one is sure quite what. Perhaps, it was whispered, abuse is inevitable in such places, and perhaps the people who choose to work in them, to spend day after day cleaning children's messes and wiping their bottoms, are, by definition, depraved. The Boston papers published editorials calling for both closer scrutiny of centers and for more careful prescreening of day care teachers and staff. Insurance companies took a cold, hard look at day care centers and either stopped covering them altogether or raised insurance rates in anticipation of further legal actions. And, with its new beefed-up staff, the Office for Children got serious — at least nineteen other day care facilities around the state were investigated for alleged abuse. Among these was Cambridgeport Children's Center.

MARK Johnson was a student at the University of Massachusetts at Boston when he applied for a job at Tot Lot in the summer of 1984. Mark was articulate, competent, and experienced, and he had excellent references from two other day care programs, including the one at the university he attended. He was also serious about child care; his ambition was to pursue a permanent career as a day care teacher. He was hired in July as a part-time teacher in the preschool room. Some parents recall him rather vaguely as a "nice guy and a good teacher." Their recollections are vague not because Mark was a shadowy person but because he didn't teach at the center for very long. Things were a bit strained there at the time, and no one was entirely surprised when Mark gave his two weeks' notice after teaching for less than four months. But Mark didn't last the two weeks. Within days of giving his notice, he was suspended with pay and ordered to leave the premises immediately. A parent had charged Mark with sexually abusing her four-year-old daughter.

Mark vehemently denied the allegations, and the other teachers backed him. Mark was a good kid; there was nothing the least bit weird about him. Besides, there was no place for sexual abuse to occur unnoticed at Tot Lot. With the exception of the diaper-changing area, where Mark, being a preschool teacher rather than a toddler teacher, rarely went, the school was wide open, and the parents were welcome to visit at any time.

But DSS insisted that it was not only possible but probable that Mark had committed the act. The agency called an emergency meeting of parents and staff to explain Mark's suspension. The parents were told at that meeting that little children do not, cannot, lie about sexual matters, that they don't know enough to lie. The officials implied that the child's accusation substantiated Mark's guilt. Then the child's mother took the floor and offered stomach-wrenching details of her daughter's ordeal, details that made it impossible for other parents to raise any doubts about its occurrence. The emotion-choked meeting adjourned with everyone feeling betrayed.

The parents were divided. On the one hand, the accusations dovetailed nicely with some strongly held preconceived notions. Some parents found the idea of a man teaching preschool a bit hard to take. What made a young man turn to working with children? That, in itself, was suspect. One parent mentioned that she'd been suspicious of Mark ever since she'd seen him sneaking off with a little girl toward the bathroom. The fact that taking preschoolers to the bathroom was part of his job did nothing to diminish the horrors the woman could envision taking place during this particular trip to the john.

But other parents came forward with information that raised doubts about OFC's aspersions. First of all, the child in question had grown up in a troubled home with an older sister who herself had been the victim of sexual abuse. Sexually explicit language was not foreign to this four-year-old; in fact, it would have been hard for her not to have picked up the rudiments of whatever jargon was necessary to make the claim she made. The child also had a history of telling tales and acting out to get attention, so much so that, just weeks before, a team of teachers, Mark among them, had advised her mother to get the child professionally evaluated. It was no secret that the mother was enraged by this advice. Anger is a common response of parents confronted with the possibility that they themselves are responsible for their children's difficulties. It is also common for such parents to attack the bearers of these disconcerting tidings, to blame the teachers for their children's behavior. Mark, being the center's lone male employee, was the obvious target.

Still, the state "experts" continued to speak of Mark's guilt as if it were a proven thing, and this verdict seemed to take on a life of its own. More "evidence" of abuse at Tot Lot trickled in. Another mother accused Mark and two other teachers of physically abusing her son. Few of the other parents believed her claim — one of the accused teachers wasn't even at the center at the time she was said to have committed the abuse. Nonetheless, the accusation was troubling. Then another mother reported that she had noticed her son acting out a good deal lately and that the cause of his misbehavior was abuse he had suffered at the hands of yet another Tot Lot teacher. Almost no one believed this claim, but it served to fertilize the seeds of doubt that had begun to sprout and poke holes in Tot Lot's legendary solidarity. The parents split into two warring factions, those who believed there had been abuse and those who didn't.

"This was an incredibly divisive issue," says Sally Benbasett, whose daughter was a student at Tot Lot at the time. "DSS and OFC were so ready to believe that it had happened. Things just got hysterical."

The ensuing DSS investigation produced not a shred of evidence to substantiate charges that either physical or sexual abuse had taken place at the center. Still, it was clear that the children had been violated by someone. By putting the blame on Mark, investigators were absolved from mucking about in the private lives of families who were already in obvious pain.

Mark was indicted in the spring of 1985 on one charge of rape and one charge of indecent assault. His working-class parents borrowed money against their home to pay the fifteen thousand dollars in legal fees it took to keep him out of jail. Molly and the handful of other teachers who were as yet uncharged with abuse were summoned to Middlesex County Court to testify.

And then, suddenly, the charges against Mark were

dropped. The child's mother made it clear that she believed that abuse had taken place, but she said she also believed that a trial would do her daughter and her family no good. Particulars of the case were impounded by the court to ensure privacy for the child. And Mark was free. Free to do what, no one knew. Certainly not free to return to working as a day care teacher. News of his indictment had not been impounded — it had hit the newspapers. Guilty or innocent, his career as a teacher was finished. What all this did for his ego, or for his reputation as a human being, is unclear. All that anyone seems to know is that he left Cambridge for good and that he never showed his face at Tot Lot again.

Meanwhile, the Office for Children dropped its investigation of Mark and the other teachers. Still, the agency never officially exonerated anyone, and those teachers who remained, both the accused and the unaccused, were left numb and confused. They were afraid to pull a child onto their laps, afraid to give a child a hug. Most of all, they were afraid to say anything about a child who they believed was being mistreated at home. There was no telling when a parent might retaliate by filing a charge against them with DSS. And it was clear where DSS stood in these cases: a parent's word was taken over a teacher's word every time. Being a day care teacher meant not only hard work and lousy pay; it meant being an easy mark for disgruntled parents as well.

"After that, I became afraid to be a teacher," says Molly. "In fact, we were all afraid to go to work."

The center sank into a collective and chronic cold sweat. The teachers stopped keeping detailed files on children for fear that those files would be pulled by DSS and used against them. If they suspected parental abuse, they kept it to themselves rather than risk reprisals. And if children did poorly and were in need of help the teachers couldn't provide, it went unmentioned: two of the three parents who had charged the teachers with abuse had been told that their children needed special-needs evaluations. Several of the teachers, including one who was generally considered to be among the best teachers the center had ever had, quit.

"We saw what had happened to Mark," Molly says. "Being a teacher just didn't seem worth it anymore."

DAVID Finkelhor is Professor and Codirector of the Family Research Laboratory and the Family Violence Research Program at the University of New Hampshire. He is an expert on child abuse and has coauthored a book, *Nursery Crimes,* on sexual abuse in day care centers. He works out of a small and crowded office on the university's sprawling and bucolic main campus in Durham, New Hampshire, just north of the Massachusetts border.

Finkelhor is a sensitive man in a difficult specialty. He chooses his words, and his battles, carefully. The very fact that a book on child abuse in day care centers has been written, he says, is sometimes used to support arguments with which he fervently disagrees. One of those arguments is that day care centers are, by their nature, dangerous institutions.

While sexual abuse of children is as old as just about anything, public concern over the problem is not. In fact, little was written on the subject until the mid-1970s, when the first reports of widespread abuse became public. In 1975, 7,000 cases of sexual abuse were reported, and, to many, that number sounded horrific. A decade later, the number rose to 120,000, and that got people thinking. Maybe it was time to do something about all this. There were conferences on sexual abuse, television docudramas about sexual abuse, and talk of teaching children as young as two or three the facts of life to help them somehow keep themselves from being sexually abused. (How a three-year-old was to "just say no" to a twenty-five-year-old molester was never convincingly explained.) However, the fact that the vast majority of sexual abusers of children are either members of the children's own families or part of their families' intimate social networks was not always included in public awareness campaigns. Abuse in day care, while rare, was much easier for the public to believe and stomach; it provided a welcome distraction for those reluctant to face the unsavory fact that tens of thousands of children are sexually abused in their homes every year.

"Parents have a tendency to believe that the home is safe, that the risk of child abuse in the home is zero," Finkelhor says.

"Ironically, the risk is far greater in the home than it is in a day care center."

This is not to suggest that abuse does not occur in day care centers, only to point out that abuse can happen anywhere and is most likely to occur when a child is alone with an adult, not in the company of other children and a multitude of caregivers.

Unwillingness to face reality has caused many parents to become unwitting accomplices to the relatively rare cases of abuse that do take place in day care settings. Finkelhor has studied many such cases and found that it is not uncommon for the problem to be perpetuated by parental negligence and disbelief.

"No one wants to confront the possibility that their child has been abused," he says. "They can't face the idea that they've put their own child into an abusive situation, so they'd rather believe that the abuse did not occur."

Many parents have such a hard time finding day care that they are reluctant to remove their children from a center where things appear to be going okay.

"They don't want to go back to the drawing board and search for a new day care center," Finkelhor says. "Finding good day care is just too tough."

So, all too often, parents respond like those parents at Fells Acres who at first seemed to focus more on their job security than on the possibility that their children were being raped. When it became clear that abuse was rampant at Fells Acres, parents responded with outrage, not at themselves for having inadvertently subjected their children to a sentence in kiddie hell, but at the teachers, whose psychopathology had somehow escaped them.

In Massachusetts, the Fells Acres case, as well as nationally publicized cases such as the McMartin Preschool case in swank Manhattan Beach, California, where as many as three hundred children were said to have been abused, led to a public outcry for protection against such horrors. In August 1986, a state law was passed in Massachusetts requiring criminal-records checks of all newly hired day care teachers. Many day care teachers, including Molly (who was not subject to the checks), objected to this. They argued that public school teachers undergo no such scrutiny, nor do social workers or pediatricians or even workers in the foster-care system. It seemed that, for whatever reason, day care teachers had been singled out as particularly likely abusers. And, Finkelhor says, research shows that this simply isn't the case.

"Criminal-records checks aren't very effective because day care sex offenders tend not to have criminal records," he says. "They also tend not to be habitual pedophiles, to have a history of child abuse. I imagine almost everyone who interacts with children regularly feels sexual at one time or another. People who are exposed to children all the time, such as in a day care center, are faced with many seductive opportunities. What distinguishes sex offenders from the rest of us is that they succumb to these opportunities. Generally, they have large, unmet emotional and sexual needs, and the children offer them an outlet. But there is no acid test to ferret these people out."

IN 1987, three years after Mark Johnson had left Tot Lot and shortly after the center had managed to scrape together enough money to purchase the garage and begin its slow crawl toward autonomy, Susan answered a knock on the door and was unceremoniously handed a summons. Susan had worked at Tot Lot for only three months, and what she read in the summons made her sweat. The summons stated that a boy, now six years old, had been brutally assaulted while a student at Tot Lot in 1984. The summons said several teachers, Mark among them, had taken part in these assaults. The child, his mother claimed, had been battered, bruised, scraped with a knife, and sodomized repeatedly at Tot Lot. The woman said her son, now a first grader, had not spoken of these atrocities sooner because he had been warned by Mark and the other teachers that both he and his mother would be killed if he did so.

"I read this thing, and I thought, 'God, this is disgusting, how could this have happened here?' " Susan says. "I mean, I knew there were problems, but I had no idea that they went this deep."

Included in the summons was an affidavit from the child's pediatrician stating that there was physical evidence of abuse.

The fact that there was no evidence that the abuse occurred at Tot Lot — or at any day care center, for that matter — did not dissuade the doctor from adding that it was "probable" that the abuse had taken place at Tot Lot. The boy was deeply troubled. He wet his bed, had terrible nightmares, refused to sleep with his windows open "even on the hottest nights," and was under psychiatric care that, in all probability, would have to continue for some time. The mother mentioned in her statement that psychological counseling was costly and that she, being single and a student, could not afford to pay for it. The underlying theme of her appeal seemed to be that Cambridgeport Children's Center, now the proud owner of valuable Cambridge real estate, was in a better position to foot the bill than was she. Tot Lot was slapped with ten counts of neglect. The mother sued for half a million dollars.

It took three years to decide the claim. Meanwhile, Tot Lot's assets were frozen by the court. Insurance company lawyers tackled the school's end of the case and neglected to tell even Susan of their progress. She says she still doesn't know how it was settled. It was considered best for all parties to keep things confidential. Mark Johnson, though he was mentioned explicitly in the suit, was not involved in the settlement. In fact, it is likely that he was kept ignorant of the details. At that point, Mark didn't really matter anymore. He had run out of money.

IN July 1989, less than a year after returning from her tour of Sweden, Linda de Lissovoy decided to cut the cord binding her to the Office for Children. Her timing was prophetic; she left shortly before the Waltham field office was closed for lack of funds. Linda's former boss says that Linda's departure was inevitable. He says that Linda took too much upon herself, felt too strongly about her cases to last any longer in the job.

Linda plans to go back to graduate school to study film and drama and literature. From now on, she says, she's not even going to think about her ten years at OFC.

"I did all I could," she says. "And all I could do was definitely not enough."

Given that there were no funds to fill Linda's position, Tot

Lot was assigned to another licenser, an articulate, no-nonsense woman in her late thirties who, unlike Linda, insists on criminal-records checks of all day care employees who spend time alone with children. Susan, who understood the regulation to include only recent hires, is stricken by the announcement. She knows that many of her teachers, Margaret and Molly in particular, will be angered at what they believe to be a breach of their civil rights. She is worried that they may refuse to be checked or, worse yet, quit. Susan cannot afford to lose staff. On the other hand, Tot Lot is up for a license renewal this year, and she can't afford to play fast and loose with the rules. She decides to break the news of the crackdown as tactfully as possible at a staff meeting, pointing out that she must run the records checks or endanger the center's future. When she finally gets the courage to make her announcement, Molly and Margaret respond as anticipated. They bristle. Molly points out that the Civil Liberties Union has gone on record as objecting to the checks, and she thinks that Tot Lot and other centers should join in the fight. Susan sighs; she's tired of fighting.

Susan quietly sends OFC the paperwork to get criminal-records checks on all current and new employees. But, as it turns out, her effort is a token one. OFC is too overwhelmed with work to run the checks. And the new licenser fails to make even one trip to Cambridgeport in the next year to inspect Tot Lot's files or play areas or teaching materials or teachers. She doesn't have the time. Tot Lot's license is extended by mail, without an inspection. This time, the Office for Children settles for leaving well enough alone.

Nine

SOLSTICE

MOLLY lacks patience for all holidays, but there's something about Christmas that makes her particularly grumpy. Maybe it's the forced frivolity or the commercialism she can't afford. Or maybe it's all those football games flickering across the television screen and into the corner of her eye when she visits with relatives at her parents' house in Medford. Whatever the reason, Molly strives not to waste perfectly good schooltime commemorating Christmas. In fact, she strives to ignore it. This takes a good deal of willpower, given how many of her students' parents expect to see the toddler room decked with something like candy canes or paper wreaths toward the middle of December. But Molly holds fast — there are no errant Santa figures in her classroom.

This is not to say that Molly is entirely devoid of holiday spirit. She has planned a party. Her class will celebrate December 22, the day when the sun shines directly over the Tropic of Capricorn at noon. There isn't much precedent for the celebration of the winter solstice in Cambridge or, for that matter, in the world, so Molly takes the liberty of improvising. Given that December 22 is the shortest day and the longest night of the year, she usually throws a pajama party.

It's difficult to describe the kick two- and three-year-olds can get out of wearing their Doctor Denton's out of context. Even sleepy Carlos seems to wake up and take notice. And sleepwear that is just short of abhorrent at home, such as fussy, high-necked nightgowns, becomes de rigueur in the classroom. Max struts around the gray rug in his fuzzy blue "feet pajamas" beaming like a new father. Rosa looks sweetly sure of herself in her shoulder-to-floor nightie. Marcia, bundled like a babushka into a stylish Care Bear ensemble, seems almost relaxed.

And then there is Claude. As a committed Jehovah's Witness, Claude's mother, Madeline, disdains holidays even more than does Molly — she has not packed Claude's pajamas. But Molly anticipated that at least some parents would forget their children's nightwear and has brought extras. Claude's parents did not explicitly forbid his participation in today's event, so Molly tosses him a size Large T-shirt emblazoned with the visage of a giant pig. Claude wiggles down into the shirt through the neck hole, like a fox. It drapes over his thin shoulders and down to the ground. He giggles and flaps his arms, revved up with nervous excitement.

The teachers are not to be outdone. Molly, brow furrowed in concentration, darts from child to child in her fuzzy pink bathrobe and slippers, playing the mad housewife. Linda looks sleek and sassy and oddly sexy in one-piece pajamas that, like Max's, come equipped with feet. But it is Julia, the afternoon teacher, who steals the show. She has rigged herself out in curlers, long johns, and the second of Molly's T-shirts, this one adorned with a cow. Lolling on the floor like a sorority sister at an all-night soiree, she pats her headful of rollers and purrs, "I hope Susan doesn't fire me for my appearance."

At circle time, Molly draws the children down onto the gray rug for the lighting of the lamp. She sticks eight multicolored candles into a menorah and lights them, reciting a much abbreviated version of the Hanukkah story that leaves out all of the violent parts. The children, mesmerized by the flames, sit in stunned silence. Then Molly tells them all that toddlers need to know about the winter solstice.

"What's nice about the winter solstice," she says, "is that

it's about light. And Hanukkah and Christmas are, too." Holding up her finger for silence she leads the children in a few rounds of "This Little Light of Mine, I'm Going to Make It Shine," as José hangs brightly painted papier-mâché blobs from the ceiling. The children sing the spiritual for all they're worth, expending their last drop of energy after a most exciting morning. And then David starts to droop and yawn, and Claude starts tugging at his pig T-shirt, and Dawn tries to walk off with the menorah. Molly smiles and pushes to her feet, pulling her bathrobe tightly around her. It's time for snack.

DECEMBER is bleak, and the late afternoons flicker dim and then dark, forcing the toddlers to spend more and more time inside. Without sunlight, the universe of little children becomes tiny. The longer they are confined, the wilder and more willful they get, until, on some late afternoons, the teachers lie flat out on the floor, eyes fixed on the dropped, acoustically tiled ceiling, while the children dance around their heads, like whirling dervishes. Tot Lot, like most day care centers, is a kiddie ghetto. The needs of happy, active, constructive, well-organized children as construed by adults were all that was taken into consideration in the design. The needs of tired children, and stressed-out adults, were not much considered. While there are plenty of books and records, plenty of art supplies, plenty of opportunities for stimulation and interaction, there are few isolated, protected, quiet spaces for children to relax and dream in. There is no wide-open space for children to stretch their legs on cold or rainy days or when the afternoons are dark. And other than Susan's well-worn office, there is no place for teachers to take a break or make a phone call or sit on an adult-sized chair, even for a minute. In winter, the teachers regard making snack as a privilege, an opportunity to slip into the kitchen, which is off-limits to children, for a moment's peace. In winter, the kitchen is frequently overcrowded.

And winter brings other unwelcome side effects. The donning of coats and snow pants, boots and mittens, is a time-consuming ritual, one that often results in the older and quicker children becoming overheated and sweaty as the younger, slower ones get swaddled. The center is a hothouse, breeding germs by the trillion. Most of the kids have colds, and many also have more serious maladies requiring the frequent ingestion of antibiotics. This doesn't prevent them from coming to school. There are seven notes from parents taped to the refrigerator door today, each one bearing instructions for the administration of some type of medication. Pediatricians and child psychologists say children should be at home with parents when they are ill, but, by their policies, most employers show that they disagree — few parents have the luxury of being allowed to take time off when their kids get sick. It is unclear to doctors whether children in day care build up a biological resistance that gives them a head start on coping with contagious illnesses in grade school, but the toddlers at Tot Lot would make an interesting case study: their exposure levels seem high enough to confer a lifelong resistance to disease. Molly jokes that, at this time of year, she often feels more like a nurse than a teacher.

Of the toddlers, Christopher has suffered more than most. He has been absent from school for going on two weeks, the only toddler to miss out on winter solstice. As with his mother, a tendency toward asthma complicates and worsens each bout of flu. Today he has a temperature of 104 degrees and has started to wheeze and to gasp for air. X rays of his chest show signs of pneumonia. Bundled up on the pullout couch wedged between the closely set walls of his living room, he is pale and thin and nearly mute from exhaustion. Holly says she finds his silence particularly frightening. The tiny apartment resounds with it, making a mockery of anything she can say to comfort him. Holly, too, is ill. When she brought Christopher to the clinic for tests, the doctor took one look at her blotchy skin and tissue-chapped nose and ordered X rays for her as well. Her chest was clear, but her throat was not; she had a very bad upper-respiratory infection. Holly is allergic to antibiotics, so the infection rages on. Holly's mother and brother come to take care of Christopher each day but not to give Holly a rest. Despite her illness and Christopher's, Holly continues to go to work.

"You're not supposed to get sick when you work for the telephone company," she says, hacking out a sardonic laugh.

"They keep tabs on you, and if you're sick too often, they send you up to talk to this person who tells you to take better care of yourself, to eat better and take vitamins." So far, Holly has managed to stay clear of the vitamin man.

Still, things have gotten a little easier for Christopher and Holly since the telephone company strike broke on November 21. For one thing, Christopher wakes up to his mother's face each morning. Neither his grandmother nor his uncle nor Holly's friend, Kevin, have to sleep on the foldout couch so that Holly can trot off to work at 3 A.M. Christopher eats breakfast with his mother and, when he is well, walks with her to school. Sometimes, when she doesn't have grocery shopping to do, Holly even drives to Tot Lot on her lunch break to be with him. Perhaps as a consequence, Christopher has stopped waking up in the middle of the night and poking his mother awake. He has stopped grabbing her leg at 3 A.M. each morning and begging her not to leave him. And he's stopped bad-mouthing the black kids in the toddler room.

For some reason, Christopher turned racist during the strike. He picked fights with Claude and Marcia and said Claude's dad and Marcia's mom were "bad." This attitude strained even Molly's tolerance.

"Racism is a learned thing," she says. "Somewhere Christopher has gotten the message that black people are not okay."

Holly still isn't sure where the message came from, but she knows it didn't come from her, unless her penchant for watching the nightly news for word on the strike had something to do with it. On the news Christopher saw a good number of black kids getting rounded up by police after shootings in Dorchester. Holly says this could have scared him into thinking that all black people were "bad guys."

But Holly can't quite convince herself that this reasoning holds. After all, how likely is it that a toddler would make note of the skin color of people on television? If the truth be told, Holly has no idea where this weird behavior came from, but she is very grateful that it appears to be gone.

Still, Christopher continues to be aggressive at Tot Lot at times, yanking toys from other kids and demanding attention.

He also talks a lot about dying or getting hurt or killed. Molly says that Holly is simply not dealing with this aspect of her son, that she refuses to see it. Generally, Molly is loath to judge parents, but she thinks that Holly needs guidance. Holly, Molly says, is too indulgent of Christopher; like many parents, she focuses too much on his achievement and too little on his behavior.

"Every time I sit him down to talk about his acting out, he falls apart," Molly says. "He bursts into tears and says he wants his mommy. Discipline is just too scary for him. Holly has a very hard time putting limits on Christopher. She lectures him. You can't lecture a two-and-a-half-year-old. You have to be short and sweet, and you have to act. All Holly does is talk, talk, talk."

Holly does indeed like to talk, and she sometimes worries about using Christopher as too ready an outlet, especially now that Frank, her husband, isn't around. Holly met Frank five years before, at work. She was hanging around outside the office one night, hungry and thinking about what to get for dinner, and Frank offered to buy her a pastrami sub. Holly says the sandwich was awful but Frank was great. He was different from the other men she'd dated. He was romantic and family oriented. He was devoted to his mother. He was meticulous. She remembers he wore three-piece suits to work nearly every day, even though, as a telephone company clerk, he didn't really need to. In the morning, Frank would stop by her office with coffee and apple croissants. And he sent her flowers.

"We were the office romance," she says.

Holly and Frank were married in East Boston, in Saint Joseph's Church. Holly says the church is imposing, like the Sistine chapel in miniature. Her wedding dress was satin and cost six hundred dollars. "It weighed about four hundred pounds," she laughs. "I looked like a marshmallow."

Frank was in his element at the wedding, and at the reception, where he bantered with his wide circle of friends like an Italian don. In their wedding photos, Frank and Holly make an unusually attractive couple, clear eyed, smiling, and very much in love. Two years later, Holly was pregnant, and Frank had cold feet.

"I noticed Frank seemed really unhappy around my eighth

month of pregnancy," Holly says. "He started saying things like 'Maybe we shouldn't have done this' and 'Maybe we should get a divorce.' I had eclampsia my last month and couldn't get out of bed. Frank didn't stick around much to lend moral support, but that didn't bother me; I just assumed he was at work. Anyway, he promised we'd spend two weeks together after the baby was born, and I really looked forward to that time."

Holly was nearly two weeks overdue when her doctor recommended that she have the labor induced. Frank went with her to the hospital. But the baby refused to budge, and Holly was told to settle in for what might be a long haul. Frank went back to work, and Holly's mother took over. Holly's labor lasted for three days, and Frank visited her each night. The second night, he looked deep into her groggy eyes and broke the bad news: he would not be able to take any time off after the baby was born. Holly was stunned. Frank explained that some bureaucratic screwup or computer error had bilked him of his vacation time. Holly had put up with a lot from the phone company, but this was too much. Between labor pains, she told Frank to call his boss and demand that things get straightened out. Frank stalled and balked, got angry, and said there was no way he was going to take orders from his wife, that he knew what he was doing. But Holly persisted, and finally Frank broke down and admitted that he'd been lying, that he'd actually squandered his vacation weeks before, hanging out with his buddies in East Boston. Holly hadn't been much fun when she was sick, he said, and he'd needed a break from the drudgery.

Holly gulped hard, reined in her temper, and proceeded as if everything was normal, or as normal as it could be two days into a three-day labor. After Christopher was born, she asked Frank to take a week off without pay, just until she was back on her feet. From then on, she said, she'd be able to handle things on her own. Frank agreed.

Holly stayed home to care for Christopher for two months, and she recalls it as the most blissful time of her life. She and Christopher would dream away the day together, waiting for Frank to come home each night to tell them how things were going in the outside world. It was a beautiful time.

Holly went back to work the day after Christopher was christened. Her life went from peaceful and cozy to hectic and crazy. In order to spend most of the day with her baby, she swapped her day hours for the swing shift, working 4 P.M. until midnight. Frank worked days, getting home at 5 P.M. to relieve the baby-sitter.

Holly hated to leave Christopher, but she had no choice; they needed the money. On Saturdays and Sundays, she'd cook, filling her freezer with the Italian delicacies Frank liked best. After work, she'd go home to unwind with the David Letterman show and a breast pump — she was determined that Christopher would consume nothing but breast milk until he was six months old. Holly enjoyed the early morning solitude. The house was peaceful then, and she had time to think. She thought a lot about Christopher and what a joy he'd turned out to be. She hadn't expected motherhood to be this good — Christopher filled a need she never knew she had. But she worried about Frank. He paced nervously around the apartment on weekends like a tiger in a cage. He clearly did not enjoy coming home from work to a needy infant every night. He started getting his mother or a baby-sitter to stay with Christopher and then going out. Gradually, he started going out on weekends, too, leaving Holly alone with Christopher while he joined his friends in East Boston. Sometimes he'd stay away all weekend, coming home on Sunday night feeling no obligation to tell Holly where he'd been. East Boston became his refuge, a place where he felt safe and needed and in control.

Gradually, Frank's drinking, always troublesome, got worse. He came home drunk on Sunday nights. Holly was quick to criticize this but slow to make judgments; that is, she would attack Frank's behavior without casting aspersions on his character. She was no prude when it came to alcohol. She remembered sitting at the kitchen table as a child watching her father sip Manhattans out of a stemmed bowl designed to hold ice cream sundaes. Holly's father was a heavy drinker, but he held down a steady job all his life and kept his family intact. Still, when she rolled the living room couch away from the wall to vacuum and found the empty vodka bottles hidden underneath,

Holly got worried. She started asking Frank questions about where he went and with whom and why. He told her to back off, to mind her own business, to leave him alone. And then, almost by accident, he told her that not all the buddies he hung out with on Saturday night were men. And, for Holly, that was too much. She phoned a lawyer and asked if she had the legal right to take Christopher and leave. The lawyer said yes.

"It was January fourteenth and bitter cold, fifteen degrees below zero with the windchill," Holly says. "But I was out of there."

The divorce took a long time to come through, and it was painful. Frank at first refused to sign the papers, and he and Holly would argue. Sometimes, after Holly picked Christopher up from school, she would arrive home just in time to get one of Frank's frequent phone calls. The conversation usually started out okay but ended up in a fight, often over Christopher. If the argument got really heated, Christopher would act out and try to grab the phone from Holly's hand. The next day, at school, he'd pick a fight. Still, Christopher was amazingly resilient through the strike and through the divorce and tremendously supportive of his mother. She says he kept her from being lonely, from thinking too much about herself. Sometimes Holly wonders out loud just who is parenting whom in her little family. And then she bundles Christopher up and takes him to the library.

TOT Lot has a policy of sending teachers into homes to talk with parents about the progress and problems of their children. This gives the teachers a chance to touch base with parents and to gain access to the home, to see which of the child's behaviors can be explained by circumstances outside the classroom. Not all parents agree to the arrangement. Some are just too shy or too private to allow teachers into their lives. The teachers at Tot Lot think this is a shame, but they don't push. They have learned not to go where they are not welcome.

But most parents look forward to spending an evening mulling over their children's strengths and weaknesses with a teacher. Holly, for one, anticipates Molly's visit with excitement and pleasure. Molly comes on a drizzly Monday evening, the kind of night working parents may be tempted to bring home pizza or a take-out order from a Chinese restaurant. But Holly has prepared for tonight with a feast of lasagna and salad and garlic bread and wine. She apologizes for having to heat up a casserole, explaining that work prevented her from whipping up something fresh. She apologizes because she has only home-made brownies for dessert, instead of something "really good." Molly smiles and, waving away Holly's offer of red wine, picks her way through the toys on the chipped linoleum in the living room. Holly apologizes for the condition of her floor and out-lines her intention to get a hardwood floor installed. Molly smiles again; she wonders when Holly is going to stop all this apologizing.

Christopher stands near Holly in the living room, a toy tool belt strapped tightly around his waist and a plastic work helmet yanked down hard on his head. He is busy drilling a pretend hole in the floor with his plastic drill. He is absorbed in his work and seems not to notice Molly, sitting less than a yard away on the pullout couch. Molly takes a glance at her notes. She says that Christopher has adjusted very well to the daily routine at Tot Lot and seems to have no problem making the morning tran-sition from home to school. She says he takes pride in his work and in himself, often congratulating himself out loud on the good job he's done.

Holly beams, delighted that Christopher has avoided what she says is her family's tendency toward low self-esteem. Then, as if the session were over, she launches into a monologue about the funny things Christopher told her last week.

Molly is prepared for this and cuts in to caution that not everything is hunky-dory for Christopher at school. He seems to miss his mother a lot and asks for her repeatedly during the day, usually out of the blue. He'll be sitting there, playing with Legos or reading a book, and suddenly start chanting "I want my mother." Molly doesn't quite know what to make of this. She doesn't know why he hasn't made a better adjustment to daily separation. She is also concerned about Christopher's gross motor skills; she wonders about his muscle tone. Christopher trips a lot, and a few weeks ago he fell down the stairs to the roof deck, which was quite a long and potentially dangerous tumble. Molly doesn't think he is inherently uncoordinated, but he does seem distracted at times. Molly thinks he fell down the stairs because he was so intent on chatting with her that he lost track of his feet.

"Christopher seems to focus on language so much, and he is so good with words, that he distracts himself from other things, like walking," Molly says, laughing. "He's quite a talker; I have to admit he can be quite entertaining at times."

But not always. Molly says that Christopher's periodic bouts of aggressive behavior are quite disturbing. He sometimes pushes and even hits other kids and can be a regular bully.

Holly rushes in to explain. Christopher's pediatrician thinks that the problem might stem from her divorce, which was finalized in late October. Holly is not too proud to admit that she was jarred by the divorce. She says it made her feel lonely and lost and as though her youth had ended. She finds it difficult to leave Christopher with his father on weekends, and she isn't all that confident that he's getting good care. She knows that Frank has a girlfriend and that Christopher has met her. And she knows that Frank leaves Christopher with a sitter and goes out on Saturday nights from time to time. Given that Christopher is with his father only two nights a week, leaving him with a sitter seems unnecessary and potentially hurtful. Christopher's life, she says, has been turbulent; it's no wonder he acts out.

Molly sits staring at her notes and then takes a quick look at Christopher. If he has heard any of this, he doesn't show it. He's finished with his drill and with a stack of picture books and stands squarely in the middle of the living room, aiming a foam-rubber basketball at a pint-sized net that Holly has mounted on the front door. His accuracy is uncanny; he barely misses a shot. Molly watches, amused; clearly there is nothing wrong with this boy's motor skills, at least when he's at home. Christopher grabs a lawn mower and buzzes it up and down the linoleum, while Holly, noticing an off odor, dashes off to find a diaper. She returns to the room, diaper in hand, looking hopeful. But Christopher has no intention of having his diaper changed and throws a toy screwdriver at his mother. Holly laughs, throws up her arms, tosses Molly a "see what I have to deal with" look, and smiles as Christopher sticks his *Bambi* tape into the VCR.

"Really, I have to admit that tape scares him," Holly whispers to Molly. "You know, the part about Bambi's mother dying. Sometimes, when I go to work or leave him with his dad on weekends, I think he worries that I won't come back, either."

Molly tries once again to pick up the thread of the evaluation. She says that Christopher shows no interest in toilet training, which is fine, but that she is just a little concerned about his acting out every evening when Holly comes to pick him up. She's used to this, of course; children often fall apart at the end of the day, and they feel safe acting out in front of their parents. Still, Christopher seems to go overboard at times, throwing toys and sometimes hitting other kids. Again, she wonders about all that pent-up aggression.

"He's mad at me," Holly cuts in. "Sometimes he just gets mad at me."

As if to demonstrate, Christopher picks up a stuffed frog and smashes it through the basketball hoop. The frog's eye pops out, and Christopher howls with frustration. Holly finds some glue and reattaches the eye, warning Christopher that the glue will have to dry before he can resume playing with the frog. Christopher grabs the frog, and the eye falls off again. Christopher demands that Holly sew the eye on this time. Holly tells Christopher that she doesn't have time to sew right now, that he can either wait for the glue to dry or deal with a one-eyed frog. He agrees to the latter, and she hands the frog back to him. He takes one look at the cyclopean frog and yells that he wants the eye put back. Holly steps into her bedroom and finds a piece of paper and a pair of scissors. She cuts out a half-circle of paper and hands it to Christopher, telling him to color it with his crayons. The frog, she says, will wear a paper eye patch, like a pirate. Christopher looks delighted with the idea and runs off to find his crayons. Holly invites Molly to join her in a glass of wine.

This time Molly accepts. She looks grateful that the evaluation seems to be over. Everyone piles into the tiny kitchen for lasagna. When Molly swears she can't eat another bite, Holly packs her brownies to take home. Then she grabs a stack of books for Christopher and points him in the direction of his pajamas. It's late, but she wants to squeeze in at least a couple of stories before bedtime.

AFTER New Year's, things begin to unhinge in the toddler room. The photos of parents pasted on the wall start to curl at the edges, the Play-Doh has lost its allure, and the kids, especially the older ones, have grown restless, mischievous, and edgy. The days are still dark enough to cast a shadow across the gray rug most of the time, making it look even grayer and dirtier than it is, and some of the teachers are starting to droop, as if for want of sun. Lilian, a teacher who started fresh out of college the previous summer, seems to be sinking further and further into a funk. She's taken to wearing dark, dingy clothes and to neglecting her strawberry blonde hair, which settles limply around her face in a tired compromise. Although she was active and outgoing when she was hired as a temporary summer replacement, she has become increasingly complacent and passive since having been put on permanent staff in the fall. And she gets even more distracted when José is around.

José's enthusiasm seems greatest at noon, when his half-time shift comes to an end, and at eleven, when Lilian comes in to work. These days, he seems to speak more Spanish than English and, as a result, has distanced himself from most of the other teachers. But Lilian is fairly fluent in Spanish, which she learned in addition to Portuguese during the seven years her family lived in Brazil, and she and José seem to have a lot to say to each other. They speak mostly in whispers, exchanging sarcastic looks every time Molly opens her mouth. When Molly leaves for a quick break at eleven, the toddler room inevitably breaks down. When she returns, she finds the kids wandering around or bunched around Nancy, who is frantically attempting to entertain them while José and Lilian chatter away in a corner. Save for Claude, who is drawn to Lilian, the kids usually run to Molly whenever possible. They seem to have less and less interest in the other teachers, sometimes even losing track of their names. Molly has no idea what's going on between Lilian and José, but she knows that their alliance is not doing the children any good. José and Lilian sense her disapproval and respond by convincing Nancy, who at one time was devoted to Molly, to form a sort of anti-Molly coalition with them. The coalition calls a group meeting and, in Susan's words, "roasts Molly" for being unnecessarily authoritative and unresponsive to their suggestions. Nancy, who is studying Montessori techniques, complains that Molly has no interest in trying new things. Molly, Nancy says, is rigid and cramps her creativity. She and the others would like to do many things with the children that Molly seems not to approve of — though what those things are, exactly, remains unclear.

José says growing up oppressed in Mexico has given him his fill of dictators and that he will not tolerate being ordered around. He says Molly's casual criticisms of him are evidence of her small and prejudiced mind, of her lack of creativity.

All the toddler teachers accuse Molly of resting on her laurels, of being afraid to try new things for fear of losing control.

Molly listens patiently to the criticism, twisting a strand of hair faster and faster around her forefinger, until the strand is as tight as a bow string. She can't believe that these people, each of whom has less than three months' experience as a full-time teacher, are criticizing her for being rigid. She can't believe that she's spent close to twenty years in the field to end up being lectured to by, among others, a twenty-two-year-old. She's fuming, but she knows a setup when she sees one. She holds her peace. After the meeting, she slams on her boots, jams on her coat, and heads out.

"I think the other teachers think Molly isn't working as a member of a team," Susan says. "But, the point is, she's a real heavy in the classroom; she's so experienced, and the other teachers just aren't. The other teachers think she's taking over, but it's not because she's bossy. It's because she knows the ropes so well. And they don't."

Susan says the new toddler teachers were hired despite their lack of experience because, quite frankly, she had no choice but to hire them. The parents on the hiring committee liked them, and, besides, the pool of teaching talent for preschools and day care centers is small and growing smaller with every budget cut. She took what she could get.

Massachusetts has among the most stringent requirements for day care teachers of any state, yet these requirements do not include a high school diploma. (In some states, any person over the age of eighteen can legally be given full responsibility for a classroom full of preschoolers, whether or not he or she attended high school. This contrasts vividly with the system in, for example, Scandinavia, where day care teachers are required to have three years of specialized training.) In Massachusetts, anyone twenty-one years old or older with three credits in what is called "child growth and development" and nine months of experience working in a day care center as an assistant teacher is qualified as a full-fledged teacher. (Any warm body sixteen years old and older is qualified to work as an assistant teacher.) A college graduate who majored in, say, business administration or chemistry, needs only six months of work experience to qualify as a day care teacher, and anyone with a degree in early childhood education is qualified to become a lead teacher, a teacher of teachers, with just nine months of day care experience.

Teachers like Molly, with many years of experience, are rare — there's not enough prestige or stability in day care to keep most people in the field for more than a few years. And then there's the question of money: after six years at Tot Lot and nearly two decades in day care, Molly's income remains very low indeed, just over $9 an hour, less than $270 for a thirty-seven-and-a-half-hour week after taxes. Molly does, however, earn substantially more than the average American day care worker, whose wage is $5.35 an hour. Day care workers in Boston are among the highest paid in the country. But the cost of living in Boston is also high, about 50 percent higher than the national average, so this salary doesn't go far. On average, day care teachers in the greater Boston area earn one-half as much as comparably educated women and one-third as much as comparably educated men in other lines of work. This means that while Molly probably makes twice as much as a day care provider in, for example, Mississippi, she does not earn enough to put a down payment on a house or to buy a car or even to pay for her own dental work. She earns less as a teacher than she would as a manager of a fast-food restaurant or as a secretary for a plumbing supply company or as a cocktail waitress. After twenty years in the business, Molly is able to keep her head above the poverty line, but barely. As a rule, Molly doesn't complain about her salary, except to say that it is reflective of this country's commitment to its young.

Molly is one of those rare plums, a teacher with knowledge and experience and loyalty, and Susan needs to hang on to her. Susan realizes that Molly is often reluctant to innovate, that she is not eager to tamper with a system that has worked so well for so many years. But Susan also knows that if Molly gets insulted and leaves, the toddler room will be left in the hands of a trio of teachers who, among them, have a total of less than two years of professional teaching experience.

"Molly's not perfect," Susan says. "It's hard for her to try new things, and the other teachers feel like they're in a rut. We don't talk about curriculum in the toddler room, and maybe that's not a good thing."

This is a criticism that Molly has heard before. She does not believe that a formal curriculum is important for toddlers, and she resists setting long-term plans in stone. She is willing to scout out a field trip or a celebration or an activity, but she wants the freedom to approach most weeks as an empty pad upon which she and the other teachers can sketch out their plans more or less spontaneously, keeping in mind the particular needs of the kids at that particular time. Molly is an excellent classroom manager; it is only when she leaves the room in the hands of others that things slip out of control. But sometimes it is hard to fathom where all her tightly organized activities are going. Where, for example, a half hour spent chasing soap bubbles might lead. Molly doesn't believe that it has to lead anywhere.

Some parents and teachers argue that Molly's weekly routine, which has barely changed since she began at Tot Lot six years before, is predictable to the point of being boring, that it soothes but does not challenge the kids. It's not that they want two-year-olds doing calculus, or even reciting the alphabet; it's just that they can't figure out what mucking around with corn-meal or hand lotion has to do with school. But while Molly is not averse to running a weeklong program on, say, civil-rights leaders in the sixties, she is loath to organize any systematic teaching of lessons. And while she's never set foot in a college classroom or cracked a textbook on child psychology, her think-ing on this point is precisely in line with the thinking of most early-childhood theorists.

PSYCHOLOGISTS and educators have debated the question of what place a rigorous curriculum has in the preschool classroom for close to a hundred years. It is a furious debate fueled by much passion and little data, an animal of the "more heat than light" species. Some debaters cling to the notion that the earlier kids are exposed to letters and numbers and the names of things — like colors and shapes — the better off they'll be when they start school. Their idea is that early-childhood educators must either introduce children to these concepts before they enter school or lose them later on to an uncaring system. This logic makes sense to many parents but not to a majority of experts in the study of early childhood. They subscribe instead to the child-initiated ap-proach to learning, in which children learn by participating in activities rather than memorizing and reciting. Advocates of this approach support the contention of Swiss psychologist Jean Pi-aget that the cognitive development of preschoolers centers on their thinking about and manipulation of the physical world of objects, not the symbolic world of words and numbers. Child-initiated learning is play, but purposeful play carefully organized to keep children involved and challenged. It relies on the child's natural curiosity, not the teacher's coaxing or enthusiasm.

Given that most teachers are taught to teach, not to relax and let children take the lead, it is not all that surprising that many highly trained teachers feel uncomfortable with the child-initiated approach. They feel that it somehow puts them out of a job. Their instinct is to tell or show a child the right way to do something, not simply to put out a slew of materials and let the children find things out for themselves. And, typically, parents prefer the teacher-directed approach. They want proof of progress, that scribbled worksheet or carefully colored cutout that says, "Your child has spent the day in constructive play." Even those parents who are convinced in theory that the less academic approach is right sometimes become uneasy and demanding of change when they see a next-door neighbor's toddler counting off by fives or reciting the colors of the spectrum. Parental demand and teacher pressure have led many preschools and day care centers to adopt a structured approach, one that focuses on the product rather than the process of learning.

Demand for the more structured "back to basics" approach waned in the 1970s but returned with a vengeance in the 1980s, when the pursuit of excellence eclipsed the pursuit of happiness in the public mind. *A Nation at Risk,* a report prepared by the Department of Education that suggested that the way to remedy the nation's ailing educational system was to demand accountability of educators, fueled the "pushing down of curriculum," resulting in the teaching of second-grade skills to first graders and first-grade skills to kindergartners and preschoolers. Given that self-confidence and intellectual curiosity are not measurable on an objective scale, promoting such qualities has, in many preschools, become less important than the teaching of testable skills, such as counting and letter recognition. But, the question remains, what can tests really tell us about the cognition of a three-year-old? As Harriet Egertson, an early-education specialist at the Nebraska Department of Education, puts it: "Just because a child can give the Latin name for every tree in the forest doesn't mean that he knows what a forest is." Because they cannot grasp abstractions, very young children can only memorize, not internalize, symbolic concepts, and children in structured preschool programs often memorize not because they are intrigued by the idea but because they sense that their parents and teachers want them to. Children who are externally motivated rather than motivated from within risk having their natural curiosity compromised — they may work hard for approval, but not at all for themselves. When adult approval becomes less important, say in the teenage years, these children no longer have a reason to learn or achieve and often don't. Molly's job, as she sees it, is to motivate children to seek out their own questions and their own answers, not to cram facts down their throats or provide them with a constant stream of "creative activities" designed by adults to stimulate little minds. This attitude makes her unpopular with staff who feel uncomfortable without a game plan. To them, she stands as a threat.

THE feud between Molly and the rest of the morning toddler-room staff rages on well into January. José and Lilian no longer sit with the other teachers during staff meetings but huddle off by themselves, all but ignoring the discussion as they dig into pizzas coated thickly with José's dried hot pepper flakes. And their criticism of Molly becomes more and more pointed. When she steps out for her break, they accuse her of abandoning the class. When she makes a suggestion, they raise sarcastic eyebrows that silently accuse her of bossiness.

One day, when the thermometer has crept far enough above the freezing mark to cause a slow leak in the carpet of snow in the play area, the teachers decide to risk an extended venture out of doors. While Molly helps a child into a particularly bulky snowsuit, the other toddler teachers stand in a clump in the play yard, stomping their boots and griping about Molly's lack of dependability. As they chat, the kids wander the play area in search of a game. About half the children are without mittens, which makes snowball production a particular challenge and results in several of them sobbing with cold. The teachers manage to ignore most of the fuss until Claude reaches down and grabs a mittenful of dirty snow and carefully rubs it in Dawn's face. Dawn looks thoughtful, then worried, and then lets loose with a howl that brings Molly, child in hand, to the door. Seeing Molly, the other teachers become galvanized with frantic activity, none of which results in the children being calmed. Nancy climbs to the top of a large wooden structure and dumps fistfuls of snow down on the few remaining dry children. Her goal is to attain a sort of winter wonderland effect, but she does not achieve it — still more kids scream. The kids, seeing Molly, start chanting her name, like tiny fans rooting for their football hero. She strides into the snow, picks Dawn up in her arms, and slides her slowly down the front of her parka.

"Look how slippery my jacket is," she says, steadying Dawn on the ground. "We're so slippery together, I can't even get a grip on you."

The other children beg for a try, and Molly spends the remainder of outdoor recess lifting and sliding kids down her jacket while the other teachers look on and scowl, as if Molly's behavior were somehow subversive. Getting ready to leave later that afternoon, Molly looks tired and upset.

When asked how they feel about the turmoil in the toddler room, most parents say they haven't noticed. Some admit to having an inkling that something is amiss but add that they have neither the time nor the inclination to get involved. The general response is that their children are doing okay and that Molly seems to be doing a good job of holding things together. The other teachers, Lilian, José, Nancy, are barely acknowledged. It is Molly whom these parents turn to, Molly whom their children talk about. What these parents don't consider, however, is that even Molly has a limit.

"The other toddler teachers have made me want to quit this job," she says, late one drizzly afternoon, over coffee in her apartment. "I've worked at Tot Lot for so many years, and this is my community. But, at this point, it's either them or me."

The showdown comes quickly and, for Molly, is fairly painless. For some reason that is clear to no one, both José and Lilian refuse to take the child-development courses on which their hiring at Tot Lot was contingent, and Susan has no choice but to let them go. Both are furious and resentful and accuse Molly of forcing Susan's hand. They are gone within two weeks. Nancy follows them about a month later, leaving Molly where she has been by default all semester, completely in charge.

After José leaves Tot Lot, his son, Julio, a student in the preschool room, draws further and further into himself and starts yanking out his hair even more furiously than before, leaving one side of his head completely bald. One day, well after his departure as a teacher, José appears at Tot Lot, silently removes

Julio from the play area where he is wrestling with his friend Quy, and returns him an hour later with the other side of his head shaved to the scalp, leaving a thick strip of hair down the center of his head in the Mohawk style. Julio is proud of the effect. That is the last time José sets foot inside Tot Lot. The next anyone hears of him, he has left Cambridge and his family and has gone home to Mexico. And he has taken Lilian with him.

Ten

IT TAKES A VILLAGE TO RAISE A CHILD

THE Brissetteses go to the Kingdom Hall on Monday and Wednesday evenings as well as Sunday mornings. On Monday, the service lasts one hour; on Wednesday nights, it lasts two hours, from seven until nine. Today is Wednesday. Lucien has just returned from picking Claude and Luke up at Tot Lot, and everyone is tired and cranky. Lucien got stalled in rush-hour traffic, and the boys made a fuss, poking and kicking each other in the back seat while Lucien rolled his eyes and pounded the horn. They are late getting home, and Madeline ushers them to the dinner table directly from the door. Lucien and the children stand silently forking mouthfuls of rice, chunks of spicy beef, and shreds of lettuce and tomato salad into their mouths while Madeline keeps an eye on the clock. Nobody sits. The telephone rings constantly, and Lucien lunges to grab the receiver, shouts a few words of Creole, and hangs up before losing his fork's rhythm. In minutes, dinner is over. Madeline piles the dishes in the sink and drags Claude into the master bedroom. The bedroom is neatly furnished in thickly varnished woods and bright fabrics. Framed family photos are clustered on the dresser. Madeline shuts the bedroom door firmly behind her, but Claude's chatter leaks through the thin wood. He is complaining, in English, about the tight fit of his dress slacks. Madeline answers him back in rapid French, warning him to hold still or risk untold consequences. Though spoken to in Haitian Creole and French at home, both Claude and Luke are reluctant to speak or respond to any language but English. Madeline is not altogether unhappy about this; she understands her sons' need to assimilate. Also, while she intends to teach them French, she is not concerned that they learn Creole. Creole is the language Haitians most often speak together, but it is also a language of bitterness. A mix of French and various African dialects, it is the lingua franca of slavery.

The bedroom door opens, and Claude struts out wearing a white shirt, a black clip-on bow tie, and slightly scuffed black dress shoes. His trousers, if anything, are baggy, but Claude whines and claws at the waistband as though he were shackled around the middle with a band of iron. He bolts for the television, takes a quick flip through the channels, and, finding nothing on but the local news and "Sesame Street" reruns, turns his back to the tube and joins Luke in a quick roll around the living room floor. Lucien scoops Luke to his feet before things get too heated and steers him to the bedroom and Madeline, closing the door in Claude's giggling face. Minutes later, Luke emerges dressed much like his brother, with the exception of his necktie, which is straight and stockbroker red. Lucien takes a couple of swipes at Luke's head with a flat, oval hairbrush, clucks his tongue disapprovingly at the effect, and disappears behind the bedroom door to change out of his corduroys, leaving the boys to amuse themselves.

Madeline and Lucien are not great believers in toys. They come from a country where children depend on each other rather than on things for entertainment. In Haiti, they say, children grow up playing the game of life. In Cambridge, Claude and Luke do have a handful of trucks, a couple of plastic superheroes and dinosaurs. They do not have games or picture books or crayons or paper. Generally, they make do with their bodies and their imaginations. Tonight they kneel on the couch and squint out at the Alewife Station train yards. They count the trains sitting like frozen ducks on the short strips of track. They ogle the moon, which is just starting to emerge from behind a cloud on the horizon. They look wistfully at the bedroom door, willing their parents to appear. Then they cut loose. Luke gets to his feet and jumps methodically from the couch onto the floor and back again. Claude joins him, the two giggling and falling into each other, their shirts pulling out of the back of their pants, their ties working loose. Claude, suddenly smitten with a fierce thirst, dashes into the kitchen to get a drink. He comes out with a cup of juice, trips, and spills it down his shirtfront. Luke is overjoyed. He can't wait for his parents to see the mess. Claude stands paralyzed, holding his cup and staring down at his shirt. Lucien comes out of the bedroom wearing dress slacks and a sports coat and knotting his tie. He is handsome but not composed. Luke, hooting and doing a little war dance, jabs a tattletale finger in the direction of his brother, who stands with one hand on his crotch and his head deeply bowed. Lucien slaps his hand to his forehead and throws a look at the ceiling. Madeline, dressed in a black-and-white coatdress with two-toned shoes to match, hurries to the kitchen to get a cloth while Lucien hurries Claude back to the bedroom to change his shirt. Claude comes out wearing a clean shirt, his head still bowed over his lopsided bow tie. Lucien takes one last frantic swipe at Luke's hair with the oval hairbrush and, with a grunt, pronounces the family ready to go. Madeline hands Lucien and Luke their briefcases, picks up her own, and hustles Claude out the door. Next year, Claude will have a briefcase of his own.

The nice thing about living on the twenty-first floor is that the elevator is usually empty when it arrives. The downside is the twenty opportunities the elevator has to stop on its descent to the ground floor. Madeline and Lucien ponder this as they stare at the brown metal doors while the boys do mock battle in the hallway, which smells strongly of onions and spices and faintly of urine. Finally, the doors open, and the family clambers into the empty car. Three flights down, the doors open again, this time for a pair of young men dressed in jeans and hooded sweatshirts, the hoods pulled into tight frames of their faces. The Brissetteses push back to the rear of the elevator, and the young men shove in, filling the space. They wear "pump" sneakers, hightops that can be pumped up with air with a tiny ball in the tongue for a snugger fit. Luke recognizes the sneakers; he has seen them advertised on television, and he admires them. He can't keep his eyes off the feet. The young men are talking business, loudly comparing the price of cocaine in Boston with the price of cocaine in New York City. Apparently Boston has become a less favorable market, and this is in some unspecified way bad news for them. On closer scrutiny, it becomes clear that the young men are not men at all but boys of around fourteen. Lucien listens to them with mild interest, as if to a weather report, his eyes resting lightly on their lips. The boys don't blink, and they don't stop talking. They fix Lucien with a razor-eyed stare. Lucien smiles politely. The teenagers take a quick look at Madeline and the children and give Lucien a "fuck off" glare. Lucien keeps the smile steady. Madeline clenches Claude's hand and lowers her eyes to her imitation patent leather pumps, which are polished to a high shine.

The elevator drops slowly, opening its doors at half a dozen more floors on its fitful descent to the lobby. Every time the doors open, the people waiting take one look at the young men with the pumped-up sneakers standing inside and make a quick decision not to crowd them — they step back to wait for the next car. When the elevator finally clatters to a stop at the ground floor, the doors stick for a moment. The teenagers keep their eyes fixed on Lucien, as if daring him to make a move, then kick the doors with two quick chops. The doors open. Madeline clamps Claude hard by the shoulders and pushes him out, between the two boys. But Lucien stays back to let the teenagers pass, and Luke stays with him. The teenagers give him one more hard glare, then leave, glancing skittishly over their shoulders as they push through the double glass doors of the apartment building and into the night. Lucien and Luke follow, joining Claude and Madeline in the lobby. They walk slowly and in silence through the glass doors and into the parking lot, which glitters with broken glass. The Brissetteses pile into their car, and Lucien cranks the engine. It takes several turns to catch, and with each crank Madeline catches her breath. The children bounce lightly in the rear seat. The engine grabs hold, and Lucien directs the car out of the lot. The drive to the Kingdom Hall takes less than ten minutes. By the time they get there, Madeline is smiling.

There are about 6,000 Jehovah's Witnesses living in Haiti, and Madeline became one of them when she was eleven years old. There was a big surge in membership in the sect at that time, not only in Haiti but all over the world. The surge was due, at least in part, to the prediction of Armageddon in 1975. As prophesied in the Bible, Armageddon is the scene of a great battle to be fought between good and evil that will conclude in the end of time. Only 144,000 true believers from the whole of history will be born again as spiritual children of God and go to heaven to rule with Christ. For the rest, there is hell.

To the people of Haiti in 1975, the battle of Armageddon must have seemed like a done thing, with evil triumphing decisively. Four years before, the enormously fat, notoriously stupid nineteen-year-old "Baby Doc" Jean-Claude Duvalier had replaced his father, "Papa Doc" François Duvalier, as chief of state and had since shown himself to have all of the cruelty (though not the finesse) of his father. Haiti, already brutalized by a reign of terror under Papa Doc, an unspeakably murderous man who made no secret of his admiration for Nazi tactics, was dragged deeper and deeper into depravity by Jean-Claude, who treated his country and its populace as trifling playthings. Port-au-Prince, where Madeline lived, was crowded with petty bureaucrats lording over hordes of starving peasants, farmers who had been forced off their land by misguided economic policies. Lucien recalls that, under Papa Doc, Haitians were able to live off the fruits of their labor, the sugar, coffee, bananas, cocoa, rice, cotton, and maize harvested from the fields of their small farms. Under Baby Doc, the farmers were forced off their small farms and into the pursuit of agribusiness. Following an informal policy that became known as the "American Plan," the United States gave Haiti food aid that so reduced the price of locally grown crops as to make their small-scale cultivation impractical. Haiti switched to an export-driven economy in which agricultural goods like coffee, fruits, and tomatoes were grown for sale to the United States. Displaced farmers poured into Port-au-Prince looking for jobs. Some of them found work in factories that manufactured finished goods like baseballs, bras, and radios, also for export to the United States. Those who could not find work stayed anyway. The slums of Port-au-Prince, already crowded, became so crammed with bodies that several families shared single rooms, with the men sleeping in shifts on the bed while women and children made do on the floor. Those not fortunate enough to have room for a bed made do with *domi kanpe*, a Creole expression that roughly translates as "sleeping on one's feet." Unemployment in the country soared, leveling out at around 80 percent.

The Catholic church, of which Madeline's father was a member, seemed to Madeline to have done nothing to stave off the systematic decimation of her country and its people. The streets were patrolled by prowling Tontons Macoute, the all-powerful secret police force known for extortion, torture, and chopping people's heads off with machetes for any reason, or no reason at all. The name Tontons Macoute derives from a Haitian folktale in which a bogeyman crawls out of the night, grabs up handfuls of unwitting children, and stuffs them into his *macoute*, or straw shoulder bag. Tontons Macoute were recruited from among the hungry unemployed of the Port-au-Prince slums and from outlaw societies, desperate people. Madeline had seen what they could do, and, like most Haitians, she was terrified of them. There was no political force that seemed able to stave off or even control the cycle of injustice and corruption that had flourished under Baby Doc. Attempts to take action under such a system seemed futile and silly. To Madeline and her mother and many other Haitians, the Jehovah's Witness sect, which preaches neutrality in worldly affairs, carried great appeal.

Jehovah's Witnesses do not join independence movements, sign on to political parties, or salute national flags. In Haiti, as elsewhere, their goal is to preach the faith, keep a low profile, and contribute as little to the prevailing status quo as possible. This attitude has led to their persecution, particularly in parts of Africa such as Malawi and Zambia, where their passivity and unwillingness to pledge loyalty to one-party regimes has been interpreted as insolence. In Haiti, Jehovah's Witnesses have declined to participate in any reform movement or to serve in the armed forces, with the result that they are broadly mistrusted and disliked. As a Jehovah's Witness in Haiti, Madeline learned to pull into herself, smug in the confidence that the world would come to an end soon enough and that she would be among the few prepared for the battle.

"I made my choice," she says. "When you are a Jehovah's Witness, you are separate from the world. We know that government can do nothing. That's why when other religions got together to overthrow the regime in Haiti, we didn't get involved. We're not supposed to do that — our job is to teach others about Jehovah's kingdom. Men have tried all sorts of governments, yet there is still suffering and hunger, even in the United States. Only the kingdom of God can save us."

Madeline has no patience or sympathy for those who, to her mind, bring poverty or sickness on themselves. "Jehovah says, 'If you don't work, you don't eat,'" she says flatly. "People should learn to live on what they have. If you don't drink, you don't smoke, you don't gamble, look at all the money you save." When the Food and Drug Administration announced that Haitian blood would no longer be accepted at donation sites because it was considered more likely than average to be contaminated with the AIDS virus, the greater Boston Haitian community rose up in protest. But not the Brissetteses. Madeline says that the AIDS epidemic would not have happened if more people had followed Jehovah's preachings. Taking blood into the body is a breach of Jehovah's laws, as are drug use, homosexuality, and promiscuity. As far as she's concerned, AIDS is just one more way for God to enforce His laws: people who obey stay healthy.

But Lucien does not agree. He is outraged at the implication that Haitians are somehow tainted. He says that Haitian blood is no dirtier than that of any American and snorts with glee when a friend tells him that the Swiss, also fearing AIDS, are refusing to accept all American blood donations.

Lucien finds it difficult to stay apolitical. He has opinions, and in voicing them he can get angry and loud and, sometimes, overbearing. When that happens, Madeline sits quietly, smiling to herself, waiting for Lucien to run out of steam. Then Madeline reminds him that there is no use in ranting, that life on this earth is a fleeting thing not worth getting so worked up about. Lucien agrees, in principle. But his heart isn't in it.

The evening is chilly, but inside the Kingdom Hall it is bright and warm and moist, almost tropical. Many women have brought fans, the colorful paper kind sold in little storefronts in Chinatown. The women flip the fans open from time to time and wag them furiously in front of their faces, stirring up a breeze. Most of them appear cool and composed. The men, stiff in their two- and three-piece gray and black and navy blue suits mop their close-cropped heads with starched handkerchiefs.

The hall is nearly full by the time Madeline, Claude, and Luke find seats on a bench halfway up the aisle, excusing themselves as they suck in their stomachs to squeeze past an elderly gentleman proudly balancing his eight-month-old grandson on his lap. Lucien is an usher and stands at the back of the hall, ready to lead any stragglers to the few remaining seats. Lucien stands for the duration of the service, nodding to friends, smiling sweetly at the ladies, and handing out Bibles. The Bibles are printed in French, but there is a small pile in English for those who need them. So far, the English pile is untouched. All members of the congregation, save one, are black.

The service starts suddenly, the white man stepping up to the podium to announce the first Bible reading. Madeline explains that women are not allowed to lead these services, although they may answer questions about the Bible put to them by men. Two men with microphones walk up and down the aisles, amplifying the responses of women. The microphone comes to Madeline more than once. She knows the Bible by heart.

Luke and Claude know the Bible, too, but not so well that they care to recite it. They are hungry for diversion. Luke stares and stares at his book of Bible stories, which sits open and upside down on his lap. Claude crawls off his mother's knee and onto the floor, where he plays with a sneaker that has slipped off the foot of the chubby infant down the aisle, who now sits cooing and drooling down his grandfather's shirtfront. Neither Luke nor Claude pays any attention to what's going on at the front of the hall, which at the moment appears to be a commercial break. A woman and a man sit in chairs across from each other, demonstrating the proper technique for distributing religious literature.

The talk from up front goes on and on, and the room seems to close in on itself. The grandfather, dripping with perspiration, gets up quietly and carries his grandson to the back of the hall, where they sit down together on the floor to play. Older children, decked out in tights and dresses and three-piece suits and positioned like dolls at their mothers' and grandmothers' sides, are expected to stay put. They sink into what appears to be a state of group catatonia, staring blankly, enduring in silence occasional cuffs and pokes from parents and grandparents. But Claude can stand it no longer. He climbs up Madeline's legs and into her lap and lets out a wail. No heads turn, though a grandmother in the next row cracks a smile and pats the tightly braided head of the little girl sitting next to her. Madeline grips Claude tightly but keeps her eyes on the stage. Claude crumbles, sobbing silently into Madeline's skirt as she gestures one last time for the microphone. As always, when the microphone comes, the correct answer leaps instantly from her lips.

At 9:00, the meeting is over. Lucien joins Madeline to shake hands and clap backs with half the people in the room. One of Lucien's older brothers is here, dressed in a cool beige suit. Lucien has not been able to convince his other brother to join the church because he, as Madeline says, is more interested in having a good time in this life than in preparing for the next one. While Lucien chats with his brother, Madeline, looking relaxed and close to beautiful, bustles around the hall greeting friends. Luke and Claude, struck nearly dumb with heat and tedium during the meeting, suddenly spring to life and tumble about the hall like a pair of puppies, roughhousing with the other children. It's a school night, a work night, but no one is in a hurry to leave. The congregation spills out onto the sidewalk, where men and women stand with their children in the starlight, talking and laughing and making plans to get together after services on Sunday. Madeline and Lucien shake one last hand, then gather Luke and Claude and head back to the car. The boys sit quietly in the rear seat, exhausted. Madeline and Lucien share their first private conversation of the day.

Back at Trois Bébés, the parking lot is dark, and the benches in the play area are filled with shadows. Rap music blares from an open window. The Brissetteses walk through the double doors and into the lobby, where a clutch of men stand, their coat collars pulled up against the chill, their right hands curled around brown bags hiding bottles. An older man stands alone, smoking a cigarette and muttering to himself, staring out into the night. Madeline fixes her eyes on the floor and shepherds the children toward the elevator. She pushes the button and stands back, waiting. The children, looking hollow eyed with exhaustion, lean against her legs. Lucien rocks on his heels and smiles gently to himself. The elevator doors open, and the family gets in quickly. Lucien jabs the button for the twenty-first floor. With any luck, they'll be able to make the rest of the trip home alone.

BY winter, Luke's friend Marcel has changed. He is gentle and cooperative and has learned to share. He can sit for sustained periods of circle time and enjoys, in particular, snuggling into the old sofa cushions in the makeshift "library corner" and pulling one book after another off the shelf to be read out loud by a teacher. As the teacher reads, Marcel sits on her lap and turns the pages, his eyes drawing the words in close. He has learned to write the first letters of his name shakily in pencil, and he enjoys practicing new words, rolling them around in his mouth like wine, then sending them soaring off the end of his tongue. By the end of January, Marcel is doing so well that the teachers have almost forgotten what a handful he once was. And then Susan gets the call from the hospital.

Michel phones Tot Lot from the emergency room at four o'clock. Marcel's leg is hurt, his hip dislocated, and Michel is furious. He says it happened at Tot Lot the day before, that Marcel ran into a door, and that the teachers did nothing to help him. Susan is puzzled. She knows nothing of the incident and recalls Marcel leaving school yesterday evening happy and with no apparent problems. If an accident had happened, she says, she would have known about it; there is a formal procedure for recording such incidents, and something would have been put in writing. Susan stands behind her desk frowning, her lips pursed, listening to Michel rant on and on. Then, gradually, it dawns on her that what happened to Marcel probably had nothing to do with Tot Lot. It dawns on her that perhaps Michel has hurt his son and, under questioning from the doctors, is pinning the abuse on Tot Lot. But, of course, Susan can say nothing of this. She can say nothing of the times teachers have seen Michel speak harshly to Marcel and threaten to clobber him if he did not obey. She can say nothing of the many meetings Michel has neglected to attend or the fact that he refuses to allow even Haitian teachers to meet with him at his home or that he lied about his son's well-documented history of behavioral difficulties at his previous preschool. All Susan can do is listen quietly to the accusations and assure Michel that she has heard nothing of Marcel running into a door at school. The next day, Marcel is back at Tot Lot, smiling and dragging one leg behind him like a pull toy.

Susan and the other teachers worry that Michel is dangerous, but they are afraid to file charges with the Department of Social Services. Michel has run before, from the last day care center, and he may well do it again. Susan decides to talk to Michel's friend, Lucien. She corners him that night when he comes to pick up his sons and Marcel and asks politely if there is anything odd going on with Michel.

Lucien is incensed, furious that Susan has even thought to get involved. Michel, he says, might speak angrily to his son, might spank or slap his son, but Michel would never actually hurt his son. What Susan doesn't understand, Lucien says, is that Haitians raise their children differently. It is up to Susan to see that Marcel is educated. It is up to Michel to see that Marcel becomes a man.

There is a book, entitled *L'Expérience Ti Pye Zoranj Monte*, that was written half a decade ago by a group of Haitian mothers living in Montreal. These mothers wanted to put into words the plight of the child whose parents have been wrenched from their homes and thrown into a society that has, to their minds, very little understanding of or appreciation for Haitian culture. The following excerpt is typical:

The Haitian family is what we could call an extended family, that is, in Haiti the neighborhood, the aunts, the uncles, the cousins, the grandparents are as many "parents" available to the child. This community prevents the authority from becoming arbitrary. . . . If [the child] is in conflict with the father or mother, he/she knows he/she can find "replacements." So that we can see the very structure of the Haitian family protects the child against a certain parental exclusivity and thus attempts to spare him/her any risk of rejection. What happens to this "family" when, because of financial or political difficulties, it is forced to emigrate? The extended family explodes. The isolated nuclear family often creates certain forms of insecurity; its members are reduced to silence, even to anonymity.

The book goes on to say that a child living in isolation with his parents is a prisoner, subject to the whims of a single, often arbitrary authority. In effect, these Haitian mothers are acknowledging what few Americans will admit: that many nuclear families are emotional tinderboxes that, left alone to smolder, can, without notice, burst into flames. In Haiti, families rely on the good judgment of an extended family and friends to intervene when things get prickly between parents and children. Without the extended family, many Haitians in this country feel unprotected and vulnerable.

Joseanne Barnes is Haitian, a graduate of the Harvard University School of Education and the mother of two small boys. She came to the United States ten years ago to go to school but stayed because she could not afford to work as a teacher in Haiti, where, she says, teachers were paid seventy dollars a month while secretaries got several hundred. Joseanne teaches in the Haitian program at Graham and Parks School, the same school where Peggy Thompson teaches seventh and eighth grade. Joseanne says that Haitian parents do not believe in sparing the rod, and this can put them at odds with the status quo.

"Here, in this country, the day care center is a place for a child to be free, to play," she says. "In Haiti, centers are very structured, and children are expected to shape up. In schools in this country, the middle-class values are the only values that matter. In Haiti, the values are different."

Because Haitian parents tend to be authoritarian and do not necessarily regard children as autonomous beings, Joseanne says, they consider their treatment of their own children to be an entirely private matter, something totally outside the purview of social service agencies, teachers, or the police. Corporal punishment is not uncommon among Haitian families, but in Haiti, it is kept in check.

"A father might hit a young child in Haiti, but when he does, that child will run to his grandfather, and his grandfather will protect him, even if it means giving the child's father a good belt," Joseanne says.

But a child removed from his extended family in Haiti and cast into isolation with a pair of frustrated parents in this country may well be at risk of more serious treatment, treatment that, to American thinking, sometimes verges on abuse.

Says Joseanne, "I tell the parents of children in my classes, 'I know you have the right to discipline your children, but if I see bruises, if I see broken bones, that's too much. If your child comes into my classroom damaged, I will not keep that information to myself.'"

Susan respects cultural differences as much as the next person, but she can no longer take a chance on Marcel. She calls a meeting with Michel and tells him that Marcel did not dislocate his hip at Tot Lot. She goes on to suggest with great tact and delicacy that perhaps the accident happened at home. Michel meets Susan's eyes in a steady gaze and insists that the incident occurred at school. Susan takes a deep breath, pokes the tip of her pencil through one of the pieces of paper on her desk, and points out that Marcel has complained frequently about being beaten by his father. Michel, looking far from contrite, says, yes, he does, in fact, hit his son with a belt. Beating, he says, is a personal matter, not something to talk about with a day care teacher. Besides, beating a child and dislocating his hip are two very different things — there is no way he would ever intentionally injure his son. Susan pushes no further, for she knows she can do no more. She suddenly realizes that Michel regards Mar-

cel as property, no more Susan's business than are any of his
other possessions. Applying more pressure on Michel will only
send him running and further endanger Marcel. For now, Lucien
can provide some protection, but, unlike a Haitian grandfather,
he can only intrude so much. Unlike a Haitian grandfather, he
cannot use his belt on his friend.

By late February, Madeline has found a job in Watertown,
a working-class suburb about a ten-minute drive from Trois
Bébés. It has taken many months for Madeline to land a job. Still,
she makes no mention of the possibility of discrimination, of the
chance that some employers might be reluctant to hire a black
Haitian mother with a thick Creole accent. She is grateful that
she has been given the opportunity to work, and she has every
intention of making the most of it.

At work, Madeline sees to the switchboard, takes care of the
time cards, and handles personnel problems for the company,
which specializes in the production of bread crumbs for the coat-
ing of fried foods. Madeline has brought home a handful of company fliers, which she proudly fans out like magazines on the
coffee table and hands out to visitors. The new job starts early,
and the Brissetteses have only one car, which means that the
entire family has to be ready even earlier to take Madeline to
work in the morning. But Madeline has no complaints. She loves
her job. Besides, she is accustomed to getting up early and juggling schedules. Madeline remembers leaving her bed at 5 A.M.
in Haiti to squeeze in two hours of English classes before starting
high school. After school, she took French lessons and often
didn't get home until dinnertime. Haitian women, she says, are
raised with the expectation that their lives will be hard. Haitian
women, she says, expect to work.

"I spent three years not working, after I had Luke, and,
believe me, it drove me crazy," she says. "My mother worked
for the government in Haiti. I see no reason, really, why women
shouldn't work, especially now, when everyone needs two pay-
checks to get by."

In fact, the Brissetteses have only one paycheck, for Lucien's
only income comes from the bit of disability compensation he
gets for having had a car fall on his chest in auto mechanics

school. He is still in school studying air-conditioning and refrigeration technology. He lugs a thick textbook filled with charts and diagrams everywhere he goes, like a ball and chain. These days, he appears more stressed than happy and complains constantly of not getting enough sleep. When the children wake with nightmares, he says, they come into his bedroom. Recently, he says, they've had a lot of nightmares.

Lucien can't seem to get used to the United States, can't seem to rid his mind of memories of tropical beaches and mango trees. It's particularly hard for him this time of year, when the night wind blows so cold and the roads are smeared with slush. Lucien spends much of his time mushing through that slush, chauffeuring Madeline back and forth from work and the kids back and forth from Tot Lot and everyone back and forth from the Kingdom Hall. On weekends, he takes care of the children while Madeline goes door to door preaching or to other people's apartments to help them with their Bible studies. Every night, he brings his family to a home that he can't convince himself is safe. And all the while, Lucien has to keep an eye on Michel and on Michel's family. Lucien says little of Michel, except to point out that his friend is not like him.

Often Lucien thinks of going home to Haiti. Sometimes he can't help thinking that there are worse things in life than living in a dictatorship — for instance, living around drug dealers and muggers and children who squeal on their parents. America, he says, is great for many people but perhaps not for all people. He says he has had two children in this country and will probably have more but that he does not approve of the way children are taught here to question authority, to question, even, their parents. He doubts that he will ever feel truly free here. To be free in America, he says, you have to be part of the system. At this point, it seems unlikely to him that he will ever be eligible for that distinction. He wonders if his children will.

AT school, Claude seemed nervous without his diapers. He slunk around the periphery of the toddler room with a skittish half-smile, trying not to make a big deal of the fact that he was wearing underpants. And then, just before naptime, he wet them, the pee dripping down his legs and onto the floor before Molly knew what was happening. Molly took Claude by the hand and led him into the bathroom and changed his clothes and sent him back to the gray-rug room. The next day, Claude wet his pants again, and again the morning after that. Claude had been among the last boys in the toddler room to speak. Now Molly had to bring his parents the disappointing news that he was not going to be the first to be toilet trained.

When parents of two-year-olds come to Molly and tell her that they want their kids out of diapers, Molly listens sympathetically, nodding her head like a therapist. But over the years she has learned that, ultimately, it is not parents who make this decision. Those who try, like the Brisetteses, are destined for disappointment.

Molly is concerned that Lucien will threaten or coerce Claude and therefore defeat his own purpose. She consults with Edith, the early-childhood expert who visits the center each month. Together they decide to tell Lucien to start all over again with his son, as though the thought of parting Claude from his diapers had never entered anyone's mind. Lucien smiles broadly when Molly brings him this advice and agrees enthusiastically. But secretly he is not certain that this is the best approach. He believes Claude is too old to be in diapers and that discipline, not psychology, is the key. To his mind, it is stubbornness, not immaturity, that has caused Claude to fail. Still, he agrees to give Molly's idea a try. Claude is put back in diapers, and everyone waits for him to show his own signs of readiness. Toward the end of February, Madeline proudly announces the news that she has bought her last diaper. Claude, it seems, has made his decision; he is proud of his Ninja Turtle underpants.

About once a month, Molly meets with a small group of women to sip coffee, eat store-bought cookies, and hash out ideas about teaching. Everyone in the group started out as a day care teacher, but Molly is the only one who stuck with it. The others went on to get advanced degrees and jobs at public schools and colleges. They have elaborate theories about how to teach children from diverse backgrounds, and Molly listens to these theories respectfully, frowning and twisting a lock of hair in concentration. But the next day at Tot Lot, she finds herself putting the theories in the back of her mind and simply doing what works, which is listening and watching and offering all the support she can muster to both children and their parents. Molly is very careful to keep cultural differences in mind when working with parents. Parents, she has found, can be prickly if they get the feeling that their historical identity is being challenged, be it white middle-class Republican or working-class Hispanic or Cambridge lefty intellectual. But Molly does not make culture-based generalizations about children because she says she finds fewer differences among cultures than she does among individual kids. For example, as far as she is concerned, Claude's difficulties with aggression and toilet training and discipline and attention span have less to do with his being Haitian than with his being Claude.

Things have gotten a lot tougher for Claude since Lilian and José left. When asked whether Claude misses his teachers, Madeline laughs and shrugs and says that he didn't seem to notice, that everything is fine, that her son loves Tot Lot. But Madeline rarely sets foot in Tot Lot except to attend general meetings, and she doesn't see her son following Molly around, clinging to the legs of her jeans as if afraid that she will abandon him. He gets jealous when Molly spends time with other kids and tries to push them out of her lap when she reads them books. Today Molly has to carry Claude to the library during circle time to keep him from disrupting the class. When she comes to get him after circle, he kicks and bites and, she notices, has ripped a book to shreds. There is no telling where all this anger is coming from, or how long it will last, but for now it's troubling Molly deeply. She's worried that Claude might end up hurting himself or, at the least, become even more isolated from the group. Claude is already a loner. Molly sometimes gets him together with other kids on the sly, by using herself as bait. She'll sit down with Claude and loudly read a book to attract a crowd, then sneak away, leaving him to play with the others. Sometimes the trick will work, and Claude will spend a few minutes playing with a new-found friend. Mostly, though, Claude orbits the other children like a moon, keeping a constant, leery distance. He seems less interested than the other kids in knowing things — he is one of the few children in the toddler room who still can't identify colors and shapes.

Claude is lagging so far behind the others that it's easy to get the impression that something is wrong. But given that the symptoms are unclear, Molly refuses to apply a label. Labels stick to kids, she says, long after their benefit, if any, is outlived. Molly says she herself was labeled as a slow learner at an early age, and she ended up living up to that distinction, although it was clearly misplaced.

"As a kid, I always felt stupid," she says. "I was trained to take care of children and keep the house clean, and that's what I did. I didn't learn to read until I was in the fifth grade, but my mother never noticed — a teacher had to tell her. Don't you think it's ironic that my mother quit work to stay home with her kids, yet she never realized her oldest daughter couldn't read? In any case, I make a point of not comparing kids with each other, because every child has his own timetable. It doesn't really matter whether a child learns his colors at two or two and a half; what matters is that he feels good about where he is now. Once children have self-esteem and confidence, they have what they need to go far in life. There's no telling what I would have done with a little encouragement."

"Claude is normal within his world," she continues, pulling a plug of modeling clay out of a Lego block. "There's no doubt that he's bright and that he'll probably learn his colors very quickly when he puts his mind to it."

Molly puts down the Lego block and walks to the record player. She picks out something with a lively tune and a steady rhythm. The other kids go on with what they're doing, but Claude looks up from the floor and grins. Almost before the needle hits the vinyl, he's on his feet, swaying and rocking, twisting his torso and stomping out the beat. He's also singing, the melody seeping out of his nearly closed lips like a secret.

"Watch him," Molly whispers, beaming. "He knows every word of this song by heart."

Eleven

WORLDS APART

MARCH comes on mild and dry in New England, leading the teachers to indulge in heady speculations on the effect of greenhouse gases on global temperatures and from there to ease into heartfelt debate on the impact of synthetic diapers on landfills. It is a favorite topic of discussion, particularly at general meetings, where parents and teachers sit in a large circle on the floor in the toddler room and hash over the benefits of cloth over plastic both to the environment and to children's behinds. Everyone agrees that Pampers and Huggies are a sin against nature, but somehow cloth diapers never find a place at Tot Lot. Lofty discourse is one thing; the storage of large quantities of dirty diapers quite another.

Spring is a welcome gift, liberating students and staff from dank classrooms and grinding routine. The children have grown since September, and they take up more room. A few are already five years old and no longer fit into the furniture — their knees, like those of the teachers, push skyward. They have lost their roundness.

The weather is so beautiful today that the preschool teachers decide to bag the planned activity and bring everyone down to the Morse School playground directly after morning snack. The children are deemed old enough now to serve themselves, with the result that great mounds of Cheerios and torrents of milk get poured first into bowls and then down the drain. The teachers scowl and scold over the waste of "perfectly good food," and the children take on serious, regretful looks. But in their hearts they know that Cheerios are not "perfectly good" after they've soaked for more than a minute in milk. Next time they'll wait for the teachers' backs to be turned before chucking the soggy stuff.

The preschoolers make a quick bathroom run before shrugging on jackets and heading out the door. Holding hands, they walk two by two toward Hastings Square, a rectangle of grass and mud and dog droppings a block down Chestnut Street. The sight of open space sends the children into fits of high spirits, and the nearly orderly queue smears into a streak of flying windbreakers and pounding sneakers. Marina charges to the front of the blur to find Luke, Marcel, and Dylan standing with the tips of their shoes poised over the edge of a curb, as if daring each other to make an unauthorized dash across the street. Marina grabs Marcel's hand and waits for the others to assemble before moving on. The children bump up behind her like pinballs, except for Mike, whose arm is clamped in Margaret's firm grip. Mike is not allowed to run unfettered through Hastings Square or, for that matter, anywhere.

Marina raises her right hand, palm forward, and counts to three in Italian to get the children's attention. She is a commanding presence in sunglasses, black high tops, and tights, her red hair cascading down her back in loose kinks. Her voice booms, frightening a dog and turning the heads of two teenagers tossing a Frisbee on the far side of the square. Even dreamy Noel takes notice, making a much-exaggerated effort to check in both directions for signs of traffic. There is none, and the procession continues down Rockingham Street to the Morse School, where it is met by a mob of rowdy kindergartners just let loose for recess. Marina stands at the gate like a cop, surveying the scene.

"Those kindergartners are going to make mincemeat out of my preschoolers," she mutters in her sweet, Italian-flecked English, swinging open the gate and negotiating her flock around the flailing bodies. "It drives me crazy that those teachers don't supervise their kids."

A bevy of teachers stands off to one side, arranged in a circle like covered wagons in Indian territory, while the kindergartners run amok, pushing, shoving, and practically trampling each other in a blaze of rubber soles. The Tot Lotters eye the older children respectfully and from a distance — they know when not to mingle. But soon the novelty wears off and the younger kids break into clumps of two or three to scout out adventures of their own. Dylan, Moses, and Luke take turns diving headfirst into a sandbox "swimming pool." Noel and Samantha run off to hide and then to gather pine needles to stuff like prizes into their pockets. The teachers scan the action, searching out strategic positions with the eyes of combat veterans on a battlefield. Marina grips Mike's hand and leads him away from the center of things and toward a wooden climbing structure at the far end of the play area. Linda is already there, overseeing a group of preschoolers challenging each other to increasingly daring feats of acrobatics. Mike scrambles up to join them. Straddling a wooden cross beam with his sturdy legs and chanting "Rambo, Rambo, what do you see?" he does not appear to be up to the challenge. His belly bulges from beneath his parka, and his pants have settled on his hips, presumably to escape the constant press of his stomach. Mealtime seems to be the one time when Mike's attention doesn't flag. He is a hearty eater, so hearty that several of the teachers suspect that he is using food to plug a deepening emotional hole. Things have gotten harder for Mike lately.

ONE night, not long before, Mike's father appeared at his apartment with a knife and a threat. Mike's mother, Elizabeth, grabbed Mike's baby brother, fled to the bedroom, and locked the door, leaving her older son to fend for himself. Mike had scuttled under the kitchen table, where he cowered shaking and sobbing for the better part of an hour. Eventually his father left, and Elizabeth got a court order to deter him from coming back.

But Mike's father returned, and more than once. Elizabeth admits that she has started seeing him again. And Mike's nightmares have gotten worse. It's not uncommon for him to wake up from a nap screaming as though the knife was there, poised at his throat.

At staff meetings, Mike is overwhelmingly the child most frequently under discussion, and the talk of having him transferred to a school where he could have more one-on-one attention has intensified. He is more and more violent, less and less in control, and the other children are becoming contemptuous of him. But the teachers don't want to lose Mike. They have already lost three preschoolers, one because his parents lost their jobs and could no longer afford to send him, another because her mother couldn't be bothered to bring her anymore. And Peter left after Christmas.

Peter had to go. The authorities found out that he did not live in Cambridge, as his father had claimed, but was driving into the city from Boston with his dad and waiting at his grandmother's house for the bus to come to pick him up for his morning program at Special Start. The Cambridge school system runs Special Start, which is restricted to city residents and has a long waiting list. When the teachers at Special Start discovered that Peter was not a Cambridge resident, they had no choice but to drop him from the program. Peter's father enrolled him in another morning program in Boston and made arrangements for him to spend his afternoons with an elderly couple who live nearby. The Special Start teachers figured this might be for the good, that Peter would be better off not getting up at 5:30 every morning and spending the first hours of the day with his grandmother, whom they did not consider to be the best of influences. But the teachers at Tot Lot weren't so sure. One of them, Idara, went so far as to pay a visit to the elderly couple with whom Peter was to spend his afternoons. She found their apartment foggy with cigarette smoke. There wasn't a toy in the place.

Peter's father brought a cake to celebrate his son's last day at Tot Lot. It was the first cake he had ever baked, chocolate, with vanilla frosting and Red Hots sprinkled on top. Peter's social worker came to the good-bye party and stood in the kitchen watching the proceedings like an understudy hovering in the wings. She declined a slice of cake.

Peter acted out a little on his last day. He kicked another kid and used some bad language. He wasn't going to just lie down and take this, wasn't going to make things easy for everyone. When the teachers reassured him that he'd like his new school, he vowed to hate it and followed up with a promise not to make friends there. Linda gave him a Good-bye Book with pages of purple construction paper filled with crayoned renderings and photos of his classmates. Peter looked at each page carefully and closed the book gently. Then he asked if he could keep the plastic spoon he'd eaten his cake with as a souvenir. Linda said yes and gave him a hug. Then Peter left right away, with his father, holding his Good-bye Book in one hand and his spoon in the other. Linda walked out after him, telling the others she needed a short break. After Peter drove off, she sat on the hood of her car, lit a cigarette, and cried. Two months later, Linda gave her notice and, not long after, went to work for a bank.

WHEN Susan gets nervous, she smiles and nods her head and only pretends to listen. Today at staff meeting, she is nodding and smiling even more than usual. The teachers are spread across the Formica tables in the preschool room, eating separate meals rather than sharing a pizza as they so often do. Julia has her nose in an advertising flyer, and Marie, as usual, is scanning the *Globe* classifieds for a used car cheap enough to buy. So far, months of looking have yielded nothing but disappointment — seems as though, on her salary, any price is too high.

Susan pokes around the edges of her egg salad sandwich, waiting for everyone to get settled. It's clear that they aren't going to get much done at today's meeting. Everyone's got an attitude. Susan has only a few things to get through, and then she can go back to the paperwork in her office. Paperwork is looking better and better to her these days.

Susan works through the agenda quickly. She starts with an update: the ceiling needs fixing, and the estimate just came through — the repairs will cost fourteen thousand dollars that the school doesn't have. This is not news to most people. Tot Lot has a work weekend twice a year, when parents come in and paint and mend and build what needs to be built. Work weekend is a legacy of the school's cooperative past. Last work weekend, a couple of dads started poking around and noticed that the ceiling frame sagged. They took off a few acoustical panels to get a closer look and found pure bad news — the ceiling was a mess, close to a safety hazard. The fund-raising committee is scrambling to find a way to pay for a new ceiling but so far without success. Hard times have made foundation money difficult to come by, and every nonprofit agency in town is grubbing after a handful of dollars. Meanwhile, the floors are in terrible shape, and the gutters need repair. Holly Torroella and Marina have organized a fund-raising dance for the spring, but they'll be lucky to collect a thousand dollars that way. And the ceiling must be fixed as soon as possible — if the Office for Children ever gets around to inspecting the center, the ceiling could give them reason to close the place down for safety violations.

Susan drones on and on about building repair, but nobody's really listening. There's always something falling apart at Tot Lot, always something in need of fixing or replacement. It's to be expected with thirty-three kids dishing out their tiny daily punishments. The real problem, as everyone knows, has nothing to do with the infrastructure. The real problem is that teachers have left and those who have stayed are overburdened and bickering and no one is doing anything about it.

Susan is a skilled teacher and an organized manager, but somehow she can't bring herself to talk about hard truths with the staff. As a teacher, she was trained to make the best of things, to emphasize people's strengths. The thought of going one on one with individual teachers, pointing out their deficiencies, makes her uncomfortable. She prefers to see the best in people. When Mike wakes up screaming from one of his nightmares, Susan uses the opportunity to adjourn the meeting. The teachers, equally relieved, scatter to their stations.

Susan has taken out ads in the "help wanted" sections of the *Boston Globe* and the *Cambridge Chronicle*. She needs a replacement for Linda and will soon need a replacement for Margaret, who is leaving in June. Margaret has been at Tot Lot for two years, longer than anyone thought she would stay. Margaret lives in a very adult world; she is not satisfied with special moments. She needs control. It was Margaret who was most adamant about the ban on sugar at Tot Lot, demanding that even sweetened applesauce and fruit cocktail be banished from children's lunchboxes. By and large, people seemed relieved when Margaret gave her notice. Margaret was relieved, too. She never felt comfortable in the job.

"It's a running joke that people in human services are in the field because they need so much support themselves," she says. "It's like being in battle and relying on your comrades. You are up against so many things that you can't change, trying to bring your ideals to bear when the odds are totally against you. I enjoy being a teacher because I enjoy the world of ideas, experience, and discovery. But the stresses — physical, psychological, and emotional — are just enormous. I want to teach, but I no longer want to teach young children."

So far, the applicants for Linda's and Margaret's jobs, though more promising than those who applied for Ben's job the previous fall, are not quite right. A good number of former public school teachers have applied, chiefly, it seems, because the state budget crunch has made it all but impossible to land a job in the public schools. But Susan and the other teachers are leery of hiring former elementary school teachers. It's one thing to stand in front of a classroom teaching kids the capitals of states and the names of the planets, quite another to tend to the needs of entire families. Public school teachers mostly teach; preschool teachers mostly nurture and support. As of now, Susan is juggling part-timers to fill the open hours and hoping for better pickings.

"I need teachers with experience," she says. "This time, I'm going to require it. I keep telling the parents on the hiring committee that it's nice to get people from other cultures and ethnic groups, nice to have creative types, but that the most important thing right now is that the teacher have experience. I'm having a slew of problems with the teachers in both the toddler and the preschool rooms. I'm exhausted, and I can't take time off because I have no backup, no one to fill in when I'm gone. There's no one here who is head-teacher qualified except for Molly, and I can't ask her to work a ten-hour day to cover for me." Once again, Susan mentions that she's thinking of chucking it all and retiring to a tropical island, one with hot and cold running piña coladas. It's become clear that this is an idle threat; Susan would no more leave her kids than she would join the Foreign Legion.

When Linda left, very few parents knew why. There was a good-bye party and a Good-bye Book, and everyone acted cheerful and united. Most parents chalked up Linda's departure to normal turnover, as though job hopping were a natural part of being a day care teacher.

But Peggy Thompson and Glen Barth didn't see it that way. For them, a change in teachers represents a tidal wave in the ebb and flow of their daughter's life. The previous year, Peggy spent long hours at Tot Lot helping to smooth things over among the staff. But Ben left anyway. And now Linda is gone, and so are Lilian and Nancy and José, and Margaret is leaving soon. Noel is caught in the middle.

Staff turnover is a perennial problem in day care. Marcy Whitebook, project director of the ongoing National Child Care Staffing Study, says that 41 percent of day care staff changes jobs every year. The consequences of high turnover for children are not good. Children in centers with high turnover spend less time socializing with peers and more time wandering aimlessly around the room. Their language skills are also less well developed than those of children attending more stable centers. And one can only assume that the constant loss of caretakers is not a positive influence on a child's developing sense of trust.

Like Linda, Ben, and Margaret, the majority of day care workers leave not only their jobs, but the field. Perhaps the reason for this is that, as a nation, we are reluctant to compensate people adequately for performing a job that, subconsciously or not, many of us believe we should be doing ourselves. The idea that caring for and teaching small children is a profession requiring special skills, education, and talent has not yet penetrated the public psyche. Yet, in child care as in everything else, we get what we pay for. We accept in child-care workers what we would not accept in, for example, automobile mechanics or hair stylists or physicians. We could tolerate unskilled, untrained people in those positions if we chose to, but, of course, we do not.

The staffing study found a good deal of variation in turnover among centers, and this variation was entirely predictable — those offering the highest wages had half the turnover of those paying the lowest. For-profit centers, which generally offer lower salaries, had higher turnover than nonprofit centers. Tot Lot, with its relatively generous pay scale, four weeks of vacation, and high teacher autonomy actually holds on to teachers longer than most centers. Indeed, low turnover is one of the reasons why the center is so popular. Everyone expects that, no matter what, Molly will be back year after year to take care of their children and that Susan and Julia and others will be there as well. That is more, much more, than can be said for most day care centers.

THE Graham and Parks School is an alternative public school named for Rosa Lee Parks, the civil-rights activist who refused to give her seat on a bus to a white man in Montgomery, Alabama, in 1955, and for Sandra Graham, a former Massachusetts state representative from the Cambridgeport district who lost her job soon after her son was charged with selling cocaine out of their home. Graham and Parks is a progressive school, a place where students call teachers by their first names and learn more about Harriet Tubman than they do about Abraham Lincoln.

Peggy Thompson Barth teaches seventh- and eighth-grade social studies and language arts at Graham and Parks, and she specializes in breathing new life into old subjects. For example, for today's lesson on World War II, her purpose is not to fill the students' heads with dates and names but to get them to think hard about social responsibility. To inject some immediacy into the lesson, she plans to offer a firsthand taste of Third Reich discipline by assuming the role of a Nazi teacher.

There was a slush storm today, many Boston thoroughfares are clogged, and several teachers have called to say they will be late or absent. But Peggy comes early to arrange the desks in stern quartets, each grouping far enough away from the next to convey a feeling of isolation. As she pulls and pushes furniture across the floor, she looks anxious, as though uncomfortable that this little role-playing session is a deception. Peggy has built a reputation around playing it straight.

At 8:45, the students trickle in and raise eyebrows at what appears to be the new geometric order. They smile weakly, or smirk, and look knowingly at Peggy, who rebuffs their greetings and orders them to be silent and take their seats. She tells them that there will be no talking and no questions and that anyone who is not prepared for the day's lessons will be automatically put on detention. The students eye each other. Peggy is a notorious soft touch, not the type to give students a hard time. The kids sense something is up, but they aren't sure what. They giggle and poke each other nervously. One boy leans so far back in his chair that it tips over, spilling him onto the brown linoleum. He grins, takes a bow, and resumes his seat. Peggy ignores the stunt and proceeds with the lesson, trying like crazy to play the hard-boiled Nazi. But the kids don't buy it. In her Reeboks, flowing purple dress, and loose string of black wooden beads, Peggy looks no more a Nazi than she does a sumo wrestler — she can't help smiling every time she tells a kid to shut up. Fifteen minutes into the exercise, she gives up on the Frau Führer act, admitting to the class that it was only an exercise designed to make them think. The idea, she says, is to understand what education would be like in a dictatorship, where obedience is the ultimate virtue and the expression of free thought is a punishable offense. The kids yawn, stretch, and assume empty "what else is new?" looks. They get the picture, but they'll be damned if they'll let Peggy know it.

At lunch, a hunk of cheese and an apple sliced with a Swiss Army knife at her desk, Peggy explains that she had more than history in mind when she planned today's lesson.

"Teaching kids just to follow rules is dangerous," she says. "My goal is to make them lifelong learners and to get them to question and test. A lot of these kids come from an authoritarian culture. I want to reach these kids, to get them to challenge authority rather than to sit back and pretend to accept it. Democracy is a process that you can't ever not be involved in. A big part of my job is teaching kids to believe that."

GLEN was also a teacher once, but he saw the limits of the profession all too clearly. His interest is in making policy, not implementing the policies of others. As dropout-prevention specialist for the Massachusetts Department of Education, he helps to set the pace. The problem is, most school systems aren't prepared to keep up with the pace he sets.

Glen spends a good deal of time in meetings. Today, for example, he has five. The first meeting is in Boston at nine o'clock, so Glen rushes Noel through breakfast even more emphatically than usual and gets her to Tot Lot just after Molly unlocks the front door at eight. There are no preschool teachers around, so Noel happily follows Molly into the toddler room, where Marcia is already wandering around, foraging for attention. Noel is usually one of the first children in school, and Glen is usually the one to bring her. Like many fathers, he uses the drop-and-run technique, whipping Noel out of her jacket and into a teacher's care before she shows any signs of noticing the trade-off. But Noel always notices. She smiles her Cheshire cat smile and stares dreamily at her father's back as he trots out to his car. Then she gives her teacher a hug and wanders into the toddler quiet area, which is piled with cushions and scattered with reading material. Noel loves books and she is especially fond of books about music. Often she'll mouth a made-up story as she turns the pages and hold the book out to show the pictures, as though to an imaginary friend. If grown-ups look over her shoulder and attempt to correct her interpretation, she scowls and barks at them to go away. Noel prefers not to take her reading too literally.

Meanwhile, Glen folds himself into his Hyundai and drives it to a parking place within walking distance of the subway — parking in Boston is too expensive. As he walks to Central Square Station he thinks out loud about Tot Lot, about why the place is pissing him off these days. He's particularly pissed off at Susan. It was Glen who offered Susan her job four years ago, Glen who, as a member of the hiring committee, made the call to persuade her to sign on as director. And he doesn't regret that decision one bit. In fact, he's grateful to Susan, grateful that she pulled the place out of the fire after the Mark Johnson affair, grateful that she helped Tot Lot get back on the good side of the social service agencies, grateful that she saved the place from almost-certain ruin. But while Susan was calm and steady in a crisis, she seems to Glen to lack the leadership skills to keep things moving on a day-to-day basis. He says that Susan sweats the small stuff too much, that she has no vision. He doesn't regard her as a true educator. And he knows she's lost control of her staff.

"Susan doesn't really get what it means to have teachers working in a team," he says, stabbing around in his pocket for a subway token. "Certainly, you have to run the place democratically, but democracy does not mean everybody running around doing their own thing and pretending everything is okay."

Glen says he hopes that Susan will improve after her evaluation, that is, if the coordinating committee ever gets its act together to do the evaluation. It's already months overdue. The coordinating committee is made up of parents and teachers, and Glen has a hunch that no one on it will have the guts to tell Susan how much she needs to change. After all, there are vested interests all around. The teachers depend on Susan for their jobs, and the parents depend on Susan for the care of their children. They want to stay on her good side; they are reluctant to speak out. He's not, though. He's told Susan several times that he thinks she should take a course in team leadership techniques, and she agrees. But she never seems to find the time to actually take the damn thing.

Glen takes the Red Line train to Park Street Station. He ignores the escalator, bounds up the stairs two at a time to the street, and race-walks the four blocks to the fourth floor of an office building where his first meeting is just getting under way in a large, windowless conference room. A committee of teachers, administrators, and others concerned with the plight of the Boston public schools has gathered to discuss budgets and what they call "learning environments" over coffee and muffins spilled out of ripped paper bags. Glen shakes a few hands, then grabs a seat near the head of the table. He starts one foot tapping and pulls a dollar bill from a coat pocket to finger like a string of worry beads. He is already impatient; he knows that the meeting will bring no surprises.

The dropout rate in the Boston public schools is unspeakable — more than one out of three kids drops out of high school. This is not a new situation, but it is one that Glen believes is being made worse by the growing emphasis on accountability in the schools. Teachers are made accountable for the performance of their students, but they aren't being given the authority to shape improvements. Instead, they are pushed to flunk kids who can't perform at grade level, with the result that about 20 percent of ninth graders in the Boston public schools were held back the previous year. Some of those ninth graders are getting pretty old — old enough to, among other things, drop out. More students drop out of ninth grade than they do any other year, and Glen says this correlates neatly with the particularly high ninth-grade retention rate — kids who flunk feel so bad about themselves in particular and about school in general that all they want is out.

"We're punishing the victims," he says. "Making the kids pay for bad administration and planning." Glen says that, after ninth grade, kindergarten is the most common year to hold kids back. Flunking kids out of kindergarten is a little like flunking kids out of life.

Some of Glen's ideas come from the work of Dr. James P. Comer, a professor of child psychiatry and the director of the School Development Program at Yale University. Dr. Comer, a black man born and raised in East Chicago, contends that low-income and minority children will not reap the full benefits of the American educational system until the gap between what they are taught in school and what they see and experience at home is closed, or at least made smaller. As Dr. Comer wrote in the November 1988 issue of *Scientific American:*

> Current educational reforms deemphasize interpersonal factors and focus instead on instruction and curriculum. Such approaches reveal a blind spot: they assume that all children come from mainstream backgrounds and arrive at school equally well prepared to perform as the school expects them to. . . . Most educators do not challenge this assumption, however, and the approach has never been systematically modified.

Glen finds Dr. Comer's article particularly telling in light of what's happened in the Boston public schools over the last twenty-five years or so. It used to be, he says, that the schools were run by white Irishmen who were proud of being tough enough to kick a low performer out of school. Now, there are so many low performers that kicking them out is no challenge and getting kicked out is not necessarily a stigma. More than one-third of the students in Boston schools are poor, and close to a third are members of a minority. They come from homes that, almost by definition, do not hold middle-class values and standards. Yet the schools continue to run on the old white middle-class assumptions Dr. Comer describes. Instead of trying to force children to conform to a system that is totally alien to them, Glen argues, the schools should change to accommodate the realities of the children.

"Traditional education is not working for low-income people," he says. "That's because the things that improve education for low-income kids are not traditional. Minorities feel that they don't have a voice in education, and, frankly, they are right. That's why we work so hard to make parents feel empowered at Tot Lot. . . . At least they get a taste of what it's like to be in control. And some of them continue to demand control when their kids enter public school. Anyway, it's a start."

At 4:30, Glen heads back to the Red Line and to his final meeting in the library of the Kennedy Elementary School in East Cambridge where colleagues sit in folding chairs, munching chocolate chip cookies and drinking apple juice out of paper cups, like a circle of preschoolers at snacktime. Peggy is among them. Glen gives her a nod, then takes a seat several chairs around the circle from her.

The meeting begins with a vice principal passing around a copy of a new report entitled "The Impact of State Human Service, Health and Education Budget Cuts on the Cambridge Community." The report announces a reduction of twenty-five hundred day care slots, as well as substantial cuts in early-childhood intervention programs, in food subsidies for infants and young children, in literacy programs, and in the budget for books and other materials for elementary schools. The Office for

Children has cut nineteen positions and will close eleven of its offices by the end of the year. The implications of all this are clear: children will come into the Cambridge elementary school system less well prepared and less well cared for than they have in years past. The teachers will be expected to pick up the slack.

Glen is revved up, hyped to speak out, but Peggy's thoughts are elsewhere. She's heard most of this stuff before, from Glen, and she's got other things on her mind. She has a pile of blue books on her lap, and she needs to read at least a few of them so she'll have time to attend yet another meeting after dinner. The blue books hold essays written by her language arts students. She reads and writes comments on three or four of them, and then one essay, scribbled in a hasty hand, stops her short. The student, a girl, has written only a handful of sentences. The last one reads: "I'm depressed, I need help. Help me." Peggy is taken aback but not shocked by the message; she's received such pleas before. In fact, if she wanted to, Peggy could fairly list "suicide-prevention specialist" on her résumé. She adds the student to the mental list of people she plans to call that night.

At 5:30, the meeting starts to break up, and Peggy gets ready to go. She's in a hurry; Kate is in her afterschool program, and Peggy doesn't feel comfortable keeping her there this late. The program is generally well run, and Kate usually has a good time there, but she tries hard not to let Peggy know that. Kate makes Peggy pay for all the time they spend apart.

"Last night, I had a meeting, and I couldn't pick up Kate until six o'clock," Peggy says, pushing toward the exit. "So we had this forty-five–minute screaming battle over nothing before dinner. It was awful. The kids really need to be home earlier."

There's a movie, *A World Apart*, that Peggy finds particularly moving. The film tells the story of Diana Roth, a character based on Ruth First, the journalist and political activist who was the first white woman to be arrested under South Africa's infamous Detention Act. First was thrown into solitary confinement for ninety days for her work in the antiapartheid movement. Her husband was living in exile at the time, and her three young daughters were cared for by their grandmother. Peggy showed this film in her class and used it as the basis of discussion about apartheid. But what really gets her about the story is something she doesn't discuss with her students. What really gets her is how First could feel so deeply about a cause that she would abandon her children in its name.

"I just couldn't do that," Peggy says. "I just haven't been able to feel that strongly about anything, though I respect like hell people who do. To me, the children have to come first."

Twelve

CUTTING BACK

DRUMLIN Farm was an actual farm once or, rather, five small subsistence farms purchased and merged into a sprawling estate by Donald and Louise Gordon, a wealthy couple with no need to eke out their living from the soil. The Gordons maintained a small gentleman's farm to provide both food for themselves and their staff and a wholesome, educational diversion for guests invited from the city some twenty-odd miles to the east. When Mrs. Gordon died in 1955, she left the property to the Massachusetts Audubon Society, with the understanding that the farm be opened to the public. It is the sort of low-key, environmentally correct attraction favored by school groups and upper-middle-class families that prefer their rusticity in small doses.

The road that leads to Drumlin Farm, Route 117, winds through some of the choicer bits of real estate in the greater Boston area, sprawling historic homes on two-acre lots and cedar-shingled contemporaries with vaulted ceilings and decks designed to merge tastefully with the surrounding countryside. The farm itself is in Lincoln, a tony and rather far-flung bedroom community favored by tenured college faculty and seasoned executives with relaxed schedules. The farm is set well back from the road on 175 acres of rolling green pasture that, minus the pig sty, goat barn, and corrals of horses and cows, might easily pass for a golf course.

The parking lot is busy this morning, half filled with Volvos and Saabs and Japanese station wagons. A chartered school bus, showing more rust than yellow paint, pulls in, cranks open its door, and dumps its load. The kids from Tot Lot fall out like puppies set free from the pound. The fresh air hits their lungs like a drug. They roll on the balding turf, dash after each other in fits of tag, and all but forget to whine. The teachers fold their arms and smile — this is the way it is supposed to be.

The locals, preschool-age children from Lincoln and nearby Weston and Sudbury, observe all this from a cautious distance and then move toward the admission booth. The day is bracing even for March, with a chilling wind, and the local kids are bundled up in warm natural fibers: well-padded Patagonia jackets, sturdy leather hiking boots, and gleaming white cotton skullcaps imported from Sweden. Mothers and nannies in tow, they proceed from one exhibit to the next as though at an art gallery. They have a sense of decorum.

The children of Tot Lot gawk at this well-groomed procession as though at some genetic improbability. Most have forgotten their mittens, and few have boots. They wear thin, hand-me-down snowsuits, nylon hats, and sneakers. The most scantily dressed, wearing T-shirts and windbreakers, do an improvised routine of calisthenics to stay warm. Their noses run.

Marina and Molly count heads and then sort the preschoolers and toddlers into manageable clumps, each with teacher chaperones. Parents are here, too, having somehow managed to cop a sick day to share a breath of fresh air with their kids. Holly Torroella is one of them. Holly is still on the night shift at work, so it is sleep, not the job, that she is compromising this morning. She looks groggy and ruffled, as though pulled too quickly from her bed, which, in fact, she hasn't seen for close to twenty hours. But she wouldn't miss this chance to be with her son. She and Christopher join Max and Max's mother for an inspection of the sheep barn and poultry pens. Max is three, large for his age, and, like Christopher, a quick thinker and fluid talker who is rapidly outgrowing toddler-room status. Christopher appoints himself leader of the little group and yanks his mother and friend from barn to barn, loudly outlining what he contrives to be the sleeping and eating habits of the various occupants.

In the sheep barn, a woman in a baggy sweater with a smile that reveals several missing teeth demonstrates the art of carding wool. Christopher grabs the carding tool, gives a few good swipes, and hands it back. The sheep are okay, but they're not what he came for. He grabs Holly's hand and, losing Max and Max's mom, drags her, laughing, out of the sheep shed, past the mule barn, and straight to the pig house. The pigs are outside, lolling in the half-frozen mud. They are grotesquely obese and entirely oblivious, both to the squirm of piglets nuzzling at their teats and the battalions of flies crawling across their eyes. They seem supremely satisfied with life. Christopher pushes through a knot of bundled-up locals to get a closer look, then scrambles up the wooden fence, and hangs headfirst over the edge of the pen, stretching his arm out to pet a snout. Holly grabs him by the waist and holds on tight. Christopher flails and pushes hard with his feet, as if trying to throw himself overboard. Holly shrieks and pulls him back into her arms. Christopher looks up at her and laughs. Wouldn't it be nice, he asks, his long eyelashes batting, if she and he could always be together like this? Holly rolls her eyes.

"This kid," she mutters, lowering him to the ground, "really knows how to push my buttons."

HOLLY Torroella was brought up a Catholic, but her parents didn't make a big deal out of it. She's glad of that now, because she'd hate to spend time on her precious days off sitting in a church. Not that she has anything against church — it's just that she doesn't believe that churches are necessary. She believes that people can practice their religion quietly, without making a show of it. Holly's mother-in-law disagrees. Her mother-in-law takes Christopher to church every chance she gets. Holly says her mother-in-law thinks that not bringing a Catholic boy to church on Sunday is tantamount to child abuse.

Holly and Christopher spend most Sundays in Weymouth, about an hour's drive southeast of her apartment. Weymouth is a working-class town of fifty-five thousand made classy in parts by its proximity to the ocean. There is a Navy air station there, and at one time a good number of residents worked at a nearby shipyard, but the yard closed several years ago. Now the major employers are the South Shore Hospital and Electroswitch, a maker of heavy-duty switches. There aren't a lot of glamour jobs left.

Holly's folks, Larry and Betty Michaels, live in Weymouth on a street of small, well-kept homes in a modest neighborhood. Many of the houses in their area were built in the Cape Cod style, and some seem to exude a certain seaworthiness, as if uneasily moored to their foundations. The Michaelses' house is one of these, and it is all but dwarfed by a thirty-foot pintail yawl in the side yard.

This particular Sunday, Holly and her mother have plans. They and her brother, Ted, are taking Christopher to Nantasket Beach. It's still too cold to swim, but there's a boardwalk to stroll on, and Betty plans to pick cattails.

"There are so many things children aren't allowed to touch," Betty says. "I like to take Christopher where he can touch the trees."

It's freezing on the boardwalk, the wind blowing in off the ocean in deep, pungent gusts. Betty and Holly keep their heads low and their hands in their pockets, walking in long, easy strides while Christopher rides high and proud on his uncle's shoulders. Christopher's eyes tear with the wind, and Holly has to keep wiping his nose with a tissue. After half a mile or so, Betty steps off the walkway to the edge of the marsh and pulls out a handful of cattails, roots and all, for Christopher. Ted and Holly recoil; they are both allergic to the plant. But Christopher grabs one and swings it around his head, twirling it like a lasso. Ted bucks and whinnies obligingly, then turns away from the marsh and toward the warmth of a nearby video arcade, just across the road.

Holly says she used to come here years before to ride the roller coaster at Paragon Park. She and her brothers had a great time, buying full day passes and eating junk food and getting sick on the rides. But the amusement park was torn down to make room for luxury condominiums (Betty ventures a guess that the developers went so far as to put whirlpools in the bathtubs), and Holly says this arcade is a sorry substitute. Christopher and his uncle run around poking quarters into the video games and then into the money slot of a toy race car. The race car doesn't do much, just jiggles around a little, and Christopher gets out before it stops. He's tired, and suddenly the arcade is noisy and confusing, with teenagers dominating all the good stuff. Betty takes Christopher's hand and walks him outside toward a low, white building with boarded-up doors and windows. She explains that this is all that's left of the old amusement park, then lifts him up for a peek through a side window. He puts his nose to the glass, and a circle of snorting wooden horses with manes like sea glass stares back at him. Holly goes on and on about how much fun he'll have when the carousel opens for the summer. Christopher watches until the horses fade behind a fog of his own hot breath, then squirms out of his grandmother's arms, and runs toward the car. He's had his fill of deferring gratification.

Back home, Betty makes toasted cheese sandwiches, tea, and cocoa in the kitchen, while Holly and her brother sit in the breakfast nook bickering. Ted is bored with his current job, which is driving a van for a photo-finishing lab, and he talks about quitting. Holly has no patience for this: she has worked at jobs she's hated most of her life, and she sees no reason why her younger brother should continue to sponge off their parents rather than endure a little paid boredom. Ted chuckles and takes a long sip of cocoa, pleased that he, like Christopher, can still yank his big sister's chain.

Holly's father comes in from outside, stamping his feet and pulling a blue knit cap from his head. He wears coveralls over thermal underwear and thick leather boots. He has icy blue eyes that melt quickly at the sight of his grandson and a healthy shock of hair that even a much younger man would be proud of. Like Christopher, he is quite handsome. Despite the cold, he's been working outside all afternoon on the yawl. Ever since Holly can remember, her father has been tinkering with one boat or another. He can bring almost any boat back to life. He bought a lobster boat for a dollar once and turned it into a cabin cruiser. The yawl he owns now was honed from a battered hull he bought fourteen years before. He spends almost every spare moment working on it, or in the backyard, messing around with the swimming pool, or in the driveway, with his truck.

Holly's father started out in the Coast Guard, then left the service to marry and go to work as a mechanic in his father's automobile repair business. The family lived on Myrtle Avenue in Cambridge then, in a tightly knit neighborhood just on the edge of Somerville. Holly remembers being close with the neighbors and spending her afternoons chasing balls in other kids' backyards. There was no such thing as day care in those days, not as far as she knew. She went to Mass on Sundays, usually with her grandfather. But when Holly was five, her dad felt the pull of the water. He got a job as an insurance adjuster and moved his family to Weymouth, where, in their neighborhood anyway, people kept pretty much to themselves. There were fewer kids to play with, and Holly felt lonely for the first time in her life. Holly's father got busy with his boats, and the family stopped going to Mass. For a while, they even lived in a house on a boat yard. Holly can remember waking up in the morning, walking out her front door, and seeing nothing but the ocean and boats for miles.

Holly's dad is retired now, which gives him even more time to spend tinkering and dreaming of the sea. He plans to sail to the Florida Keys next year and stay there. He's tired of the cold. But Holly's mother likes the change of seasons, and right now she's refusing to go with him. Holly isn't sure what her mother will do after her father is gone, but the prospect of her parents separating bothers her less than she thought it would. Even Betty admits that she and her husband don't always have that much to say to each other, especially now that most of the kids have left home. After forty years of marriage, Holly says, any couple is entitled to a break.

Holly's father takes a seat in the kitchen slightly apart from the rest of his family. He pulls out a cigarette, then, thinking the better of it, taps it back into the pack. He takes a long, affectionate look at his grandson, who is hunched over on the floor, intent on his coloring, then asks Holly how things are going at work.

Holly snickers. She says that Christopher rarely misses the opportunity to show her how fed up he is with the constant changes in her schedule. It just throws him for a loop, makes him cranky and insecure and hard to live with. She's just started working on this insane third shift, from 11 P.M. until 6:30 in the morning. It's good in that it allows her to see Christopher every afternoon, bad in that it has turned her into a zombie. She never manages to catch up on her sleep.

"Talk about power struggles," she says, slicing Christopher's cheese sandwich into perfect quarters and handing him a napkin. "There were two women, including myself, and three men on the day shift in the computer room. Two of the men are married without kids, and the third one is a bachelor. Both I and the other woman are single mothers. When the shift change came, guess who got moved to nights? Right. . . ."

Holly tried hard to make her boss change her assignment. She argued that she had worked tirelessly through the strike and that she was already paying $170 a week for child care. She just couldn't afford a baby-sitter at night. But her supervisor told her to keep her personal life out of the office.

"I told her, fine, I won't bring my personal life in, I'll bring my son in," Holly says.

Holly's supervisor began to get the picture. The image of a three-year-old messing with the disk drives catapulted her into compassion. She looked at Holly with sisterly understanding and suggested that she find a relative to help out.

"I told her that the only relative I had who didn't work was my sister but that she lives in Nova Scotia," Holly says. "That was a mistake. My boss said, 'Well, that's great — send Christopher to your sister for three months. That way, it would almost be like being single again; you could really have a good time. With the money you make on the pay differential, you could even fly up to visit your son on weekends.' Do you believe that? This kid is my life, and she's telling me I can visit him on weekends? I wanted to quit."

But Holly couldn't afford to quit; the telephone company

pays her more money than she would dare ask for anywhere else. On the other hand, there was Christopher. She settled the matter by pocketing her pride and convincing Christopher's father to let Christopher spend weeknights with him in his apartment in East Boston. Now Holly drives Christopher to his father's place after dinner before going to work and picks him up at 6:30 the next morning to drive him back to Cambridge for breakfast. Most mornings, Christopher wears his pajamas on the way home. He dawdles over his oatmeal or eggs and makes what seems like a conscious effort to be late. If Holly tries to rush him, he says he doesn't want to go to school at all. If she nags, he throws a tantrum, and then, sometimes, he throws up.

"That's how he tells me he doesn't like the situation," Holly says flatly. "I tell him it's okay to be mad, that we'll still love each other no matter what. But, you know, he's put up with an awful lot for a little boy."

Holly's father listens to all this silently, then shakes his head. He doesn't approve of his daughter's life-style, doesn't think it's right for the mother of a three-year-old to work full-time. But he figures that there's nothing he can do about it, so he might as well keep his mouth shut. He pushes back from his chair and goes to the living room for a smoke. Holly throws her mother a knowing look, and Betty rustles back to the toaster oven to pull out the next batch of cheese sandwiches.

Later, Betty asks Holly how things are going at Tot Lot, whether Holly still likes the teachers. Holly says, yes, she pretty much likes most of them, especially now that José's gone. José gave her the creeps. But she's concerned about staff turnover. The other parents seem not to have noticed. This, Holly says, is a testament to Molly, who has managed to make things run smoothly despite everything.

"Molly is the person who the parents turn to for support," Holly says, stirring Christopher's third mug of cocoa. "Molly is the glue that holds that school together."

MOLLY anticipated her appointment with the Mad Russian with great optimism. But as the time approached, her optimism melted into dread. She knew he would change her life forever, and she wasn't sure she was ready. Today's the day, and Molly is really getting nervous. She stands outside Tot Lot at 3 P.M., inhaling a Marlboro and waiting for her ride to show. She smokes the cigarette down to the filter, taking one last lung-filling drag before grinding the butt carefully into the sidewalk. She can't believe this cigarette will be her last. But she knows it will be. The Mad Russian is said to have a 95 percent success rate, and Molly isn't about to screw up his record.

A Toyota Camry pulls up, and Molly gets in. She feels lucky that her friend Ginger could take the time to drive her this afternoon. They head over the Cambridge line and through a corner of Boston and turn onto Beacon Street in Brookline. Ginger double-parks beside a maroon Honda with a parking ticket flapping giddily from its windshield. There's a yellow brick town house with a large display window and a sign that reads "Boston Oriental Rugs." Molly steps out of the car and rushes up the steps of the town house, through the front door, and up another flight of stairs to the second floor. The hall is dimly lit and covered with oriental rugs that, she speculates, are probably on loan from downstairs. She and two-and-a-half dozen others are ushered into a boardroom-sized meeting hall filled with metal folding chairs. They all sit down.

The Mad Russian comes in and takes a seat behind a desk, facing his audience. Molly had seen him running around the hall earlier, though she didn't know who he was then. He is short and round and is losing his hair, not at all the look Molly had imagined, especially of a man whose real name is Yefim Shudentsov and who bills himself as a "bioenergetic consultant." Molly expected a much more exotic figure, a tall, dashing, charismatic man with a touch of mystery about him. She has no idea why she thought this, but she did, and she is disappointed: this chubby old man doesn't exactly imbue her with confidence. Still, she is hopeful. She has friends who swear by this guy, and even her internist spoke highly of him.

The Mad Russian gets up slowly from behind his desk, as though pushing back from a heavy meal, and walks methodically around the room, rattling off a well-practiced monologue. He talks about the sanctity of the human body and how shortsighted it is of anyone to pollute it with dangerous foreign substances. Molly is skeptical; after all, it looks like this guy has put a little too much of something into his own body for quite some time now. The lecture drones on for forty-five minutes, and then an hour. It is all too much. Finally, the Mad Russian is done. He tells everyone to leave the room and to wait outside in the hall and that he will call them back in one at a time for a private consultation.

Molly stands waiting in the hall, nursing a powerful urge to smoke. What, after all, will this man have to tell her? She knows just about everything there is to know about her habit, save how to shake it. And she doesn't think she can stand another lecture. That's what she hated about school, the lecture part. Lecturing is no way to get a message across; anyone who works with kids knows that. When Molly's name gets called, she walks slowly back into the room, prepared to be patronized. Instead, she's surprised.

The Mad Russian tells her to focus on a mental picture of herself smoking a cigarette and to raise her hand when the image is firm in her mind. Molly thinks back to two hours before, when she was standing outside of Tot Lot. She zooms in close on that last drag and focuses. She can savor the gritty taste of nicotine, smell the sulphur, feel the heat of the burning paper on the tips of her fingers. She closes her eyes in reverie.

Suddenly there is a noise. "Poof!" Molly opens her eyes. The Mad Russian has performed his magic. He has broken the spell with a single word, a single syllable. Molly is dumbstruck. She can't believe the man actually said "pouf," like some schlock magician at a kiddie sideshow. The Mad Russian looks intently into her eyes and tells her that she has a lovely body and she shouldn't destroy it by smoking. Then he tells her to leave the room and to pay the receptionist forty-five dollars on the way out.

Molly stumbles into the sunlight, half-dazed but, somehow, elated. She believes she will not smoke again. On the way home in the car, she and her friend calculate that the Mad Russian probably makes more money in a week than a day care teacher makes in a year. And then they laugh.

*   *   *

MOLLY no longer talks about leaving Tot Lot. Things have been going much more smoothly since Lilian and José left, and she feels that she's got her grip back. A new teacher and a teacher's aid have been hired; neither has much experience, but they are mild mannered and accommodating, and the children like them. Still, sometimes Molly feels her tolerance for her job being stretched. Like the time she got a stomach bug, threw up all night, crawled into school at 7:45 A.M. to let Marcia in, and told Susan she wouldn't be able to last the morning. Susan was sympathetic but said that there was no one available to cover. That day, a new toddler spent the entire morning crying for his mother, and, at 11 o'clock, when Molly was scheduled to leave, Nancy marched into Susan's office and resigned. It's days like that, Molly laughs, that make her think she should have gone into another line of work. But then she thinks about the twins falling all over each other and Claude dancing and Dawn hiding her toys, and she knows she won't. She is needed here in a way that most people are never needed. There's so much she has to share with the younger teachers, so much that they need to know. She's seen them make so many mistakes.

"There's more to being a teacher than coming up with creative art projects," she says. "There's classroom management. These kids are little; you can't stand back and expect them to control themselves. If you expect that, you should go into teaching adults. When I see a clump of teachers standing around the kitchen chatting, I know why the class is going wild. You've got to entertain them, keep them engaged.

"For example, it's a proven fact that kids love unrolling paper towels and toilet paper. Some of these kids are five years old, and the teachers seem to be thinking, 'Whoa, this kid's ready for college, surely he can keep his hands off the toilet paper.' Well, he can't, and he messes with it, and he gets yelled at. But all the kids need supervision, even the five-year-olds. If they don't get it, there's going to be pushing and shoving and all sorts of trouble. It's not my position to tell the other teachers that, but sometimes I think they set themselves and the kids up for a not very happy time."

It's true that the other teachers, Marie and Marina and

Margaret, are less expert in their handling of the children than is Molly. Molly's experience seems to far outweigh the fact that she is the only teacher in the school not to have attended college. It's teachers like Molly who get child-care experts thinking about precisely which credentials child-care workers really need and which are simply add-ons to make parents feel better. Some studies have found that the more relevant education a day care teacher has the better, but these studies are not conclusive. In any case, as one expert put it, "if you assume that, to do day care properly, a person needs to become an early-childhood educator, meaning four years of college, then you have created an impossible fiction, for example, that competent people will take a job paying less per year than what they paid for college. What we need is both coursework and an apprenticeship system, whereby people can learn the profession on the job from a mentor."

Molly is one of those rare mentors, and, as such, she is highly valued by parents. There has been quiet talk of offering her a pay differential, a little extra to compensate her for her loyalty to the center and her experience as a day care teacher. At the last general meeting, one parent, an educator herself, went so far as to question whether all teachers should be treated as equals. This was a real shocker: Tot Lot was built on a nonhierarchical philosophy, whereby everyone contributes and gets paid the same. Of course, Tot Lot was founded close to twenty years ago, in those halcyon days of peace and love, before money meant so much. A lot of things have changed since then; parents no longer work as teacher's aides, they no longer supply the toys, they no longer attend meetings two or three times a week to bicker over political correctness. Most of these parents work long and hard for their money, and they recognize that the teachers do, too. So rather than dismissing the idea of a pay differential as heresy, the parents and teachers vote to break into small groups and talk about it.

The discussion is heated. Some parents, among them an outspoken psychologist who has seen four of his kids through Tot Lot, are totally against a pay differential; they believe it would destroy the character of the place. Others argue that it is unrealistic to ask teachers to work without a monetary incentive.

"I, for one, would get burned out really fast if I thought I'd never get a promotion," says one. The teachers look uncomfortable. The idea of promotion is alien to them. Promoted to what? Head teacher? What does that mean, exactly? They have not trained as managers, and, besides, there's not enough psychological space to set up a hierarchy — everyone has to do everything. Still, they realize that, without a ladder, day care will never be considered a career. And they wouldn't mind looking forward to higher pay down the road. The parents and teachers emerge from the small-group discussions an hour later without consensus. But there is a nagging sense all around that sooner or later Tot Lot will have to change.

IN May, the budget committee gets together for a hard look at the numbers. The meeting is set for 5:30, and the parents and teachers who make up the committee are rumpled and hungry and in no mood for prolonged discussion. They sit in the tiny chairs in the preschool room, slumped over the Formica table like beanbags. The smell of pizza wafts over from the toddler room, along with occasional shrieks of anger and laughter. The children of meeting parents are enjoying an early dinner while their parents talk. By the time the meeting is over, some of those children will have spent the better part of a dozen hours at Tot Lot today.

Susan takes a seat, throws everyone a smile, and opens a legal-sized file folder. She sifts through the pile of yellow, lined paper and legal documents, looking for she doesn't know what. She, too, is exhausted; it's been another one of those days when she can feel control slipping away. The dishwasher is on the fritz again, and the man from Sears never showed up to fix it. The sink is filled with dishes left over from afternoon snack, and it looks like she'll have to wash them. If only the teachers would use paper plates, just this once. But the environmentalists would freak, and Susan figures it's not worth the battle. She'd rather wash dishes for an hour than spend five minutes arguing with Margaret about landfill.

Susan starts the meeting on a cautionary note. She has planned the next year's budget on the assumption that finances just can't get any worse. But she now sees that this assumption might have been presumptuous. The state has put her on notice that times could indeed get tougher. Right now, the Department of Social Services will commit to only three months of funding at a time. Whether even more cuts will be made over the next quarter is anybody's guess, but Susan is not optimistic.

The parents wince. Most of them assumed this meeting was going to be about budgeting repairs for the ceiling and the floor. Instead, they're hearing that Tot Lot's future is on the line. It's like going to the doctor for a checkup and being told that you need triple bypass surgery.

Susan says that Tot Lot needs to take drastic measures, and she mentions a couple of alternatives. One is to reduce the number of toddlers in the school from thirteen to nine, or even to zero. Toddler care is much more expensive than preschooler care, largely because the state allows ten preschoolers but only six toddlers per teacher. And toddlers wear diapers, at a total cost to the center of roughly forty dollars a week. As it stands now, the preschoolers are actually subsidizing the toddler room.

(In fact, toddler care is always more expensive than preschooler care, and infant care, which Tot Lot doesn't offer, costs even more. Some centers provide infant care as a sort of loss leader, a way to lure in preschoolers of the future. But there are far more centers that offer no infant or toddler care at all. In Massachusetts, and nationally, it is care for the youngest children that is in shortest supply.)

Susan's other cost-cutting idea is to eliminate all part-time slots. A handful of toddler parents get discounts for fetching their children at 2:30, rather than having them stay the whole day. In theory, reduced tuition fees could be compensated for by reducing staff size and, hence, salaries, but this has never worked out. Not enough children leave at 2:30 to allow the release of a toddler teacher. So, in the afternoon, fewer toddlers are tended by the same number of teachers paid from a smaller tuition pool. Susan says that, by substituting full-timers for part-timers, the toddler room might actually reach break even.

The parents eye each other wearily, like survivors at sea in an overcrowded lifeboat. The mother of a preschooler says that she doesn't think the center can afford the part-time slots. They are, she says, "a luxury in these times of fiscal crisis." This mother works full-time. Patricia Weissman looks startled. Patricia has twins in the toddler room and spends three hundred dollars a week for part-time child care. Every morning, she has just enough time to dash back from Tot Lot to her home office and work for five hours at a career in landscape architecture that is stalled with the recession. Patricia has arranged her life so that she can be with her children in the afternoons. She wants to be fair, to do the right thing, but she just can't afford to pay for full-time care.

"It would just about break me," she says. As it is, Patricia figures she will spend sixty thousand dollars at Tot Lot before her twins graduate to kindergarten.

No one feels comfortable challenging Patricia; they can see her point. No one really wants to exclude either toddlers or part-timers from Tot Lot. For one thing, that would mean losing Molly; for another, it would totally change the character of the place. To enforce a full-time rule, to eliminate the toddlers, would be to capitulate, to fail.

Susan says there is perhaps a more palatable way to bridge the money gap: they could fill the vacancies she's kept open for the past two months. The parents look up, alarmed; they had no idea there were openings. With good day care centers at such a premium, everyone assumed there was a waiting list for Tot Lot. To be without a waiting list verges on the insulting. How the hell, their faces say, could Susan allow this to happen? Susan braces herself; she anticipated this response. Slowly and carefully, she explains that there is, in fact, a waiting list. But the waiting list is made up of white, middle-class parents able to pay for their children's care. She had hoped to fill the center's three vacancies with needy children on state vouchers. Unfortunately, that's not happening. The state has frozen the number of day care slots for low-income working parents. The only state-subsidized slots available are for the children of people in job-training programs, the so-called "E.T." (employment training) slots, which are guaranteed for a year. Ironically, parents who seek training and land jobs as a result are no longer eligible for subsidized child care, so ultimately many end up where they started, scraping by on public assistance.

"That means," says Glen Barth, "that parents will quit their jobs and go back into job-training programs to get day care. That's a terrific long-term solution."

But Susan sees it from the other side, the child's side.

"What it means," says Susan, "is that a lot of people who shouldn't be staying home with their kids will be."

The meeting lasts for about an hour and a half, with no resolution save that the empty slots at the center should be filled as soon as possible, even if it means enrolling private payers (which it does). The parents get up and stretch the kinks out of their backs and then go to peel their children off the walls of the toddler room. Susan slips into her office to check over her list of students. She's pretty sure that she won't have to kick anyone out just yet, but she's also pretty sure that she won't be able to accept several of the children for whom she's already promised spots in the following fall. That list includes Mike's brother, Benjamin, who, to Susan's mind, is in sore need of placement. She can't imagine him spending another year cooped up with his mother.

Susan leaves her office and goes to the kitchen. It's late, and the preschool room has the look of having been abandoned in great haste, like a bookie joint tipped off to a raid. Susan takes a long look around the room, at the haphazard artwork slipping down the walls and the gray linoleum patched over with duct tape and the scattered boxes of broken crayons and the rug that was wrecked by a flood two years before and never replaced. She takes a deep breath, rolls up her sleeves, walks to the sink, and turns the tap on the sink full of dirty dishes. It's times like these, she says, that make her glad she busted her hump to get that master's degree.

THE day that Mike came in with the cigarette burn on his ear, Molly and Susan and the other teachers had a meeting. They stood in the corner of the kitchen, next to the nonfunctioning watercooler, and discussed whether to notify the Department of

Social Services. A child who comes into school with a cigarette burn on his ear is clearly in some sort of jeopardy. Tot Lot is required by law to notify DSS of suspected physical or emotional abuse by filing what is called a 51A, but the teachers weren't so sure they could afford to involve the agency. They don't really trust the system.

The previous month, for example, a social worker came to observe the preschool class and noticed that one child in particular was acting out. She approached the child, questioned her, and without permission from the teachers, asked the girl to express her feelings in a picture. The social worker brought the drawing back to her colleagues, and they inferred from it that the child was angry because her parents were in the midst of a difficult separation. The social workers recommended that the child get counseling about this issue and insisted that the teachers tell the child's mother as much. When the teachers told the mother, she was furious. What right did this social worker have to test her child without her knowledge, let alone without her permission? The teachers nodded their heads; they thought the mother had a good point. So, when it came time to file on Mike, the teachers were not all that quick to include the Department of Social Services in the decision-making process. In their experience, bureaucracies tend to take on lives of their own.

Molly, ever the parent advocate, advised Susan to call Mike's mother, Elizabeth, first, to get her side of the story. Elizabeth was home when Susan called, and she seemed chipper enough. She said that, yes, she had forgotten to mention Mike's burn when she dropped him off this morning; she'd been so busy that it had just slipped out of her mind. She had moved out of her apartment over the weekend, and while she was packing, she left Mike with her brother-in-law. She had the feeling that her brother-in-law wasn't the best person to leave a kid with, but he was available, and she had to move, and she couldn't have Mike underfoot while she packed. Anyway, her brother-in-law got careless. That's what she was told, anyway. It was an accident. She was certain it wouldn't happen again. Susan hung up the phone and thought carefully about what Elizabeth had said.

Then she thought about what it would be like to have the tip of a burning cigarette applied to her own earlobe. And then she called the Department of Social Services.

"It broke my heart," Susan says. "Parents' reactions to this kind of thing are unpredictable. God forbid Elizabeth should take Mike and run. What with the guilt a parent feels over a thing like this — even parents who abuse their children don't want to lose them."

But, as it turns out, Susan needn't have worried. After hearing the story, Joe Logan, a behavior specialist with the Cambridge School Department, told her that there was little risk that Elizabeth would get hassled. Since the Massachusetts Miracle went bust, there have been so many child abuse and neglect cases reported in the state that a case as minor as this one would probably get buried. When times are tough, some parents just naturally take it out on their kids. There will be an investigation of Mike's case, of course, but it won't go deep.

"Thank God," Susan says, "that means we haven't lost him."

MARINA and Holly worked together for months brainstorming the fund-raising dance. Getting the band was easy: Marina's brother is a bass guitarist with a rhythm-and-blues band of his own, and he has enough friends in the business to keep the music going all night. The hard part was finding a place to put the bands. They finally got the go-ahead from the Middle East Restaurant, a funky kebab joint on Massachusetts Avenue with a big room in the back that sometimes passes for a nightclub. The club manager was no altruist; he offered to sponsor the gig on an off night, say on a Tuesday or Wednesday, when business was slow. Marina thought that was a bad idea. It was hard enough enticing working parents out of the house on a weekend, let alone smack in the middle of the week, when baby-sitters are scarcer than parking spots in Harvard Square. Also, who wants to get down and drunk on a Tuesday night, with the bulk of the workweek still to get through? Marina got pretty aggravated repeating this over and over to people who wanted her to give in and settle for a midweek slot. Marina knows from nightclubs;

she follows her brother's band and lots of other bands, and she knows what nights get business and what nights don't. And Holly, who hadn't been to a club for years, trusted Marina's judgment.

In the end, though, Marina had to give in. The bands wouldn't perform for free on a Thursday night, when they could be working paid gigs. So Marina settled for a Tuesday. She called in a lot of favors and got five bands to play. The deal was that Tot Lot would get all the proceeds from the door and the club would keep the take from drink sales. At first, that didn't seem fair. Tickets were only five dollars, and the bands would attract a lot of drinkers at no cost to the nightclub. But after three months of negotiations, Holly and Marina were tired of haggling, and, anyway, Holly figured, maybe it was just as well for a day care center not to profit directly from the sale of booze. Marina got the parents hawking tickets by the handful. She wanted this thing to work, and work big.

It's tropically hot the night of the Tot Lot dance, and the waitresses are sweating through their tank tops. The club is small, with a stage for the bands, two dozen tables, and a dance floor with the leg room of a king-sized bed. There are ceiling fans but no air-conditioning, and by the time the first band warms up, the place is steaming. By 9:30, just about every table is full. A row of Tot Lot parents line the back wall, clutching beers as though they were life preservers and fanning themselves with cocktail napkins. They are dressed in khaki pants and T-shirts and jumpsuits and jeans and look tired and old compared to the rest of the crowd, which, it seems, is comprised largely of Marina's friends. Marina wears a skintight strapless tank dress that clings to her like rubber, and she's working the room like a movie star, kissing cheeks and patting shoulders and buying beers. Her red hair ripples down her back like a flag. She looks sexy and savvy and totally in her element. Holly wears a sleeveless white T-shirt and a miniskirt and black hose and heels. She looks good, too, but also nervous. She sits nursing a Coke at a table near the back, chatting with a couple that she knows slightly. She's waiting for Bill.

Bill is a guy who Holly's gone out with a couple of times,

and he promised to meet her here tonight. It's been a year since Holly has had a date, and even longer since she's met a man she feels comfortable with, so she's pretty happy about Bill. Bill is a carpenter, an Irish Catholic from Maine who Holly says looks like John F. Kennedy. They've been out for pizza and for drinks together, and they seem to have a lot in common. Bill has a great sense of humor, and he says he likes kids. All this makes Holly a little jumpy; she worries that he's too good to be true. Besides, her ex-husband said he liked kids, too.

"It's been very hard trying to get into a relationship since the breakup," she says. "You get to that thing about feeling worried that he won't call you and worried that he will."

Holly has had her fill of married men who assume that divorced women with children will put up with anything for a little attention.

The second band gets on stage to tune up, and Holly orders a club soda. She takes one last glance toward the door, then makes up her mind: Bill is not going to show tonight. In a way, she's relieved. Now it doesn't matter if he's married or gay or has some terrible secret to hide; now he's just another jerk. That she can deal with. She treats herself to a beer. The band is really good, surprisingly good, and the room is filled to capacity. People are coming in off the street to see what's up, buying tickets at the door. The fund-raiser is a success; the center will probably clear at least a grand, enough to get a start on that ceiling job. She can't believe that she and Marina actually pulled this thing off. It's turned into a great night.

The music plays on until 2 A.M., though most of the parents leave much earlier. Getting a baby-sitter on a Tuesday is an ordeal; finding a baby-sitter who will stay past midnight is a miracle. One couple jokes that having a baby-sitter at all is such a rare luxury that they almost feel obliged to rent a room at the Hotel Sonesta for an hour to consummate the occasion.

Holly stays late. Christopher is sleeping over with her parents tonight (her mother doesn't work on Wednesdays), so she's free. She jokes around with Marina and the musicians until one o'clock, when the bar closes, and then walks back to her car alone. The night is still sticky but cooler and quieter, with the traffic slowed to a trickle and the air clear of exhaust fumes. Holly drives home slowly with the radio off, savoring the solitude. When she gets home, she splashes just enough water on her face to wash off the makeup, brushes her teeth, and falls into bed with fantasies of sleeping until eight. Ha, that's a laugh. Christopher wakes up at seven, and he'll be waiting for her call. She wouldn't dream of letting him down.

Thirteen

RALLY ROUND THE FLAG

FLAG Day, June 14, is not a legal holiday, but to the children of Tot Lot, it might as well be. They've been wound up tight and raring for action all morning, as though expecting Santa to drop in for an off-season visit. If Dylan were here, there would be some serious kick-boxing action, with legs flying in all directions and the more timid kids ending up in tears. But Dylan has been out all week, so the big boys, the boys who are overready for kindergarten, find other ways to let off steam. Moses, running in figure eights around the Formica tables, grabs a plastic dinosaur and waves it under Luke's nose, tempting him, and holds it high above his head like a trophy. Luke laughs his deep, deep belly laugh, lashes out a hand as quick as a lizard's tongue, and jumps, palming the toy and pulling it tight into his chest, like a football. Seeing this, Marcel gets so excited that he grabs for the toy, too, and, wrenching it from Luke's grip, throws it at the dingy glass fishtank, startling the goldfish out of their customary stupor and igniting a frenzy of finger pointing and tattling. Normally, a flying tyrannosaurus is no big deal. Normally, a teacher would tell Marcel to pick up the toy and put it back on the shelf, out of circulation. If by some chance another child's head had been in the toy's trajectory, Marcel would have been sentenced to five minutes of self-examination in time-out, but there would have been no showdown, no discussion of the infraction at the Tuesday staff meeting. This is because the teachers have come to trust Marcel, to count on his good intentions. Since starting at Tot Lot ten months before, he has grown from wild and rough to calm and considerate. He takes pains to control himself and is particularly gentle and even loving with the younger children, volunteering to hold the toddlers' hands on outings, being the first to pat the cheek and coo in the face of a visiting infant.

"Before he was a monster," says Marie. "Now he seems to fit right in."

But today Marie is not the one doling out Marcel's discipline. Today Marcel's father, Michel, is here to see the flying dinosaur. Michel grabs Marcel's arm at the elbow and pulls him toward the door. Marcel's toes reach for the floor through his sneakers, and his eyes go wide — he rolls them beseechingly toward Marie, who stands, hands on her broad hips, shaking her head at Michel's departing back. Images of what Michel has in mind for Marcel flash through Marie's mind, one after another, like slides in a child's View-Master. She shudders and then shoves the possibilities to the back of her thoughts. Michel and Marcel are already halfway down the path to the street by the time she finds the words.

Later she says what she wanted to shout was "Leave that boy alone, and go back to Miami or Haiti or wherever it is you go." What she calls out instead is "Don't you spank him, now."

Marie stands at the door as Michel's car pulls away from the curb, shaking her head and muttering under her breath. Then she steps back inside, rubs the palms of her hands lightly on her navy blue stretch pants, and walks through the kitchen and into the preschool room just in time to get a good look at Mike threatening Ruth with the receiver of a toy telephone. Ruth's eyes are wide in horror, but Marie pays no mind — she knows Ruth can give as good as she gets. Sitting down heavily in one of the tiny wooden chairs, Marie reaches down and carefully peels the remnants of an orange crayon off the sole of her shoe, shakes her head, and laughs.

"You know," she says, "sometimes you just have to let things slide."

Later that morning, the preschoolers gather on the ragged red rug under the plastic bubble skylight and practice singing "We Shall Overcome." They have sung the song many times before, for many occasions, and they know it by heart. Their voices rise high, well above the teachers', and their hands act out the lyrics in American sign language. Mike knows the song as well as anyone, but he doesn't sing or sign. Instead he clinches his eyes shut, claps his hands over his ears, stretches his jaws, and yowls like a coyote. The teachers raise eyebrows, but they don't interfere. Today his yowling seems almost on key. Besides, they don't want to break the momentum; they need to get through the song.

The preschoolers are rehearsing in preparation for this afternoon's field trip. They are going to the State House to protest the cuts in the day care budget. Most of the teachers are charged up at the prospect of organized protest. But Molly keeps her distance, going about her business as though nothing special is in store. Molly has participated in many, many rallies over the years, and she has learned to pace herself. Nine years before, for example, she went to a rally much like the one she will go to today. Michael Dukakis was governor then, too, and then, too, his administration proposed cuts in the budget that would keep needy children out of day care. Molly remembers that rally pretty well. She remembers the toddlers were so tired and hungry by the time they got to the State House that it was all they could do to eat their snacks and keep their eyes open. But Molly stood her ground, cheering on the speakers and singing protest songs, and pretty soon the kids perked up too, what with the Frisbees zipping over their heads and the guitars playing and all, and the day turned out just fine.

"What's the point of living in a country where you have the freedom to speak if you don't use it?" she asks. "Isn't speaking out what living in a democracy is all about?"

So Molly voted yes for the trip to the State House, even though she knows how much work these trips are and also that some parents are uncomfortable with them. Dawn's mother,

Sharon, for instance. Sharon told Molly the day before that Dawn wouldn't be going to the State House, that she is afraid to allow her daughter on the subway. Dawn has ridden the subway many times before on many other field trips, but Molly doesn't make a point of this. Sharon is young and is going through a divorce, and she isn't in the mood to rock boats right now — her boat is unstable enough as it is.

Other parents were not as direct as Sharon about their reluctance to participate, but it was clear from their responses when the rally came up for discussion at the general meeting several weeks before that they would not be in attendance. Sure, when it came down to a vote, their hands went up in support of the majority, but their eyes were cast to the floor. Each of these parents had personal reasons for not wanting to go, but what it really boils down to is fear or apathy. It is the parents who have the most to lose, those who rely on public money to pay for their childrens' care, who are most reluctant to act. These parents seem to be in a state of denial, as though the proposed budget cuts are political abstractions that have nothing to do with them or their families. In fact, the state has threatened to cut twenty million dollars from its day care budget, enough to slice out subsidized day care for any number of these families and force them onto welfare.

It is the children of these parents, the parents who won't be at the rally, for whom Molly is most anxious that today's protest have an effect.

AS a rule, day care in this country has enjoyed only timid and erratic political support. Arguments that children have an inherent right to decent care have, until recently, simply failed to impress the private sector or the federal government in any meaningful sense — that is, the money sense. There's been lots of talk, of course. Most politicians strain to portray themselves as allies of children, even as their voting records belie their rhetoric. Congress passed the first bill authorizing federal funds for care for children of the working poor, the Child Development Bill, in 1971. But President Nixon saved Congress from having to find a way to pay for the bill with a veto, arguing that such legislation would institutionalize the care of children and erode the role of the family. A second child-development bill, sponsored by then Minnesota senator Walter Mondale and others in 1974, sparked a heated debate that focused not on the needs of children but on how day care would weaken the family bond. The fact that 46 percent of the nation's mothers were working at the time seemed not to sway this reasoning, for the bill was quickly killed. Meanwhile, parents kept working and paying for child care as best they could, which, by and large, was not very well. With the exception of meager subsidies for the children of poor parents in work-training programs or trying to get off welfare, things have been pretty much the same ever since, with the result that day care in this country is in many respects a national disgrace.

Child advocates have lobbied tirelessly to rectify this, calling for minimum federal standards for day care centers and child-care providers and demanding penalties for those who fail to comply. But their arguments have been overruled by legislators convinced that federal standards would usurp the rights of individual states to decide what is best for the children of their constituencies. What's good for kids in Waco, Texas, they say, may not be good for children in Port Byron, New York. There is also talk that regulation would interfere with the natural order of things, with, for example, the care of children by their aunts or grandmothers. While it's unlikely that caring for relatives in one's home would ever be subject to government regulation, the fear of such regulation is frequently capitalized on by opponents of day care standards. (On the other hand, toddler Jessica McClure was in the care of her aunt when she fell down that well in Texas, where she lay trapped for fifty-eight hours. The fact that her day care provider had nine children in her charge at the time had a lot more to do with the quality of Jessica's care than the fact that she was Jessica's aunt.)

Child-care regulations are left to the discretion of the states, and many states have been slow to take a stand for quality care. According to the Children's Defense Fund, based in Washington, D.C., thirty-one states do not regulate group size for pre-schoolers in day care centers, and twenty-six states do not regulate group size for infants. Seven states require absolutely no special training for child-care workers. And states vary widely in setting limits on child-to-teacher ratios. In Idaho, for example, a provider can legally "care for" twelve infants under the age of six weeks.

The day care lobby, such as it is, is not a cohesive or powerful entity. Tales of the boredom and neglect experienced by children in day care centers are commonplace, so much so that they have worn down public resolve. The problem of providing decent care for children seems daunting, impossible. Perhaps, as some suggest, the problem lies in the fact that children cannot vote, and it is up to their parents to vote for them. Working parents with preschool-age children have little time to lobby, and the few who do manage to squeeze out the time often lose interest when their kids move on to kindergarten.

But as the shortage of decent care for children is increasingly perceived as posing an economic threat, the call for improvements in access to care and higher standards becomes more powerful. Harry L. Freeman, executive vice president of American Express, testified before a Senate subcommittee that "provision of proper care for young children is a matter of supreme, bottom-line importance to us today." What he meant was that parents cannot work effectively when they are worrying about their children, and, all too often, given the sorry state of child care in this country, parents cannot help worrying.

Such rhetoric, coupled with the growing legion of working (and voting) mothers, has sparked an upsurge in interest in child care in Congress, resulting in more than one hundred pieces of day care legislation being introduced over the past several years. Among these, the Act for Better Child Care Services (or ABC bill) sponsored in the Senate by Christopher Dodd of Connecticut came closest to realistically addressing the needs of working families as well as the delicate issue of setting national standards. A piece of that bill is included in the complicated, unwieldy Child Care Block Grant authorized by Congress and signed by President Bush in 1991. This measure is a compromise, authorizing money to be doled out in bits and pieces to states. Just how far this legislation will go toward improving the lot of the nation's children and how seriously the standards it sets for day care will be taken by the states is yet to be seen. Already, the standard-setting portion of the bill is under contention. And the grant certainly does not provide the blueprint or the funds for anything that could be called a national day care system or plan. But it's a start and a significant one, in that it represents the first time Congress and a president have negotiated, albeit contentiously, in support of a piece of child-care legislation. As such it's a land-mark achievement, an act to build upon.

IT is going on naptime on rally day and Molly is working the diaper assembly line, hustling the kids to the table, peeling off the old, slapping on the new, telling a joke or giving a tickle, and then lowering them heavily to the floor where another teacher directs them to their mats. The line is considerably shorter now than in September, when none of the toddlers was toilet trained. Now nearly half the kids wear underpants.

Dawn lies on her mat, wrapped in three blankets and look-ing around for more. She sees one in Crystal's cubbie and reaches out, grabs a corner, and sneaks it under her pile of covers before anyone notices. It's a cool day, but not cold, and Dawn doesn't need another blanket. She just likes to play it safe, taking what she can get when she can get it. There are books stuffed under Dawn's mat, too, and a couple of contraband toys. Molly is al-ready down on the floor, at eye level, and she has caught Dawn in the act. She crawls over to Dawn's mat and gently extracts Crystal's blanket from the tangle. Then she positions herself be-tween Dawn and Claude, props her head up on a stuffed animal for a pillow, and rubs their backs. Claude has wrapped his blan-ket around his head Lawrence of Arabia style and is howling softly, not in anger, but for diversion. Molly ignores the howls and just keeps rubbing. She figures that Claude must have been up late at the Kingdom Hall the night before and that he's just overtired. One of her sisters-in-law is a Jehovah's Witness, and Molly even studied up on it once herself, when she was pregnant with Patrick. She knows how exhausting the practice of that re-ligion can be. Sure enough, Claude is soon snoring as loudly as a man. But Dawn stays wide-awake. She reaches under her mat, pulls out a pop-up book, and scrutinizes the pages, furrowing her brow like a scholar. Then she jabs the book back under her mat, swings her feet up, pulls off her socks, and plays with her toes, singing to herself. Then she asks for a cuddle toy. Molly gets up, walks to Dawn's cubby, gets the toy, and brings it to her. Then she lies down, props her head in the crook of her arm, and stares across the room, lost in exhausted daydreams, resuming the back rub and telling Dawn to close her eyes and go to sleep. Surprisingly, this tactic works. Just as Dawn's eyelids start to flutter, though, a large woman in a black jumper and white T-shirt, the mother of one of the preschoolers, bursts through the door and announces that a cameraman from Channel Five is on his way. The mother corners Susan and tells her in a loud whisper that she has convinced Channel Five to tape at today's rally and that a producer there says she will use footage of Tot Lot as background for the piece. Susan squeezes her elbows and crinkles her nose with pleasure. For Susan, any distraction from the daily routine is welcome; she craves novelty.

A van pulls up, and a cameraman unloads his equipment and walks up the path and through the front door, a rush of plaid shirt and work boots and wires. The preschoolers spring from their mats and swarm at his feet, reaching toward the camera like a clutch of clumsy basketball players blocking a jump shot. The cameraman smiles, looks through his viewfinder, and starts the tape rolling, while nearby the producer paces the floor, a microphone limp in her hand. She's not sure whether this shoot is going to work, whether this day care rally will make much of a story. She smiles nervously at Susan and says she's sorry she can't do an interview but she has so little time — she needs to be downtown in twenty minutes to get pictures of something completely unrelated. Susan nods her emphatic "not to worry" nod and stands grinning, hugging herself with her arms, watching the kids go berserk for the camera.

Mike rolls around the floor, Tamara boogies suggestively, Samantha and Noel flash peace signs, and Jacob and Luke embrace, launching into an irresistible "Ebony and Ivory" dance routine that ends with them tumbling over each other like hamsters. The teachers stand back, admiring their work. They are proud that their kids know how to make the most of a photo opportunity. The camera keeps rolling, and, for a moment, the producer takes her eyes off the clock.

"I'm really going to try to be there for the rally," she says as much to herself as to anyone. She toys with the hem of her suit jacket and then adds, in hushed, confessional tones, "I have a baby myself."

The television crew packs up and is gone as suddenly as it came. The teachers go through the motions of trying to get the kids to calm down, to go back to their mats for a rest, but their hearts aren't in it. They, too, are ready to go downtown.

It's a great day for a protest, crisp with brilliant sunshine. Molly predicts that the turnout will be good. Tot Lot parents and teachers organized the rally, and four other centers have agreed to close their doors for the afternoon and join them in front of the State House. With the weather so nice, the others are more likely to make good on their promises. The outing is being billed as a field trip to avoid hassles by state agencies that may not consider attendance at a protest rally suitable fare for preschoolers.

Molly helps her toddlers through the exits and up the escalator at Park Street Station, past the street vendors and musicians, and onward toward the gleaming golden dome of the State House. The preschoolers, sturdy and independent, proceed pretty much on their own, with the exception of Mike, who is flanked by teachers, each of whom holds a hand. Marina looks down at him, smiles, and says, "My hand is married to yours." Many of the children have cardboard signs strung around their necks, printed with slogans like "Read My Lips, No More Cuts" and "Day Care, Not Welfare" and "Stop Cutting Our Future" and "We Want Our Money." Four-year-old Jacob, all curly red hair and freckles and baggy pants, wears one that says "My Mommy Needs to Work." The Boston Common is swarming with office workers on coffee breaks and tourists hunched over maps of the Freedom Trail. A young couple spots Jacob's sign.

"Isn't that just the saddest thing you've ever seen?" the woman whispers, her voice dripping pity.

Jacob, whose mommy is a successful urban planner, smiles

broadly, showing a couple of missing teeth. He feels like a tourist attraction.

The State House, an imposing structure of neoclassical design, looms large as the Emerald City at the summit of Beacon Hill. The children meander toward it, parents and teachers worrying them from all sides, like sheepdogs. It takes a good fifteen minutes for everyone to climb to Beacon Street, where a steady stream of afternoon traffic clogs the interchange. The scraggly group waits and waits for a break in the line of cars, but there is none. The traffic light seems not to be working; it's jammed on green. The drivers keep their eyes well over the heads of the two dozen small children with signs around their necks. Finally, Marina steps to the center of Beacon Street and holds up her hand, palm forward, forcing the sheet-metal blur to an impatient pause while the children, teachers, and parents scurry across the street.

The State House gate is open, but the children wait outside, pushing their toes into the concrete barrier wall, craning their necks for a good look at the gleaming bronze statue of Horace Mann, described on a plaque as "the Father of Public Education." Molly steps forward to explain the group's mission to a man in uniform, but the man shakes his head and waves her on, pointing past the gate to a side lawn that is out of view of the main entrance. The policeman says they cannot have their protest on the State House steps that day. It's Flag Day, and the American Legion has already claimed the front steps for a ceremony.

"I'm sorry," he says. "It's scheduled. Something to do with a big flag."

"They're probably worried that we're going to burn it," Molly cracks, pulling Claude with her as she makes her way around the corner and through a side gate.

A group of about fifty women and children and a sprinkling of men are assembled on the lawn, perched precariously on the small patch of steep hillside overlooking Beacon Street. You can sense the grass stains seeping steadily into their sundresses and jeans. A handful of technicians from local cable television stations squeeze through the crowd, pointing microphones and video cameras, foraging for color for tonight's news show or tomorrow's neighborhood special. There's not much going on, just some low-level slogan chanting and a little picket-sign jouncing. Mainly, things are quiet. Everyone's waiting for the first speaker to arrive.

The hill is too congested and precipitous to allow for running, let alone Frisbee tossing, and the kids are restless. They complain of thirst and hunger and of the urgent need to use a bathroom. The teachers cast about in mild panic; there are no bathrooms, not even a discreetly placed bush to duck behind. Mustering their wits, they respond the only way they can, with distraction, doling out slices of raisin bread and coaxing the kids into a rousing sing-along. Everyone's spitting out the second verse of "If I Had a Hammer" through mouthfuls of crust when a car pulls up to the curb.

The car door opens, and a large man dressed in a rumpled gray suit steps out. He mingles with well-wishers, shaking hands and patting shoulders, looking pleased with himself and with them. He seems to have a lot of friends here. He says that he's been on a low-calorie diet for the past week or so and that, while he's got a long way to go, he's already lost eight pounds. He pulls out the waistband of his pants to show the slack. He pats his stomach, says he sure could do with a sausage and pepper sub, and chuckles. Then he straightens his tie, clears his throat, and steps up to the microphone. His look turns serious.

"Hello, my name is Salvatore Albano, and I'm state senator from Somerville," he says. "I don't have a lot to say today, but I can tell you that the new tax package will not cover the necessary investment in our future. We'll either pay now, or we'll pay later. If we make these cuts now, we will be burdening ourselves with remedial programs for these kids in the future."

Senator Albano steps back from the microphone and waves to the parents and children, who cheer and bounce their picket signs. Then he bends down to whisper in the ear of a parent organizer that he'd love to stay for the rest of the demonstration but he has another appointment waiting for him across town. Smiling and waving, he backs into his car and drives off. The cheers go on long after the car is out of sight. There seems to be nothing more anyone can say.

The director of a Haitian multiservice center steps forward

to try to fill the void. She pulls the microphone close and talks about Haitian children in Dorchester, children whose parents work full-time but make so little that their families qualify for assistance from the Department of Social Services. Working full-time, she says, is no longer enough to guarantee decent care for one's children in Massachusetts. It takes government help.

"These cuts are unfairly impacting on the Haitian community, because Haitians refuse to go on welfare," she says. "They are afraid that being on welfare will hurt their immigration status. So what will happen to their children if these cuts go through? Should they be expected to care for themselves?"

Molly looks down at Claude, who is sitting on her lap. Claude's parents are among those who would not come to the protest today. Unlike Molly, they do not have faith in the power of political action.

A Haitian mother steps forward, grabs the mike, and shouts, "We are expected to give our blood for this government, so, government, stop lying to us. Work better for our children."

There are hoots and cheers from the audience, but not enough to attract attention from passersby. The rally is losing momentum, threatening to lose its edge. What more can be said but that the cuts are unwise, that children will be compromised and family lives torn apart? It's an old, old story, one that has lost interest in the telling and retelling. In an effort to spice things up, an organizer calls children down from the hill to testify. Children are always crowd pleasers. Those willing to talk come boldly, like witnesses at a Baptist prayer meeting. They toy with the microphone and squirm and try hard to think of something clever to say, then give up and blurt out things like "Give our day care center money so that our parents can work." These are not entirely appealing appeals, and soon the grown-ups tire of them. People are restless and anxious to go, but no one quite seems to know how to end things.

By now, a cluster of men in white shirts, dress pants, and ties has formed at the top of the State House steps. They are not within view of the rally, and they seem unaware of its existence. Their interest is directed at the tractor-trailer truck that sits gumming up traffic on Beacon Street. The trailer holds a mahogany box about twice the size of a large man's coffin. The box is polished and shiny and intricately carved, like a fine piece of furniture. The men stand with their arms folded or their hands shoved into their pockets, rolling on their heels, looking down at the box. A small man dressed in a short-sleeved shirt with a number of ballpoint pens clipped onto the breast pocket pushes through the group and runs down the steps to Beacon Street. He seems to know a lot about the box. He says that it contains the Mount Rushmore flag, one of the largest American flags in the world. He explains to the small crowd of tourists who gather that the Mount Rushmore flag is forty-eight feet high and eighty-five feet wide and that its stripes are three-and-one-half feet wide, as wide as a small boy is tall. He says it weighs three hundred pounds. He says the Mount Rushmore flag is a traveling flag and that it's been brought out today for the kickoff of one of its many national tours. Later, there will be a ceremony, though the flag will not be unfurled. As one might imagine, unfolding a three-hundred-pound flag is a logistical nightmare. But the mahogany box will be carried up the steps of the State House at five o'clock. Important people, maybe even the governor himself, will attend.

Out around the back, at the day care rally, the children are flushed and drained with thirst and begging for ice cream. They have done their bit. Noel Thompson Barth begs to go home, she's bleary eyed with fatigue and hunger, but Peggy, her mother, isn't finished. She grabs Noel's hand and all but drags her around to the front of the State House, through the wrought-iron archway, past the statues of Horace Mann and Daniel Webster and the great lawn planted with tulips and flaming red carnations, up the stairway, and into Doric Hall, named for its ten Doric columns, past the information desk and the portraits of Abraham Lincoln and George Washington, and up two more flights of stairs to State Senator Michael LoPresti's office. She tells an aide sitting behind a desk there that she is a mother and a teacher and that she has a message she'd like to deliver personally to the senator. The aid tells her that the senator appreciates the sentiment, understands her concerns, and will certainly read the leaflet Peggy has brought for him. He also says that the senator is unavailable right now. Then he reaches into a box beside his desk and pulls out a tiny American flag on a stick and hands it, smiling, to Noel. Noel looks at the flag curiously, as though at some exotic fish. She smiles back at the man and grabs the flag in her fist. And then she and Peggy go back down the three flights of stairs, past the lawn and the statues, under the archway, past the large mahogany box on the tractor trailer, down Beacon Hill across the Common to the subway and the rush-hour hustle, to wait for a train. A Red Line train pulls in almost immediately and just as quickly fills with commuters, leaving Noel to stand lost in the crush, clinging to her mother's skirt. The ride is short, only three stops, but it seems to take a long time. About halfway between the State House and home, at the Charles Street stop, Noel starts to fall asleep on her feet, and the tiny American flag drops out of her fingers. Peggy sees it fall. At Central Square she lifts Noel into her arms, but she leaves the flag where it is, taking care not to step on it as she exits.

ALL in all, the rally was a great success. Channel Five came through with a two-minute report for the nightly news, complete with touching scenes from Tot Lot and close-ups of Christopher sitting on Holly's lap with a "Kids Need Funding, Too" sign around his neck. The *Boston Globe* reported on the rally both in its metro pages and in an editorial. The publicity couldn't have been better. Elaine DeRosa, executive director of the Cambridge Economic Opportunity Program, said she was quite hopeful of a positive response. But the legislature seemed not to notice, at least not for the moment. The new rules went into place as scheduled on June 18, eliminating new day care subsidies for working people of low income. The Department of Social Services people told the *Boston Globe* that they felt terrible about having to make the cuts but that with a seven-million-dollar budget reduction they had the choice of closing open slots or throwing children out of centers. They chose to eliminate slots, which means current vacancies for subsidized children at Tot Lot and elsewhere will go unfilled indefinitely. There is talk that the policy might change over the summer, but for now the only children eligible for new day care subsidies are those with parents in job-training programs and those who are being protected from what the Department of Social Services determines is "a potential risk in their living environment," meaning, usually, that they are endangered by their own parents or guardians. The home environment has to be pretty bad to be designated as risky — no one attending Tot Lot, for instance, qualifies as coming from a high-risk home. Without subsidies, Tot Lot is destined to become victim to the vicissitudes of the open market, a facility that, like private schools and country clubs, is out of reach for all but the monied classes.

The Monday after the rally, Marcel has still not appeared at school, and the teachers are worried. They have called Marcel's apartment and his mother, who is home caring for her new baby daughter, reports that everything is just fine. Michel has decided to keep Marcel home for a while, she says, to teach him some manners. Everyone speculates about which school of etiquette she's referring to, but they don't press. There is no precedent, no procedure for getting to the bottom of situations like this. The teachers can only hope for the best and, in particular, that Lucien, Michel's friend and confidant, will keep things in check. Susan questions Lucien daily on how things are going at Michel's place, and when she asks, Lucien's eyebrows shoot up, and he lets a long, low whistle of impatience slip through his teeth before gathering together a smile and saying everything is fine. He tells her he's in a hurry, that he's late for school and needs to leave, and that Marcel will be in the following day.

Lucien resents these intrusions into his friend's business, resents having to play along. And the little game makes him uncomfortable, causes him to steal as far into the background as he can, pulling his family with him. Before, Lucien and Madeline not only attended general meetings but stayed late, after the other parents had left, to sweep the floor and straighten up while their children drooped in their chairs with fatigue. Lucien has a deep sense of obligation and justice, and he thought it only fair to contribute steadily to his sons' school. He even found time to sit on the coordinating committee, where he helped set center policy. But now he says he has no time. Suddenly the Brissetteses are keeping a low profile. For the first time, Lucien and Madeline have taken to skipping general meetings, pleading time conflicts with their church. When they do attend, they come late and stand in the back of the room, as quiet as shadows.

So Susan wasn't all that surprised when one late afternoon, after Molly had left for the day and Claude was acting out, biting and kicking and on the edge of a temper tantrum, she was unable to convince Madeline to come in to help deal with it. Nothing she could do could calm Claude down, not even calling in Marie, who bent down and took Claude's hands and spoke Creole in his face. Claude hates this, hates Marie's too-loud voice, hates the feeling of being singled out from the other kids and dressed down in a language that he wishes he didn't know. And so he lashed out harder, biting and screaming and fighting until Marie dragged him back into Susan's office, where he sulked and kicked at the black file cabinet while Susan tried to summon his parents. Madeline wouldn't come, and Lucien couldn't be reached, but he came at closing time and gave Claude a look that sent the boy drilling a hole in the floor with his eyes. Lucien said he didn't want to talk here but that he would fix things himself at home.

"We just looked at each other," Susan said. "And I wondered what he meant by fix things."

Claude came to school the next day unscarred. But the temper tantrums became more frequent, and he seemed to sink deeper and deeper into himself. Even Molly is perplexed by the boy's attitude, an attitude she can no longer attribute entirely to vague cultural differences. Claude is slowly changing from an enigma to a problem, a problem for which the teachers realize they do not hold the key. Molly thinks it might have to do with the staff turnover, with losing Lilian and then José. Lilian, she says, was Claude's favorite teacher, and then José took him under his wing. When they left, he fell apart. Molly thinks that Claude is afraid of losing her, too, that he is insecure. But his parents deny that there is any problem. They say that it is lack of discipline, not sadness, that is causing him to act out. In any case, nothing anyone does seems to make a difference. Claude is silent and stubborn beyond all reason and, because he's a loner, does not respond to peer pressure. He'll have to work out whatever is bugging him for himself.

Luke, on the other hand, is doing fine. His language skills, like Marcel's social skills, have improved enormously, and there is no doubt that he understands a good deal more than he admits to. Language seemed to have come to Luke suddenly, in a burst, but that impression was an illusion. Luke had been working on his words secretly for some time, when his speech therapists' backs were turned. It was as though he simply made the decision to speak, for the words just spilled out one day, fully formed and clear, in a song. It was circle time, and the children had just finished reading the pasta pot story. Luke acted bored and restless during most of the reading, ignoring the jokes and the teacher's questions, as though he didn't understand. But then, when the book was finished, Luke started to sing, pushing out every word in a clear and distinct cadence. He listened to his voice, enjoying the sound, grinning as though he'd been granted a wish. From that day on, Luke has talked up a storm when he wants to but continues to stutter and play dumb when he deems it necessary. Any mention of his family, or even of Michel, is enough to make him forget his words. He has learned to use language for protection.

Luke will start kindergarten in the fall, and Madeline, his mother, is leaving nothing to chance. She has already decided that Luke will attend classes taught in English, rather than go to the Creole bilingual program at Graham and Parks School. Madeline believes that children in bilingual programs are coddled and patronized and expected to do poorly. She does not expect special treatment for her children, only that they be taught to make the most of opportunities.

"I don't want a Haitian program for Luke," she says. "If you want to learn English, you have to think in English. It's not French they teach at Graham and Parks, it's Creole, and there is no reason for Luke to learn to think in that language. I can speak French or Creole to my kids if I want to; I can teach them about their culture. They go to school to learn other things. I have a niece in Graham and Parks school, in the bilingual program. She is in third grade, and she doesn't know proper English. She thinks in Creole. She can't read. She learns nothing, she is confused."

Madeline has been told that there are better elementary schools in Cambridge than the school near Trois Bébés. She has been told that the best is Peabody School, the school closest to Harvard Square. Traditionally, Peabody has been the school of choice for Harvard people, particularly the postdoctoral fellows and graduate students who cannot afford to send their children to private schools. Real estate agents use the Peabody name as bait to lure unsuspecting newcomers to buy into the area, where homes can sell for a million dollars or more. But the truth is that children come to Peabody from all over the city — there hasn't been a specific elementary school district in Cambridge since the city voluntarily desegregated its schools twenty years before. At that time it was decided that any child should have the opportunity to attend any Cambridge school regardless of his address. The Peabody student population was almost entirely white and Asian back then, and a parent recalls how, at a school committee meeting, the then principal declared that it was unthinkable that children from Central Square attend his school because they "could not be taught to read." That principal is long gone, and people laugh when they tell the story, but they take it as a cautionary tale. Today Peabody, like all Cambridge schools, has nearly 50 percent minority students, a fact that has done nothing to detract from its reputation of academic superiority. In fact, Peabody is the most requested school in Cambridge, and many parents who want their children to go there are disappointed. But Madeline is determined to get her son in, and she has every confidence that she will. After all, she says, she has the highest authority on her side.

"It's God's law to educate our kids. . . . Think how much easier it is to preach the Kingdom when you have a good education," she says. "The education Luke will get at Peabody will help him help other people. We believe in a new world, of course, but right now, we're living here."

Fourteen

SAVED BY THE KIDS

THE dishwasher is on the blink again; it's getting to be a sick joke. Susan is no mechanic, but somehow she's certain that the motor is shot (if the damn thing has one) and even more certain that Sears will not send someone out to replace it before late afternoon, when the preschoolers' parents and siblings and aunts and grandmothers will pile in, expecting a gala celebration. Susan paces back and forth between the stove and the empty watercooler, trying to second-guess whether she can slip the paper-plate option past the more sympathetic and flexible core of her staff without alarming the rabid environmentalists among them. It's worth a try. Things really must run smoothly for once. Today is graduation day.

Graduation has been scheduled early this year to coincide with Margaret's leaving. Susan and the parents thought it would be better if the children regarded yet another teacher's departure as part of the natural ebb and flow of things, rather than as a desertion. One of Susan's closest friends at the center, Idara, is also leaving, to start a career in business. Idara is a vibrant, intuitive teacher, and the children adore her. She loves to teach, but she has told Susan that she cannot afford to make a career of it, that she has a pile of bills to pay, and that right now she has to follow the money. Idara has been accepted into a summer internship program at a retail clothing outlet in London, a wonderful opportunity. Susan feels left behind. She's not ready for a drastic career change, but she wouldn't mind working at a day care center with, for example, a more reliable dishwasher.

Escape is never very far from Susan's mind. Last week, she took the first, tentative step in that direction; she applied for the director's job at a center recently set up for the employees of a large computer software firm near MIT, a center with new equipment and a squeaky clean space, a center that is offering a director's salary of over thirty thousand dollars a year. Molly would blanch if she knew Susan was thinking of moving to a place like that, a corporate center where most of the kids are certain to be white and middle class. Corporate centers don't serve communities, they serve corporations; their bond with the children is only as strong as the parents' bond with the company. But Susan isn't Molly. For starters, her boyfriend of six years is a certified public accountant. She likes nice clothes and vacationing in warm places. One day, she wants to have kids of her own. Susan needs something to build on. Still, of course, she feels guilty.

Susan's thoughts are interrupted by the phone, and she hurries into her office to grab it before the answering machine picks up. It's Marie, calling to report that she is stranded on a street corner in Roxbury. Susan, taking care not to sound upset or intrusive, gently probes for details. Marie is only too glad to pour out the sordid tale. Susan holds the receiver a few inches from her ear, and Marie's voice booms out, loud and clear.

Marie says she borrowed her cousin's brand-new Grand Prix to drive to Stop and Shop this morning to pick up some flour and yeast and sugar to make bread for tonight's graduation ceremony and to get back to her apartment in Dorchester to pick up the props and costumes for tonight's preschool performance of *The Little Red Hen*. She pulled over on the way home to make a call at a pay phone and just as she was about to drop her dime, got a flash that something was wrong. So she walked back to the car, looked through the window, and saw the keys still dangling in the ignition. The car was locked. That was two hours before.

"I called Triple A, and they said that they'd send someone

over, but it's going to cost me sixty dollars," Marie says. "They haven't come yet, and I've got the script for *The Little Red Hen* on the front seat, and I don't know if I'll make it back in time. There was this kid hanging around, and he said he'd get the door open because he breaks into cars all the time, but he can't. So he had one of his friends give it a try. I mean, I got all the thugs in Roxbury offering to break into my car."

Susan listens to all this standing with one hand on her desk for support and her eyes on the plastic-covered chair, the one with its insides seeping out. Susan tells Marie not to panic, but, meanwhile, she's starting to look pretty worried herself, standing there wondering what parents are going to think of a school that can't even get it together to put on a three-minute dramatic performance. *The Little Red Hen* is an original adaptation of an old preschool classic, and though the children have been practicing their lines for days now, only Marie knows enough to orchestrate the performance. Susan tells Marie to "hang in there" and lowers the phone receiver gently into its cradle. She goes back to the kitchen and pauses to glare long and hard at the dishwasher, as though commanding it to heal itself. Then, tripping lightly on the bruised and cracked patch of linoleum pushing up through its bandage of duct tape, she tiptoes into the red-rug room. Circle is already in session. Susan sits down at what is normally Marie's place, crosses her legs, and pulls the closest child onto her lap. The paperwork will have to wait.

Marina and Margaret are leading a discussion about what it means to say good-bye. The kids are not particularly interested in this concept; it will be at least two months before most of them actually graduate. Only the teachers, Idara and Margaret, are leaving today, Idara to get ready for her trip to London, Margaret to prepare for her new life as a graduate student. Margaret, in particular, looks weary and, despite herself, a little sad. She looks older and prettier, too, with her long hair cropped into an attractive bob that shows her features to be finely shaped and even and her eyes large. She wears a loose-fitting red cotton top with the sleeves folded up and a long khaki skirt and leather sandals, the outfit of a somewhat rakish monk. She sits cross-legged on the floor, her arms around Luke, who is squirming slightly and daydreaming, passing the time while Marina talks about leave-takings and good-byes that aren't really forever good-byes. Marina is doing her best to make this moment poignant and memorable, but the kids aren't biting. They live in the here and now, and, as of now, Margaret and Idara are here. After a while, Marina stops talking and presents Margaret and Idara with their Good-bye Books. The books are made of construction paper held together with brass paper fasteners and filled with photos of the children and poems written to the teachers from each of them. Margaret's eyes fill with tears as she turns the pages, but she brushes them away before the children take notice. Idara lets the tears fall where they may.

Later, the preschoolers practice for that evening's performance. They sing "We Live in a City Built by Human Hands," a song that is a sort of anthem at Tot Lot. The first verse goes:

> Black hands, brown hands, white and tan,
> All together built this land,
> Black hands, brown hands, white and tan,
> The working woman and the working man.

Luke loves the song, and he sings it with exaggerated gusto, his head thrown back and his eyes beaming into Margaret's. Margaret beams back; she makes no secret of the fact that Luke is a favorite, and she is proud of the progress he has made. She sees in him a dignity and an undaunted spirit that she greatly admires and sometimes covets. Luke, she says, has come a long, long way this year, and she is confident he will do well in kindergarten. His sense of humor will serve to smooth over the inevitable rough spots.

Margaret casts an annoyed glance at Mike, who sits on the other side of the circle screaming out the lyrics, his hands over his ears. Unlike the other teachers, Margaret does not see the whole picture when she sees Mike; she cannot bring herself to feel sorry for him. Margaret has lost all patience for children who take and take and give nothing in return, children who suck up all the oxygen in the room. Today, watching Mike act out, she feels helpless and angry and, most of all, guilty. Her eyes narrow slightly, and, finally, she quietly but firmly orders him out of the circle, to sit by himself in time-out. Mike grins maniacally, pushes himself up on his black high-top sneakers, pulls his orange polo shirt snug over his bulging stomach, and thumps noisily, kangaroo style, out of the room. Idara follows and sits down next to him on the steps. Unlike Margaret, Idara checks her ego at the door when she comes to work. That is why, Susan says, losing her is so sad. After a minute or two, Idara reaches over and pulls Mike up onto her lap. Mike is one of her favorite children.

"Mike is tired of his life," she says, stroking his hair and rocking him. "Wouldn't you be tired if you lived his life?"

By lunchtime, the children have slipped into a chronic state of naughtiness that gnaws slowly at the teachers' patience like acid on slate. Tamara, dressed up for graduation day in a frilly white dress, white tights, and white patent leather buckle shoes, warns the others to "keep quiet or I'll call the cops," then collapses in a fit of giggles that sends a stream of juice gushing out through her nose and onto her lacy white collar. Noel toys with her millimeter-of-peanut-butter-on-pita-bread sandwich, pulling off tiny bits, and rolling them into balls to balance on the tip of her tongue, which she offers, eyes blinking coquettishly, to Dylan. Dylan gives her a withering look which he threatens to escalate into a karate chop if she doesn't "quit it." Luke carefully peels the skin off his hot dog and just as carefully nudges the hot dog from the table onto the floor, where it bounces slightly before settling into the grime. Shaking his head as though bemoaning a terrible loss, he bends down, picks up the hot dog with thumb and forefinger, and, holding it at arm's length, marches as though to a funereal drum to the wastebasket, where he drops the offending object and grins, breaking into a knee-slapping victory dance and moon-walking back to his seat. Everyone is on edge, excited about that night's ceremony but at the same time wanting it to be done with.

After lunch, Idara slides a tape of New Age sounds into the boom box, smooth, synthesized music composed to soothe. She tells the preschoolers to get ready for nap, and they reluctantly oblige, crowding around the sink and jamming elbows into each other's guts. Luke and Tamara toothbrush fence, jumping around the room like miniature Zoros. Marina breaks up the rumpus with a bark. The kids reluctantly pull their blankets and sleep toys out of the cubbies and head back into the red-rug room, where they throw themselves on their mats. The teachers sprawl among them, Marina between Jacob and Ruth, Susan (pinch-hitting for Marie) between Marcel and Luke. Dylan, who has decided to be Batman today, wraps himself in his heavy orange blanket and tells Mike to "go to sleep, Robin." Flattered and excited to be considered one among superheros, Mike kicks at his Sesame Street sleeping bag and lets go with a roar that sends Idara crawling on all fours to his side, warning him to "make a choice to calm down" before she makes the choice for him. Mike tosses and turns and bites his pillow, considering his options. Then, almost in midtoss, he falls fast asleep. Luke and Marcel are already snoring, and the others are down for the count. Except for Noel.

Noel shows no signs of fatigue. For Noel, naptime is a trial to be gotten through with fantasy and daydreams and what mischief she will allow herself, which generally is just a little. Today, she enjoys an animated conversation with her stuffed rabbit, making sure to keep it to whispers. Noel, the teachers sometimes say, is almost perfect.

PEGGY and Glen thought long and hard before signing Noel up for another year at Tot Lot, and they still aren't sure that they made the right decision. Noel will be five next January, and she is eligible to enter kindergarten in the coming fall. (Cambridge has the unusual policy of allowing children to start kindergarten in the September after their fourth birthdays.) Public school has a lot going for it, not the least of which is that it's free. Most of Noel's Tot Lot friends are going, and Peggy is sensitive to her daughter's feelings of being left behind. But she is also aware of the controversy surrounding the sending of four-year-old children to kindergarten. She has listened to kindergarten and first-grade teachers complain bitterly about the immaturity of some of their younger students. She also recalls how difficult it was for her older daughter, Kate, to make the change.

Kate graduated with a tough bunch of kids at Tot Lot; Molly

remembers it as the toughest group she'd ever worked with. But Kate had come to a kind of joyful peace with both her peers and her school. At Tot Lot, she was left to be herself; she wasn't pushed or pulled in any particular direction. Acceptance was always unconditional. And despite the confusion and noise and seeming chaos, she knew she was always loved, that there was always a lap to sit on when she needed it, no questions asked. In public school, there just weren't that many laps to go around. Kate had lost her audience, and she felt a little pressured to perform. It took six months for her to adjust to the change.

"Kindergarten was so much more structured than Tot Lot," Peggy says. "That was a shock. I guess I wasn't ready for it, even if Kate was. Noel has the rest of her life to get structured. I see no reason why she needs to start now."

Glen disagrees. He doesn't want to treat day care like a finishing school, keeping Noel there just because he can afford to pay for it. The other kids, the kids who are funded by the state, don't have a choice; they have to go to public school whether they're ready or not. Besides, he doesn't believe in holding kids back. He says parents are fooling themselves if they think one more year of preschool will give their children a leg up on their peers. Kate did just fine after the initial adjustment, and now, in first grade, she's doing more than fine, confident and cocky and reading like a third grader. He says he sees no good reason to hold Noel back. And, as usual, he's done his homework.

"The research shows that children who enter kindergarten young might have a slow start, but by the time they're in third grade, it's a wash," he says. "They catch up and do just as well as the other kids. Children should not have to adjust to kindergarten. Kindergarten should adjust to the child."

Of course, that's the idea, not the reality, and Glen knows it. Glen talks a tough line, but actually he's relieved that Peggy has pushed so hard to keep Noel at Tot Lot for another year. The center has been a focus of family life for five years now, and Glen's not quite ready to graduate, even if Noel is. He sees problems at Tot Lot, problems of leadership and communication and fiscal management, problems that he intends to fix. He's going to get involved next year, involved in a big way. He's already signed on for a term on the coordinating committee, written a revision of the parent handbook, and is working with Susan on revamping the personnel policy. Like a Boy Scout moving on from a campsite, Glen intends to leave Tot Lot in better shape than it was in when he came.

But Peggy is burned out on meetings and fed up with conflict. Unlike Glen, she does not regard herself as an endless resource. She continues to distance herself from Tot Lot and from the difficulties she anticipates will be part of next year's agenda. She is afraid of being swallowed up by overcommitment, of losing sight of herself as a person independent of her affiliations. She is tired of running, of leading life as though it were one continuous obligation. She needs time for herself and time alone with her children. Most of all, she's looking forward to summer vacation, to hiking in the Cascade Mountains of Washington State. It will be so much easier this year. Noel no longer needs to be carried on Glen's back, she can hike on her own now, and Kate is big enough to carry her own sleeping bag. Peggy can almost taste the mountain water, almost smell the wildflowers.

Noel stays curled up on her mat throughout nap, not sleeping. She listens to the snores of Dylan and Marcel and Mike and looks wistfully up at the sky through the skylight. She knows she's not graduating today, knows that her friends will be moving on without her. But if that upsets her, she's not telling. Noel wouldn't want to worry anyone; that's not her style.

AFTER nap, Peter appears, a surprise. He shuffles in slowly, his eyes on the floor and his fingers laced tightly with Idara's. Idara has kept close track of Peter ever since he left Tot Lot after Christmas, visiting him often and talking to him on the phone. She drove into Boston during naptime today to pick him up at his new school. He looks good in a black T-shirt and jeans and with his blond hair clipped close, just a few snips shy of military style. He has grown tall and lanky in the past few months, and he towers half a head over the others. He appears older and more composed than he was, and furtive, like a prisoner out on furlough. But he makes no secret of being happy to be at Tot Lot, and when Dylan, Marcel, and Luke rush over and floor him with bear hugs, he pockets his pride and hugs them back. They start roughhousing and patting each other on the rear, and pretty soon they're rolling on the floor. Then Marina barks, and they're all sitting on the steps, serving five-minute time-outs together and grinning from ear to ear.

The afternoon drags on, one long tiresome anticlimax punctuated with occasional outbursts of misbehavior. The teachers put some rock and roll on the tape player and sit down to watch the children work out their excitement and nervousness on the red rug. The preschoolers dance halfheartedly and wildly, bumping into each other and rolling on the floor, more or less out of control. The teachers watch from the sidelines, letting the kids fall where they may. It's been a long day, and the evening will be even longer.

At 4:10, just before the parents are scheduled to arrive, Marie comes staggering through the blue door. She is hot and exhausted and fed up. She flicks a bit of bologna off the seat of one of the tiny chairs and flings herself down into it like a sack of cornmeal. She is hopping mad.

"I had a fifteen-year-old kid in a baseball cap and sneakers — the one who breaks into cars — stuck to me like glue, which got on my nerves in a major way," she says. "Anyway, eventually this kid flagged down a Ford Bronco that was cruising the block — he knew it was an unmarked police car. The detective pulled out his Slim Jim, and if he didn't know how to use that thing? Thank God, the car still had some gas."

It looks like there won't be enough time to complete work on the costumes before show time, but at least they have the script. Marie sighs hard and holds the pages over her head, like a flag.

At 4:40, the teachers drop a Michael Jackson record onto the turntable, crank it up loud, kick off their shoes, and boogie with the preschoolers, who jump around in circles screaming, "Beat it, beat it." But by five o'clock, not even rock and roll is distraction enough. The preschoolers push and shove their way to the outside play area, joining the few remaining toddlers to muck around in the dirt, dangle bravely from the climbing structure, and chase each other with sand shovels. Dylan and Marcel and Luke seem almost too big for the space. They stage mock karate demonstrations and rub sand into each other's hair. Claude hangs close to his older brother, keeping out of trouble. He is acutely aware that his parents will be here soon, and he works hard to keep from doing something that Luke would consider worth tattling on to their father.

As it turns out, Claude doesn't have long to wait — Madeline and Lucien are among the first to arrive for the ceremony. Claude runs headfirst into Madeline and hugs her legs. She laughs and hugs him back, cool and composed in a white cotton dress printed with bright red two-humped camels and orange elephants. Lucien wears wide-wale corduroy trousers and a heavy black leather jacket with a blue-and-white V-necked sweater underneath. No matter that the temperature is pushing seventy degrees; as usual he's prepared for the worst. Lucien takes Marina's hand in both of his and shakes it warmly, with respect, before turning to his children, Claude, Luke . . . and Marcel. He looks them over, clucking his tongue, then pulls out his oval hairbrush and gives Luke's and Marcel's heads a dozen vigorous swipes each. Sand scatters from their skulls, and Lucien brushes harder, trying but failing to appear angry at the boys' sloppiness. Today he is too proud to be angry.

Madeline announces that Luke was in fact admitted to Peabody School, the school so close to Harvard Yard that it practically has ivy climbing up its walls. Luke will ride a bus to school, a bus that will pass by all those grand and historic West Cambridge houses where scholars and doctors and lawyers live. He will be overdressed and, at first, awkward, but he will learn his lessons in English. He will become an American boy with a Haitian heart, and for Madeline, that is enough.

Madeline brushes the sand from Luke's shoulders and, taking Claude's hand, walks both boys up the narrow wooden staircase to the rooftop playground, where the program is about to start. Lucien and Marcel follow. The deck has been swept clean of leaves, and three rows of chairs have been set up, facing a kind of stage. Luke and Marcel run to join the other preschoolers while Madeline finds a seat for herself and Claude, pulling the boy to her lap and circling him with her arms. Lucien stands in the back, his arms folded, a broad smile fixed on his face.

A steady stream of parents and grandparents pours in, cramping their bodies into the lilliputian chairs or spreading themselves out on the wide, weathered floorboards. Dylan's extended family, his grandmother, cousins, aunts, and parents, fills an entire wall. This is the first time most of the teachers have seen Dylan's father, a handsome, muscular man nervously toying with the collar of his freshly pressed polo shirt. A couple of other dads stand in the back, awkwardly wielding video cameras. Idara can't resist walking into tight focus and introducing herself as "the sex goddess of love," before announcing the show, which begins with a rousing rendition of "We Live in a City." Mike covers his ears and screams out the lyrics as usual, but, outdoors, with a warm breeze blowing and the sunshine pouring down, his misbehavior seems more playful than malicious. Everyone laughs, and Mike laughs with them, lowering his hands from his ears and gradually toning down his voice to match the others'.

When the song is through the preschoolers break into small groups for the dramatic portion of the show. Marina pulls the long, low toddler bench to center stage and announces that, since parents go to work on the trolley, her group, the Bees, will do a skit about a trolley ride. Jacob's dad, Lon, a compact man with dark curly hair and a beard to match, pushes himself up from the floor and saunters to the bench, straddling it like a cowboy. Lon wears black pants, black shoes, a black baseball cap turned backward, and a dark gray shirt emblazoned with the logo of the San Diego Zoo — it was the closest thing he could find to a trolley conductor's uniform. He holds a steering wheel in his hands and in his teeth a kazoo, which he blows from time to time to simulate a trolley horn. Lon pretends to drive and then "stops" to pick up each of the six Bees, who are made up to resemble their favorite animals. Mike is a tiger. Noel is a deer. Lon ends the "ride" with a flourish of kazoo blowing, only to discover that he has somehow forgotten to "pick up" Jacob, his own son. Jacob bursts into tears, and Lon jumps up, grabs him, and carries him back to the trolley, where he hands him the steering wheel, shoves the baseball cap down over his ears, and yells for applause. Jacob grins through his tears.

Margaret's group, the Butterflies, is up next with a dramatization of "Oh, Lord, I Wish I Was a Buzzard," a folktale about children picking cotton in the hot sun, wishing out loud to be anything but the slave children they are. Luke says he wishes he were a snail, which sends Madeline into a quiet chuckle, thinking about the snail's pace he seems to keep every morning, when she's trying to get him breakfast and out of the house. The Butterflies have barely finished with their performance when Marie's Lifesavers push to center stage with their rendition of *The Little Red Hen*. Having no costumes, the children make do by holding masks on sticks in front of their faces. The performance seems none the worse for it; the kids remember their few lines and manage to keep a safe distance from each other. The parents eat it up, applauding wildly and whistling through their teeth.

The ceremony ends with the children singing "We Shall Overcome." Mike manages to keep his voice in check and his hands off his ears. Peter stands to one side, hands folded in front of him, mouthing the words he's forgotten and smiling shyly. May pulls her skirt over her head, and an airplane drowns out some of the tune, but no one seems to notice. Susan hands out silk-screened T-shirts to each of the graduates, and then, to be fair, Marina hands out more T-shirts to the preschoolers who are not graduating. Kate grabs Noel's to present to her. Then parents and children break ranks to shake hands, pat each other on the back, and talk, mostly about how much they will miss Tot Lot and the friends they've made there. They promise never to lose touch, promise to keep the kids together, even if it means driving them to friends' houses on weekends. Some of these promises seem genuine.

Everyone goes downstairs to eat the feast of chicken wings and Chinese dumplings and lasagna and sausage and peppers and hummus and guacamole and chocolate chip cookies and fruit salad that the parents have brought to wash down with a plastic cup or two of contraband wine. Peggy gets a paper plate of beans and rice and chicken wings for herself and a plate of pasta and fruit salad and cookies for Noel and Kate and sits down at one of the little tables to eat. She tries not to act hurried, but she is: she's needed at Graham and Parks at 7:00 for a meeting to discuss alleged marijuana use by seventh and eighth graders. Peggy calls it the reefer madness meeting. She'd rather stay home and watch the Celtics on television with Glen and the kids. Instead, she'll have to drop Kate and Noel off after dinner and spend the rest of the evening listening to a roomful of aging flower children whine about why marijuana isn't the same as crack and why their kids, good kids, should be forgiven for bringing it to school. It's pathetic. One of these kids was actually selling the stuff. At any rate, with luck she'll be home in time to catch the end of the game and see Kurt Rambis (she calls him "Clark Kent in short pants") sink a few before dragging herself off to bed. Peggy loves Rambis, even though the rest of Boston hates him. She's a sucker for an underdog.

Madeline and Lucien stand apart from the others, wedged between the library and the toddler room. Lucien eats chicken steadily while Madeline cuts Claude's dinner into manageable bites. They do not socialize, not even with Lucien's friend, Michel, who is forking up double portions of everything on the other side of the room, his face pushed down close to his plate. Michel's son, Marcel, will not be attending Peabody School with Luke in the fall, not because he was denied admission but because his parents didn't apply. He'll be going to Tobin School, the school closest to Trois Bébés. Marcel will have to face kindergarten alone, without his best friend to back him up. The teachers agree that it will be hard for him at first but Marcel has already made great strides toward independence. Like Luke, he seems destined to pull through, maybe not with flying colors, but at least with some measure of grace.

The children bolt their food and dash to the play yard, where Christopher defies gravity on the climbing structure. Christopher is still technically a toddler and therefore not really a party to tonight's ceremony, but Holly says he wouldn't miss it for the world and neither would she. It's a night out for both of them, and, besides, Christopher is graduating in a way — to the preschool room the following month. Christopher wears a new pair of high tops and his favorite T-shirt, the orange one with the dinosaur wearing sunglasses and a bathing suit. He has been sick with a stomach flu all week, but he looks relaxed and happy. Holly is back on the day shift at the telephone company, and Christopher no longer has to drive home from his father's apartment in East Boston every morning in his pajamas. He hasn't thrown a tantrum or caused a scene in weeks, and he's looking forward to a fishing trip in Maine with his dad in a month. Holly is a bit nervous about the trip, but she knows it's necessary.

"Christopher is my guy, but I'm trying to be less possessive of him," she says. "What he and I have been through this year, with the strike and the divorce and all, that's only made us stronger. I don't think I would have felt strong at all if it weren't for Christopher. I have him to thank for my sanity. Sometimes it's the kids who save you."

Molly isn't here tonight. It's the first time in six years that she's missed graduation, but this time she sees no reason to attend. Her toddlers aren't going anywhere; for them and for her, tomorrow will be business as usual. Molly doesn't say so, but she resents the early ceremony. Holding graduation so far in advance of when the children actually graduate makes no sense to her at all. She can understand why Margaret and Idara might want to have graduation before they leave, but what's in it for the kids? It will only confuse them. What does it mean to graduate if you're back in school the next day?

Besides, Molly has a dinner date that night, with a friend whom she hasn't seen for ages, a friend who lives in Japan. Everything, it seems, has changed for him, while her life has stayed pretty much the same. At dinner, she finds herself talking about her toddlers a lot and being a little impatient when he tells her about Japan, as she usually is when people talk about things that seem to have so little to do with her life or the life of her kids. They split the tab, and Molly's friend drops her at home on the way back to his hotel. Molly climbs the stairs, changes into her bathrobe, washes her face, and lights a cigarette — she's been tiptoeing around her habit for a few weeks now, copping five or six smokes a day, though she tries to hide it. The Mad Russian's spell wore off a while ago.

Molly has no idea what the new school year will bring, whether Susan will leave as she hints she will or whether the state will pull still more money out of child care or whether Tot Lot will even be able to keep its doors open. She thinks, though, that things will remain pretty much the same, a struggle from the word "go," with the only certainty being that nothing is certain. She believes that for now day care will remain no more than an afterthought on the national agenda, but she is hopeful that this will change someday, perhaps when her toddlers are old enough to vote. Anyway, it doesn't daunt her. She knows what she's good at and where she's needed, and, above all, that she's staying put.

Molly snuffs out her cigarette. It's 9:45, time for bed. Tomorrow she has to get to school early. The weatherman predicts rain, and Marcia will be waiting for the doors to open with water dripping off the hood of her raincoat and onto her nose. Molly has no idea what that child's mother is thinking, but she personally would feel terrible if the girl came down with another cold. She's had so many. Molly chuckles fondly, envisioning Marcia's sweet, wide-open face. Then she reaches over and, still smiling to herself, turns off the light.

Acknowledgments

THIS book is about people, and most of the sources I relied upon for its completion were human ones. From the very beginning, I was informed and inspired by long talks with Kathleen McCartney, professor of psychology at the University of New Hampshire, Gwen Morgan, lecturer on child-care issues at Wheelock College, and Marion Wright Edelman, director of the Children's Defense Fund. Michelle Seligson of the Wellesley College Center for Research on Women, and Fran Jacobs, assistant professor of Urban and Environmental Policy at Tufts University, were of great help, as were Joan Costley of Wheelock College, Carolee Howes of the University of California at Los Angeles, and Patty Hnatiuk, a former day care teacher and director and researcher on the National Child Care Staffing Study.

Geneva Malephant, longtime Cambridgeport resident, provided me with a humorous and colorful oral history of that neighborhood, and Charles Sullivan, director of the Cambridge Historical Commission, led me to the appropriate written ones. Bill Cavelinni offered outspoken insights into the city's rich political life.

For much of the historical background on Tot Lot, I am indebted to Linda McPhee, Arthur MacEwan, Margery Davies, Steven Miller, Pauline Clark, Noel Clark, and Beth Oglesby. For advocating for me at Tot Lot I am deeply grateful to Laura Blacklow, and for introducing me to the fine art of negotiation and compromise, to Mary Teseo. John Manning of the Massachusetts Office for Children and Naomi Davidson of the Childcare Resource Center helped me understand the state regulatory system. My talks with Senator Christopher J. Dodd helped put the national day care agenda into perspective, as did interviews with Helen Blank of the Children's Defense Fund and Ellen Galinsky of the Families and Work Institute.

For analysis and astute insights into child-care issues, I spoke with Jerome Kagan, professor of psychology at Harvard University, Edward F. Zigler, professor of psychology and director of the Bush Center in Child Development and Social Policy at Yale, and Jean Layzer, social researcher at Abt Associates.

Douglas Baird of Associated Day Care in Boston and, especially, Lucy Mitchell, founding director of Associated Day Care, spent long hours outlining the history of the day-nursery movement. Nancy de Prosse, head of the Massachusetts chapter of the national union of day care workers, filled me in on union history and activities.

For discussions on the psychological effects of day care, my thanks to Alison Clark Stewart of the University of California at Irvine, Jay Belsky of Pennsylvania State University, and Deborah Phillips of the University of Virginia.

For discussions on the effects on young children of various approaches to teaching, I thank David Elkind, senior resident scholar at Tufts University, David Weikart and Larry Schweinhart of the High Scope Education Research Foundation, Harriet Egerton, early-childhood specialist with the Nebraska Department of Education, Dorothy Stricklen, professor of education at Columbia University, Susan Bredekamp of the National Association for the Education of Young Children, Sam Sava of the Elementary School Principals Association, and, most of all, the wonderfully sensible Lilian Katz, professor and director of the Early Childhood Resource and Information Center at the University of Illinois.

I am grateful to David Finkelhor, professor of sociology at

the University of New Hampshire, for all the time he spent with me explaining the nuances of child abuse in this country and to Richard E. Connolly, Deputy General Counsel for the Massachusetts Office for Children, for a discussion of the state's child abuse laws. Dr. Marie McCormick, director of the Infant Follow-Up program at Children's Hospital in Boston provided statistics on and analysis of the risks of premature birth.

For background on and insights into the life of Haitians in the United States in general and in Cambridge in particular, I am most grateful to Brunir Shackleton, director of the Cambridge Haitian American Association of Massachusetts, and to Joseanne Barnes, teacher in the bilingual program at Graham and Parks School.

Thanks to Cam Mann for the idea, to Jean Callahan, Michaele Weissman, and Gordon Kato for their generous editorial scrutiny, and to Doug Starr for his tireless moral support. Thanks to William Whitworth and Corby Kummer of *The Atlantic*, which printed my first thinking on this topic.

Thanks to my editor, Bill Phillips, for his careful consideration and straight talk and to Karen Dane for hers.

Much thanks to Kris Dahl, agent par excellence, for her patience, persistence, loyalty, and, most of all, humor.

My deeply felt thanks to Karen DeRusha and Geri Russillo, educators, and Fiona Jones, dear friend, for teaching and caring for my children during the course of this project.

And special thanks, of course, to the parents, teachers, children, and friends of Tot Lot, most of whom will remain unnamed, but none of whom will be forgotten.

Sources

Bikales, Gerda. *Day Care: A Program in Search of a Policy.* Princeton, N.J.: Center for Policy Analysis of Political Issues, 1976.

Bowlby, John. *Maternal Care and Mental Health.* Geneva, Switzerland: World Health Organization, 1951.

————. *Attachment and Loss.* Vol. 2. London: Hogarth, 1973.

Braun, Samuel J., and Esther P. Edwards, eds. *History and Theory of Early Childhood Education.* Belmont, Calif.: Wadsworth Publishing, 1972.

Cambridgeport Survey of Architectural History. Cambridge, Mass.: MIT Press, 1971.

Comer, James P. "Educating Poor Minority Children." *Scientific American* 259, no. 5 (November 1988).

Danner, Mark. "Haiti." Parts 1–3, *The New Yorker* (November 27; December 4; December 11, 1989).

Delpit, Lisa D. "The Silenced Dialogue: Power and Pedagogy in Educating Other People's Children." *Harvard Educational Review* 58, no. 3 (August 1988).

Greven, Philip. *Spare the Child: The Religious Roots of Punishment and the Psychological Impact of Physical Abuse.* New York: Alfred A. Knopf, 1991.

Helmer, John, and Neil Eddington, eds. *Urban Man: The Psychology of Urban Survival.* New York: The Free Press, 1973.

Hofferth, Sandra L. "What Is the Demand for and Supply of Child Care in the United States?" *Young Children* 44, no. 5 (1989).

Hunt, J. McVicker. *The Effect of Variations in Quality and Type of Early Child Care on Development.* New Directions for Child Development, no. 32. San Francisco: Jossey-Bass, 1986.

Hymes, James. "The Kaiser Answer: Child Service Centers." *Progressive Education* (May 1944).

Marx, Fern. *Caring for Children*. Washington, D.C.: National League of Cities, 1989.

A Nation at Risk. National Commission on Excellence in Education. Washington, D.C.: Government Printing Office, 1983.

Roby, Pamela, ed. *Child Care — Who Cares? Foreign and Domestic Infant and Early Childhood Policies*. New York: Basic Books, 1973.

Scarr, Sandra. *Mother Care Other Care*. New York: Basic Books, 1984.

Schorr, Alvin L., ed. *Children and Decent People*. New York: Basic Books, 1974.

Schwartz, Pamela. "Length of Day-Care Attendance and Attachment Behavior in Eighteen-Month-Old Infants." *Child Development* 54 (1983).

Shell, Ellen Ruppel. "Babes in Day Care." *The Atlantic* (August 1988).

———. "Day Care: Making a Federal Case of It." *Parenting* (February 1989).

———. "Now, Which Kind of Preschool." *Psychology Today* (December 1989).

Steinfels, Margaret O'Brien. *Who's Minding the Children? The History and Politics of Day Care in America*. New York: Simon and Schuster, 1973.

Suttles, G. D. *The Social Order of the Slum*. Chicago: University of Chicago Press, 1968.

Sutton, S. B. *Cambridge Reconsidered*. Cambridge, Mass.: MIT Press, 1976.

Whipple, Guy Montrose, ed. *National Society for the Study of Education, Preschool and Parental Education, 28th Yearbook*. Bloomington, Ind.: Public School Publishing, 1929.

Whitebook, Marcy. *National Child Care Staffing Study*. Oakland, Calif.: Childcare Employee Project, 1989.

Wilentz, Amy. *The Rainy Season*. New York: Simon and Schuster, 1989.

Zigler, Edward F., and Edmund W. Gordon, eds. *Day Care: Scientific and Social Policy Issues*. Dover, Mass.: Auburn House, 1982.